Male infertility – men talking

How do men react to a diagnosis of male infertility? How are their lives affected by it? Male infertility is commonplace, yet the male experience of it has been so far neglected. *Male Infertility – Men Talking* gathers together men's stories and explores the common strands between them.

The spotlight is on infertile men as they talk about what it feels like to be infertile. As an essential backdrop to the interviews Mary-Claire Mason examines the past and present medical management of male infertility and the problems that bedevil it. This coverage is combined with the main focus on how men are affected emotionally and socially, giving a unique insight into the male viewpoint and into infertile men's desires and frustrations. Men talk about their medical, emotional and social experiences, about painful events, their relationships with families and friends, their feelings of isolation, their desire to be fathers, and their hopes for the future.

Essential reading for all professionals working with infertility as well as for infertile couples themselves, *Male Infertility – Men Talking* will enable counsellors, doctors and nurses to understand more about the man's point of view and to respond more fully to his needs.

Mary-Claire Mason is a freelance writer with a personal interest in male infertility. She specialises in health and her articles have appeared in a range of publications including *The Independent* and *The Guardian*.

Male infertility
– men talking

Mary-Claire Mason

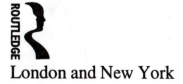
London and New York

First published 1993
by Routledge
11 New Fetter Lane, London EC4P 4EE

Simultaneously published in the USA and Canada
by Routledge
29 West 35th Street, New York, NY 10001

Typeset in Times New Roman by Michael Mepham, Frome, Somerset
Printed and bound in Great Britain by
Biddles Ltd, Guildford and King's Lynn

British Library Cataloguing in Publication Data
A catalogue record for this book is available from the British Library.

Library of Congress Cataloging-in-Publication Data
Mason, Mary-Claire.
  Male infertility: men talking / Mary-Claire Mason.
  p. cm.
  Includes bibliographical references and index.
  1. Infertility, Male—Psychological aspects. I. Title.
  [DNLM: 1. Infertility, Male—psychology. 2. Counseling.
WJ709 M411m 1993]
RC889.M373 1993
616.692—dc20
DNLM/DLC
for Library of Congress   93–11986
CIP
ISBN 0–415–07289–1
ISBN 0–415–07290–5 (pbk)

Contents

Foreword

When Mary-Claire Mason first talked to me about her idea of writing a book on male infertility, in which men themselves would describe the experience from their own point of view, I encouraged her to do so. In a support group such as ISSUE, where we can put members in touch with others who are going through or have gone through similar experiences, we find that the shared experience can do a great deal to combat the isolation that many men, and their partners, feel when faced with the diagnosis of infertility. I hope that this book, by reaching a wide audience, will also help to dispel that sense of isolation.

Inevitably, the difficulties that men have in talking about their feelings publicly have meant that the group whose experiences form the background to this book was self-selected, and therefore perhaps coped better with the feelings of being trapped, devalued, and 'less men' than, in my experience, many men who suffer as a result of infertility. Because of this, the book does not touch equally on all the stresses that men can and do undergo when diagnosed infertile and there are still many areas about which I hope its publication will stimulate further discussion. I am thinking of such important issues as the strong needs of men to have their own genetic child; the conflicts arising from the use of donor sperm; the difference between the feelings of men who have a small sperm count and those who have none at all; the problems for men who become trapped in providing emotional support for their partners and are never able truly to express their own feelings of anguish; the difficulties created by the lack of proper testing in the early stages and failure to provide a clear diagnosis; and, not least, the emotional devastation that can be caused if bad news is badly communicated.

Mary-Claire Mason's book is to be welcomed because it begins to open up a subject which has been too little discussed.

John Dickson
Director of ISSUE

Preface

Male infertility was something I had never thought about until it pushed its way into my consciousness in the late 1980s. I was ignorant about issues of sperm quality and the other factors that have to be considered when male fertility is assessed.

But that all changed when my partner and I decided we wanted children. I did not become pregnant so after a time we both went through some medical tests which indicated that my partner had a mix of sperm problems.

Both of us grappled with the diagnosis. The process of medical investigations had not been easy or straightforward and it left me feeling battered and bewildered. What did the diagnosis mean, would we ever have children? These were the thoughts that haunted me. Acute feelings of despair and anguish pushed me into reading up on the subject. I became increasingly aware that everything was largely directed at the woman rather than the man. There was a silence about the man's role in the whole business and I could see this reflected in my own personal situation. I knew only too well what I was feeling, but what was my partner going through?

The questions that increasingly preoccupied me were what did he feel about the diagnosis, how was he going to cope with it, how would I respond to him given that I was the fertile partner? My anxieties deepened because so little seemed to have been written about the man's experience.

This book was prompted by these questions. Talking to others helped me understand more about the man's viewpoint and his desires and frustrations. I started to appreciate why the experience of infertility varies so much for each person. Inevitably the book made me look at my own feelings about infertility in more depth. On reflection it has been part of my coping process, helping me come to terms with the fact that as a couple we have been unable to have our own children. This process has been painful but also illuminating.

Acknowledgements

Many people have helped me in one way or another with this book. Clinics, self-help groups, researchers, doctors and counsellors have offered words of encouragement to me, research suggestions, given me insights and helped put me in touch with potential interviewees. Friends and family have likewise been supportive. I am grateful to them all.

In particular I would like to thank the following for their support: Peter Bromwich, Alison Classe, Rachel Cook, John Dickson, Paul Entwistle, Jenny Hunt, Sammy Lee, Jackie Lindop, Jim Monach, Naomi Pfeffer, Jeanette Prevett, Geraldine Stevens and Edwina Welham of Routledge.

Any mistakes or omissions are my responsibility.

Finally this book would not have been possible without two things. Firstly those men and women who talked to me. They gave willingly of their time and shared their experiences with me even though I know this must have been sometimes painful for them to do. I am immensely grateful to them. Secondly, John gave me support of every kind whilst I was writing this book. My love and thanks to him for this.

Part I

1 Introduction

INFERTILITY IS A WOMAN'S CONCERN

Men are shadowy figures when it comes to matters of fertility. Little is still known about what they feel when confronted with the dilemmas raised by infertility generally. As Osherson says, 'we know a good deal about the turmoil women experience when couples are infertile but much less about men' (1986: 97). The picture may change again when a question mark hangs over the man's fertility, the subject of this book.

A veil of ignorance has cloaked this delicate topic keeping it hidden from view. Times may be changing but it is still women who dominate the infertility agenda. Children are seen as a woman's business and events from conception onwards her concern. She is the one who suffers when such natural matters do not go according to plan, and the one to take charge of fertility problems when they arise, regardless of whether the cause of the problem lies with her, the man or both of them. Figures from a recently established British fertility telephone helpline illustrate this picture. Some 2,582 women rang the phone line in its first year of operation compared to 326 men (Dickson, 1991), and little information is currently available about male infertility drawn from men themselves (Congress of the US, Office of Technology Assessment, 1988c).

Accounts of fertility in the past revolved round the woman. Bible stories emphasised infertility as a woman's concern. The man's reproductive potential was essentially unquestioned, impotence the only acknowledged cause of male infertility (Spark, 1988). In the Old Testament men could take on additional wives where the original ones were barren. Sterility was regarded as a divine punishment (Turner, 1984) and the ability to have children has historically been of great importance. Johnston comments 'to earliest man the propagation of the race and its survival was a source of real anxiety; a woman who failed to conceive and carry a pregnancy to term was a source of concern and she regarded her plight as a disgrace', but the man was not generally castigated. Basically his role in conception seems to have been misunderstood. The Ingarda tribe in Australia for example believed that the child was the product of something the mother had eaten (1963: 261).

More is known nowadays about male reproductive physiology and so about the problems of male fertility. Yet the assumption still lingers that it is the woman who is at fault (Stanway, 1986). Medical tests and treatments have largely been directed at her with the result that her experiences have been highlighted and the man's passed over.

Women are expected to be upset about involuntary childlessness. Infertility is seen as a tragedy for them. At the start of a book on the infertility experience, Pfeffer and Woollett say:

> In speaking predominantly to women we describe the experience from a woman's point of view because, although in at least one-third of cases male factors are heavily implicated, infertility is mostly seen as a woman's problem. Women are assumed to be more committed to wanting children and so infertility is seen as more of an issue for them. This is an assumption that we wish to question. But while this is how men's and women's motivation to have children is perceived, infertility is a greater life crisis for women than for men. This may make women more ready to talk about it. Also, it is women who by and large undergo the infertility investigations even when the problem lies with the man. So it is largely women for whom infertility becomes an issue and so we have concentrated on their experiences.
>
> (1983: 3)

A look at books and articles on infertility confirms this view. First-person tales written by women are the rule. They talk about their sorrow and anguish and the problems that beset them. Such pieces by men are exceptional. An article by John Green about his infertility grabbed my attention because it was so unusual (1988). More usually, the woman relays the man's experience, filtering it through her eyes. Back copies of *Issue*, the magazine produced by the British self-help group of that name (formerly National Association for the Childless), has letters from women writing in about their partners' problems, wanting more information about tests and treatments for male infertility. Letters from men are rare.

Likewise Ann Ferris writing about her own experience of in-vitro fertilisation (IVF) explains that her partner's sperm were found to be of dubious quality. The IVF attempt failed because none of the eggs collected from her was fertilised. Whilst mainly talking about herself, she talks about how her partner feels. 'I hate him to see me upset because I know he feels guilty. He knows he can't give me the one thing I desire more than anything – his child' (1991: 54).

But these are indirect observations of the man's experience. What do men themselves feel and think about their infertility? They have been reluctant to bare their souls in a way that women have not. The pioneering, excellent book written by Diane and Peter Houghton describes how the National Association for the Childless came to be set up in Britain. The Houghtons were unable to have their own children and towards the end of the book, Diane rather than Peter writes about her infertility experience. She explains along the way that her husband had fertility problems, yet his voice is absent from her moving story (1987). The impression is reinforced that infertility is a woman's rather than a man's business.

Men seem to have been left on the sidelines. A complex mix of social, cultural, medical and historical factors must surely account for this neglect. Reading articles and books on infertility written during the 1980s, several points emerge about male infertility. One dominates. From a medical perspective, the topic is a baffling puzzle waiting to be solved. One piece for example, talked of the lack of effective medical treatments for male infertility despite it being commonplace. There were no male specialists so men had to queue at female clinics for help, but men were also seen as partly to blame for this state of affairs as they mistakenly linked infertility to a lack of virility. Male infertility was seen as a major stigma and medical advances would only come about once the subject was brought out into the open (Hodgkinson, 1983). Another article also said men were haunted by the myth that fertility and virility were the same thing (Prentice, 1984). Philipp (who founded the British Fertility Society) blamed the lack of interest on men and doctors. The former were too proud to seek medical assistance for problems or were unaware they had any, and too few doctors took an exclusive interest in the subject (1984).

Speculation about why so little is known about the medical treatment of male infertility leads to another related area. Little is known about how men's lives are touched by infertility other than comments passed about the stigma attached to male infertility. There is a glaring gap in those studies that have considered the emotional and psychological aspects of infertility usually at the treatment stage. Women have largely been the centre of attention in these studies and men have been disregarded (Pantesco, 1986). More specifically a study on the psychology of male infertility reviewed various research pieces but found that only a minority concentrated on male patients. The author's explanation for this oddity was that men rarely showed clinical symptoms of infertility, and that the 'traditional view of confounding reproductive and sexual potency in men may have attributed to the hesitation in investigating the male patient for psychological factors' (Bents, 1985: 332).

CHANGING TIMES

Infertility has become a more talked about subject in the last decade and seems set to continue that way in the 1990s. Men are coming under closer scrutiny. One author though writing about women's particular problems acknowledges the male position – 'many men will also be extremely distressed by infertility and the associated treatments' (Doyal, 1987: 178). Infertility articles have considered the male experience, at least at the medical level, and talk of sperm counts and treatments is not uncommon in the media. A mix of factors seems to have encouraged this.

New treatments always provoke media interest. The birth of the world's first IVF baby in 1978 stimulated much discussion about how women could be helped to have children. IVF is now being used to help couples where the man has sperm problems, provoking discussion about male infertility. More recently other developments for men have attracted media attention.

Campaigning self-help groups have been established. Resolve was founded in 1973 in America and the British group, the National Association for the Childless, began in 1976. Infertile people emerged into the open according to one journalist, demanding better treatments and so gaining a higher profile. Previously they might have suffered in silence and adopted children, but changes in abortion law and improved contraception closed that route (Laurance, 1982). Inevitably such groups have wanted more effective treatments not only for women but for men and have raised awareness of the man's position.

Male health in general has been neglected and is a subject for shame argues Lyndon (1990), but it is getting more attention. Male-health clinics for example, have been established and men are being encouraged to check themselves for signs of prostate and testicular cancer. Discussion of male infertility may be part of this trend towards greater male enlightenment.

On the social side, fatherhood has become desirable (Landesman, 1991) and is something all boys can aspire to. Perhaps this has encouraged debate about what men can do if they find their road to fatherhood blocked. Male infertility was also thought suitable enough to include in a British television serial (McAllister, 1991).

A reflection of all these changes is that men are starting to talk about their experiences. Resolve has published a *Collection on the Male Perspective*. Contributors (some have fertility problems, others not) set down their feelings about infertility and talk about what it feels like from the man's standpoint. Articles are appearing where men who have fertility problems are prepared to be identified and talk about their side of the story (Mason, 1990 and Barber, 1992).

Clearly the tide is turning. The purpose of this book is to explore and air men's experiences about their own infertility. It is important to say that I am highlighting a particular group. Men experience infertility even where their own fertility is not compromised. A man, for example, may be fertile yet unable to have children because his partner is infertile, but I am looking at those whose fertility is in jeopardy. Inevitably there are shared experiences between these two groups though I believe that men's experience of infertility may be significantly coloured by the fact of male infertility.

The spur for the book was my own personal experience, but the idea for it came from Pfeffer and Woollett's work exploring the infertility experience from the female perspective. Whilst recognising that men have strong feelings about their own fertility, Pfeffer and Woollett say they did not attempt to 'tap directly or systematically men's reactions to infertility'. They think they got an indirect sense of the male experience by talking informally to women and men (1983: 3). My purpose was to go directly to men with fertility problems to find out what they had to say in the belief that men need to share their experiences with others. If their voices are heard, men are less likely to be ignored.

LAYOUT

The rest of this part of the book looks in more detail at medical issues. Everybody I spoke to had been through some sort of medical experience. Though it is only one aspect of their stories, it was for most a vital one. I have therefore devoted space to sketching out what I think is the background to the present medical treatment of male infertility, then looking at current medical management. This overview should inform and make more sense of what men had to say.

Part two, the main section of the book, is given over to mapping out what men went through. I start by explaining how I contacted people, who they were and the purpose of our discussions. Medical experiences are then described followed by reactions to the diagnosis. The importance of fatherhood and ways to it come next with subsequent chapters on coping, support and resolution of infertility. The closing sections chart men's ideas about whether their experiences are different from women's and explores thoughts about the future.

THE AUDIENCE

Finally this book is written for those people whose lives have directly or indirectly been touched by male infertility, for those who work in the area and people interested in the subject. Though the stories come mainly from men living in Britain, I believe their experiences are not peculiar to this country and will be of interest to others elsewhere.

2   Setting the scene

This chapter explores the background to the medical management of male infertility, a subject that has attracted gloomy comment in the past. Stanway for example, says that for the most part it is 'still pretty much in the Dark Ages' (1986: 97).

More optimism is voiced when it comes to the treatment of female infertility. Far more research has been done into egg production in women in the quest for a contraceptive. The links between research into contraception and infertility emerged in Vaughan's book on the pill (1972), with the result that more became understood about how the hormones involved in egg production work. This led to the female contraceptive pill and to the use of fertility drugs for ovulatory problems in the 1960s. According to gynaecologist Dr Robert Winston,

> in 1961 Dr Greenblatt and his colleagues working in the United States produced an epoch-making study of the value of clomiphene for women who fail to ovulate. Since then this drug has been responsible for more pregnancies in infertile patients than probably any other treatment in the world.
>
> (1989: 136)

Then the world's first IVF baby was born in 1978. The technology which produced Louise Brown was developed to overcome blocked fallopian tubes in women and was hailed as a great step forward for women with tubal blockages.

Male reproduction in contrast has been far less researched and the result is a lack of effective treatment options for many men, and the absence of a male contraceptive pill. Before looking at what is now on offer, it makes sense to look at the past to see what light it can shed on the present treatment of male infertility.

THE PAST

There is an awareness nowadays that men as well as women can have fertility problems, though this has not always been the case. Pregnancy and childbirth have long been considered women's business and they are the ones who have been blamed when all has not gone according to plan. Women rather than men have been held responsible in the past for the failure to conceive and miscarriages.

Mosse and Heaton point out 'until relatively recently it was popularly assumed that all men were more or less fertile, that fertility problems were a woman's affair and that every man produced enough sperm in every ejaculation to populate the whole of North America' (1990: 9).

When male infertility has been considered, it is in the context of sexual impotency. It seems to have long been held that if the man is able to have sexual intercourse, then he is fertile, and children are seen as a sign of a man's virility. Once he has done his duty, the rest is up to the woman.

For example, in pre-industrial England, the woman was assumed to be barren if she had sex with a man but failed to become pregnant (McLaren, 1984). MacFarlane remarks that

in many societies each extra child adds to its parents' social prestige: infertility is a terrible curse, and a large and growing family a blessing. The virility of the man is shown through his many children and he gains esteem through each successive birth.

(1986: 59)

The view that it is only women who are responsible for infertility has held fast into the twentieth century. Hall reviewed letters written by men and women to Marie Stopes (the birth control pioneer) for advice in the 1920s and 1930s. Correspondents reported that doctors continued to regard sterility as the woman's fault (1991).

In part this assumption may be based on the idea that the male reproductive system is more simple and straightforward than the female one and therefore less likely to go wrong. This idea is analysed and found wanting by Pfeffer who comments that people think this because they know little about male reproduction (1985).

THE MAN'S ROLE IN CONCEPTION

Lack of understanding about male infertility is clearly linked to what is known about the man's role in conception. The exact nature of this was not understood for some time, and this was also true for the woman's part in conception. Ideas changed over the years about how life began.

Aristotle, for example, apparently thought that both men and women produced seeds though the male ones were superior (McLaren, 1984). In the Middle Ages conception was thought to be due to the mingling of seminal fluids. During the seventeenth century there was a researcher who thought conception could take place without a significant contribution from the male (Spark, 1988).

Coming nearer to the present day, Mosse and Heaton observe: 'Long before the nature of a woman's cycle was understood, the role of sperm in procreation had been recognised and coitus interruptus was practised to avoid unwanted offspring.' They continue, 'even before rudimentary barriers were playing their part in female contraception in the eighteenth and nineteenth centuries, there is good evidence that the birth-rate was beginning to fall; the best explanation is that coitus interruptus was becoming widespread'. They also point to condoms being used to prevent pregnancy by the beginning of the eighteenth century. These contraceptives had been used long before then, apparently dating back to early Egyptian civilisation, but the condom was used as a protection against sexually transmitted diseases rather than as a contraceptive device (1990: 197).

THE DISCOVERY OF SPERM

The realisation that condoms might have other purposes is surely linked to the discovery of sperm in semen. In the late seventeenth century, the microscope revealed for the first time what was contained in a man's semen.

The first description of sperm was given by the famous Dutch microscopist, Antonj van Leeuwenhoek, in a letter (Animacula in Semine) to the Royal Society of London in 1677. Leeuwenhoek credited a medical student Mr De Ham with the discovery and confirmed the findings with his own microscopic observations. His description of sperm was excellent comments Kempers. Leeuwenhoek noted that he had seen at least a million sperm after ejaculation. They had thin tails almost five or six times as long as the body and moved around like snakes or eels in water (1976).

This letter ushered in the modern era of physiology of reproduction in men, say Mann and Lutwak-Mann. They think Leeuwenhoek intuitively linked the man's fertilising ability with the existence of sperm in a letter published eight years later in 1685:

> Now, when a man is unable to beget children by his wife, although his virility is unimpaired he is said in common parlance to have a cold nature. To my mind, however, it would be more apt to say that no living animacules will be found in the seed of such a man, or that, should any

living animacules be found in it, they are too weakly to survive long enough in the womb.

(1981: 1)

But there was a lot of confusion about sperm. Though they had been discovered at that stage, their function and purpose had not, says Kempers. He explains that some microscopists in those days thought that each sperm contained a miniature human being which grew once the sperm entered into the female (1976).

Nearly a hundred years elapsed before more was understood about sperm. An Italian physiologist, Spallanzani performed some experiments which made him conclude that an egg needed seminal fluid from the male to fertilise it, but he thought it was the fluid rather than the sperm which fertilised the egg. Further developments occurred in 1824 when Prevost and Dumas showed that eggs were fertilised by small cells in the spermatic fluid (Kempers, 1976). About three years later, Albert Van Kolliker demonstrated that the sperm came from testicular cells as well as also showing that sperm fertilised eggs (Johnston, 1963).

MALE INFERTILITY

Some doctors were becoming aware in the latter half of the nineteenth century that men could have sperm problems. The post-coital test developed by Dr James Marion Sims was a way of checking to see if sperm were present in the woman's vagina after sexual intercourse. In 1868 Dr Sims addressed the New York County Medical Society on 'The Microscope as an Aid in the Diagnosis and Treatment of Sterility', advocating the need to check for sperm in semen. He complained, however, that people disliked and voiced opposition to his method of collecting semen samples from the woman's vagina (Johnston, 1963).

By the early part of the twentieth century, infertility specialists such as Reynolds and Macomber advised that both the man and the woman should be examined when infertility was suspected. The man's semen should be analysed under a microscope and a post-coital test be performed to see how sperm were surviving in the woman's vagina (1924).

Male infertility was increasingly recognised. Hammen noted in the 1940s that for the past thirty years increasing attention had been paid to men, but his review of various studies that looked at the extent of male infertility amongst couples with fertility problems was inconclusive. He found widely varying estimates of the problem ranging from 10 to 90 per cent (1944).

Much was still not known about sperm. For example, Hammen wrote that doctors had been unaware until recently of the injurious effects condoms could have on sperm health (1944). Producing a semen sample by masturbation was not acceptable in those days, hence the use of the rubber condom during intercourse to collect the sample though it could be contaminated by rubber (Spark, 1988).

Semen analysis

The quality of semen samples is currently judged by looking at certain criteria, a practice that seems to have started in the early part of this century. Spark refers to a *New England Journal of Medicine* article in 1929 which promoted the idea that a certain minimum number of sperm were needed for a man to be pronounced fertile (1988). Interest in sperm numbers continued and in 1951 one study compared the sperm counts of 1,000 fertile and 1,000 infertile couples. Of the latter group, 16 per cent had counts below 20 million sperm per millilitre (ml.) as opposed to 5 per cent for the first group. The research however, did not establish a clear dividing line between fertility and infertility as many men who were fathers had counts of less than 20 million (Barker, 1986).

Hotchkiss, an American urologist who had a keen interest in male infertility, rejected the notion that some minimum number of sperm were needed to pronounce a man fertile and said there was no evidence for such a level. What he drew attention to was the couple's joint fertility, the implication being that the more fertile the woman the less sperm would be needed to get her pregnant (1945).

Sperm shape was another criterion used. It was not realised until the end of the nineteenth century that shape could vary enormously from man to man and in each ejaculate (Hammen, 1944).

Animal studies had led to improved understanding of sperm (Reynolds and Macomber, 1924). Spark, for example, says animal work established the need to distinguish between abnormal- and normal-shaped sperm. Bulls with bad breeding records had an average of 50 per cent abnormal sperm shapes while those with good ones had less than 17 per cent. In 1931 the concept of good or bad sperm shape was applied to men by one researcher. The conclusion was that abnormal shapes should not exceed 20 per cent. Researchers were also becoming aware of the importance of looking at sperm movement, but more importantly were arguing that criteria such as semen volume, sperm numbers and their movement and shape, should all be used together to assess sperm quality (1988).

OTHER DEVELOPMENTS

There were additional developments in the 1940s. Hotchkiss referred to a new exciting branch of science which was in a state of flux but which might eventually suggest treatment options for male infertility. He was talking about the hormonal system involved in male reproduction.

Meanwhile he estimated that husbands were responsible for one third to one half of barren marriages. The problem was being recognised, as in 1932 a male sterility clinic, a novel proposal, was started by the then head of the urological out-patient department at New York Hospital. Hotchkiss complained that it had taken a half century for Dr Sims's teachings about the need to check for sperm in semen to be generally accepted. The fallacy that ability to have sex was proof of fertility had held sway for a long time, but the urologist was now confident that the husband was involved in medical investigations (1945).

In Britain, similar statements were being made about male infertility. Various specialists wrote a book about the sorts of fertility problems dealt with by general-practice doctors. They said that in the past the husband's role had been ignored, but noted that in a sixth of cases he was so infertile as to make conception unlikely and that in two-thirds of cases his condition played a significant part in childlessness. The authors advised that the man should be physically examined and a semen sample taken (Jackson *et al.*, 1948).

Interestingly a note in the book's appendix said that when the Family Planning Association started to offer infertility services to the public, there were insufficient competent seminologists around to examine samples. So a specialist laboratory was set up in central London in 1945.

Yet the second world war and the baby boom after it obscured the advances that had been made in the area of male infertility. The scope and extent of involuntary childlessness and the part played by male infertility in this, was not appreciated in those years (Spark, 1988).

Further developments in identifying the different parts of the sperm did not happen until the 1950s and the introduction of the commercial electron microscope. Writing in the 1970s, Kempers concluded that despite the power of modern microscopes, much was still to be discovered about 'this complex cell' and 'many intriguing problems remain concerning the development of this cell' (1976: 1).

Some years on, certain doctors and researchers are confident that further progress has been made. Work was done in the 1960s on the metabolism and biochemical characteristics of sperm. Also, the broad principles of hormonal control involved in sperm creation had been known for the last 50 years with particular advances in the last 25. Despite all this they reflect that research into male fertility lags significantly behind that into female fertility, and safe control of testicular function is a long way off (Glover *et al.*, 1990).

CONCLUSION

What I think stands out from this brief excursion into the past is how much things have not changed since the 1940s. Then as now there was an awareness that male infertility had to be addressed, yet I was struck by how the comments made by doctors and researchers during the first half of this century are still being made today. For example, one book then stated that many of the factors responsible for male infertility were unknown and a full investigation of a young healthy man might well fail to show why he had a fertility problem (Jackson *et al.*, 1948).

Many doctors today make similar comments and also say that until recently men have often been ignored in infertility investigations. Winston writes that in many infertility clinics the woman is often seen by herself and 'she alone is examined' (1989: 94).

Hotchkiss seems to have been over-optimistic back in the 1940s when he wrote that men are now generally included in medical checks. He also wondered then why 'the man has remained curiously apart from any blame', deciding that ignorance was not the only reason for apathy. He wondered why knowledge gained from animal breeding had not been applied earlier to men and concluded that the reason for lack of interest in male infertility was more likely to do with prejudice, referring to the abuse met by Dr Sims to prove his point (1945: 1).

Hotchkiss definitely touched on one cultural reason why male infertility has remained a neglected subject. There has been no such distaste when it comes to women and they have been legitimate objects of study particularly when it comes to matters of contraception. Such research has resulted in spin-offs for female infertility treatments as discussed, but only about 8 per cent of the world's contraceptive budget is spent on the development of male methods of fertility control (Mosse and Heaton, 1990). The lack of research has backfired on men but things will become better, remarks Stanway, when a male contraceptive 'becomes more possible and acceptable' (1986: 97). The reverse point is made by the Congress of the US, Office of Technology Assessment. Advances in understanding male infertility will also contribute to the development of male contraceptives (1988c). Basically the lack of a male contraceptive pill in the 1990s reflects the fact that much is still not understood about male reproduction.

Undoubtedly a complex interplay of cultural, social and historical factors must have contributed to the neglect of the man. It is not the main purpose of this book to focus on these issues, only to note that they exist and have affected the present medical management of male infertility.

3 Definitions and detection

How is male infertility defined, who treats it, how commonplace is it and how is it detected? The following provides a checklist of key concepts and maps out the current position on detection issues. Such issues inevitably lead to the question of causation which is explored in the next chapter.

DEFINING MALE FERTILITY

This is no easy task. Overall several things must be accomplished and a broad definition would take in the following. The man must be able to produce enough mature good-quality sperm, have an erection, enter the woman and successfully deposit sperm inside her vagina.

Yet today descriptions of male infertility centre round sperm problems. This is in sharp contrast to the past when male infertility was generally thought to mean impotence. Perhaps in reaction to this confusion, some current definitions seem to totally exclude sexual problems though these may affect the man's chances of becoming a father.

Modern definitions probably also discount sexual causes because the main cause of male infertility concerns sperm quality. Sperm have to pass through several hurdles to fertilise the egg. Once in the vagina they must be able to swim progressively forward, go through various changes and be able to penetrate the outer shell of the egg (Hudson *et al.*, 1987). Defective sperm may be able to fertilise an egg, resulting in miscarriage, a possibility recognised by doctors some years ago (Jackson *et al.*, 1948). More recently, Hull and Glazener wondered whether such sperm might be responsible for early loss of the embryo (1984).

There is no absolute definition of fertility, and there are levels of fertility. A man, for example, may have poor-quality semen but eventually succeed in fathering a child. However, his fertility is of a different order to that of the donor whose sperm must be capable of producing several babies (Glover *et al.*, 1990). Fertility may also change over time, for example because of age or infection, factors looked at in the next chapter.

Terms used in investigations

If a man is told he is sterile, this means he is totally unable to have a child. This is an uncommon diagnosis and far more usual is a diagnosis of infertility. The word infertility is used in several ways and is a vague inexact term, as is the word fertility. A couple may be told there is an infertility problem if they have tried unsuccessfully for a child for over a year. A man who is told he is infertile may be able to father a child, but it could take him a long time to do this and he may need medical help to achieve this.

Sperm descriptions

Various terms are used to describe the state of the sperm after they have been examined under a microscope. The most common ones are azoospermia, meaning absence of sperm in semen; oligospermia, reduction in ejaculate volume; oligozoospermia, reduced sperm numbers; asthenozoospermia, sperm movement problems; teratozoospermia, increased number of abnormal-shaped sperm. Oligoteratoasthenozoospermia is the unmanageable term for semen samples where there are a mix of problems, i.e. low sperm numbers, poor movement and abnormal shapes (Jequier and Crich, 1986). Throughout the rest of the book I generally refer to sperm problems or no sperm, rather than use any of these cumbersome words. They seem vague and inexact and appear to mean different things to different people, probably reflecting the confusion that surrounds questions of sperm fertility as examined later on.

Extent and type of male infertility

Infertility is now thought to be shared equally between the man and the woman. Most people would not quibble with Mosse and Heaton when they say that for 35 per cent of couples attending infertility clinics there is a male problem, and for 35 per cent a female problem. Twenty per cent have joint problems with no cause being found in the remaining ones (1990).

Sperm problems are thought to be the main cause for concern. One study reported that sperm defects are the major type of male problem and also the leading cause of infertility (Hull *et al.*, 1985). Likewise, Leese says that 90 per cent of male infertility is due to various sperm problems and that only 5 per cent of men have no sperm (1988). Winston says 70 per cent of problems are due to low sperm counts (1989), and Lilford and Dalton report that low sperm counts are the commonest cause of infertility in Europe (1987). An American study reports that most male infertility cases are due to abnormal or too few sperm (Congress of the US, Office of Technology Assessment, 1988c).

Doctors who investigate male infertility

Gynaecologists have for a long time dealt with male infertility. Historically this seems to have grown out of the fact that infertility was normally attributed to the woman so services were dominated by these female specialists. Reynolds and Macomber remarked in the 1920s that despite the recognition of increased frequency of male infertility, gynaecologists were still dealing with men (1924).

Nowadays men may be referred to urologists. These doctors deal with genito-urinary problems and started to get involved in male infertility because they were used to dealing with the male sex organs, according to Stanway. But he says that the urinary and reproductive systems though closely linked are separate (1986). Consequently there has been growing interest in developing a speciality which is primarily concerned with male reproduction.

Andrology, the study of man, is a relatively new science (Glover *et al.*, 1990). The term was first coined by a gynaecologist called Siebke in 1951 to indicate that men played as important a part as women in reproduction (Schirren, 1985). Andrology according to Kelami deals with fertility and sterility as well as sexual function and dysfunction in men (1992). Andrology is a recognised speciality in the United States. In Australia it seems to be recognised as a legitimate area to work in but has not been formally recognised by the medical establishment and this picture also applies to Britain. In 1981 the International Society of Andrology was formed to encourage interest in andrology throughout the world.

Other specialists such as physiologists and pharmacologists are interested in the area now (Spark, 1988), as are embryologists because of their experience of seeing how sperm fertilise eggs during the IVF process.

Sperm production

Before going on to diagnostic tests, it is useful to sum up what is known about sperm production. The testicles have thousands of microscopic tubes inside them in which the sperm grow. These tubes are connected to others which then lead to one single tube, the epididymis, which is about forty feet long (Winston, 1989). The epididymis acts like a maturing chamber and this has been known since 1900 (Hotchkiss, 1945). When sperm enter the epididymis they are immature, do not move and are incapable of fertilising an egg. The sperm then undergo certain changes which bring them to maturity, but it is not clear how this all happens, which constitutes a major gap in understanding male fertility. In all, sperm manufacture takes about seventy-two days (Hudson *et al.*, 1987).

Once through the epididymis, sperm move on through the vas deferens. During orgasm this tube contracts taking the sperm into the urethra and into the outside world during ejaculation – the connection between the urethra and the bladder is closed off. A man's ejaculate may have several hundred million sperm in it, but no more than a few hundred or perhaps thousand will make it to the woman's egg.

Other considerations

The sperm have to become capacitated before fertilisation can happen (Fraser, 1992). Certain changes occur to the sperm. Fluids in the woman's uterus wipe a layer of proteins off the sperm heads. After capacitation a bag of enzymes on the sperm's head called the acrosome bursts (the acrosome reaction). The enzymes eat their way through the outer shell of the egg allowing the sperm through this barrier. Sperm also move in a whiplash way which is supposed to help them penetrate the egg's outer shell.

DETECTION

Semen analysis

This test is still done today despite many concerns about its effectiveness. The method used is basically the same as in 1929 when it was first applied to human semen (Glover *et al.*, 1990). It is the most popular measure of sperm fertility.

The analysis provides descriptive information about the semen and specifically the sperm. The volume of the ejaculate is measured, sperm numbers per ml. and for the whole ejaculate are noted and quality of sperm movement and shape assessed. Jequier and Crich say the man may find it stressful producing a sample because of possible feelings of inadequacy. They advise that he should be given relaxing surroundings in which to produce the sample because semen produced in a stressful situation may be of worse quality. Three samples should be taken because sperm quality can be so variable and the man should not ejaculate for two to three days before giving the sample (1986).

The purpose of the test is to give some idea of the man's level of fertility.

Only if there are no sperm or moving ones is it clear that the man will not father a child (Hudson *et al.*, 1987).

There is no absolute agreement currently about what constitutes a normal sample. Various guidelines are looked at, a practice as seen that goes back to the early part of this century. These markers have always been subject to change and there are variations in what is considered normal. In 1960 Hamblen said the volume should be 4 ml. with at least eighty per cent moving sperm. Eighty per cent should be normally shaped and there should be 40 million to 100 million sperm per ml.

More recently Barker advises that normal semen volume should be between 2 and 6 ml. There should be a minimum of 20 million sperm per ml. of which 40 per cent should be moving with less than 30 per cent abnormal shapes (1986). Neuberg agrees pretty much with this but says there should be 30 million per ml. sperm and 60 per cent should have progressive forward movement within one hour of production (1991).

The importance of sperm movement and the type of movement is vital though it is difficult to assess this objectively. Values from one to four can be given to describe movement quality (Hudson *et al.*, 1987). The idea that sperm have to swim up the vagina and onwards to the egg is outmoded. Healthy sperm swim round in circles and depend on other forces to move them in the right direction (Austin, 1976). They do have to get through the cervix on their own but once through are transported by the uterine muscles (Glover *et al.*, 1990).

Shape is a vexed issue. A basic description of a normal sperm is of an oval head, mid piece and a single tail piece, but sperm shape is subject to great variation in men and it is unusual to see samples which contain more than 70 per cent of the normal oval forms (Hudson *et al.*, 1987). Round-headed sperm often without the acrosome are apparently common in poor-quality semen samples (Glover *et al.*, 1990).

Is male fertility declining?

Sperm counts have been seen as an important indicator of male fertility and some writers have speculated that sperm numbers are declining resulting in lowered fertility. Bellina and Wilson refer to studies which found much lower sperm counts amongst men awaiting vasectomies in the 1970s compared to levels established in the 1950s. Stress, overcrowding and environmental pollution may account for the decline (1986).

Spark also considers the issue. Eighty to 100 million sperm per ml. was considered normal in the 1950s whereas counts of 20 to 60 million are now acceptable. Research gives contradictory results as to whether counts are falling, but he refers to a 1980 study which looked at the counts of 10,876 men in various studies. The overall result was a decline in numbers even allowing for factors such as different counting techniques. The downward trend does not however, seem to have resulted in an alteration of male reproductive capability (1988). Meanwhile a more recent review concludes that sperm counts in healthy men appear to have fallen by more than half between 1940 and 1990 (Connor, 1992). The British Poet Laureate Ted Hughes, was so concerned about the report that he mentioned it in a poem (*The Times*, 9 April 1992).

Thoughts about quantity

Basically the importance of the sperm count is unclear. It is not clear why men produce huge numbers of sperm and there is speculation about possible reasons for this phenomenon. Perhaps it ensures excellence; only the best sperm will be able to struggle past their fellows to the egg. Perhaps more sperm means that more women can be impregnated. The answer is not known and this is all conjecture.

Some biologists wonder whether there could be another explanation for the huge numbers. Their ideas come from looking at reproduction in other animals where several males mate with one female over a short period of time. Rather than looki. at sperm as simple cells designed just for conception, sperm may have different functions. Abnormally shaped ones may be designed to prevent sperm from other ejaculates reaching the egg as sperm link together to form a barrier barring the way to competitors' sperm. Some sperm may also have a mission to seek out and destroy sperm from other ejaculates (Small, 1991).

Currently there is scant evidence to support these theories in terms of human reproduction. The idea still most favoured is that large numbers are needed because so many sperm perish on the way to the egg. The more there are the higher the chances of fertilisation in what is at best a risky business.

Quality not quantity

Yet if this is so why can some men with few sperm father children whereas others with large counts cannot (Pfeffer and Woollett, 1983)?

One possible reason is that it is quality rather than quantity that counts, an idea that was aired in the 1940s (Jackson *et al.*, 1948). More recently, Winston says that if the sperm are normal but the count is low, the outlook is good (1989). Neuberg elaborates on this emphasising that quality is almost more important than count. It would be preferable to have a 15 million per ml. count with 75 per cent of sperm having good progressive movement with few abnormal shapes as opposed to a 200 million per ml. count where only a few were normally shaped and most were not moving. The man will get his partner pregnant faster, the more good-quality sperm he has (1991).

There is another confusion. It is not clear how often men have low, good-quality sperm counts for when the count is low, sperm may also have movement and shape problems. But sperm movement which is the single most important indicator of sperm quality could be a compensatory factor in men with consistently low counts (Hudson *et al.*, 1987).

A further indication that count is not everything is suggested by Wardle, as treatment that boosts sperm numbers is not necessarily linked to an increased chance of conception (1990).

A glimpse at this debate illustrates just how fraught the issues are and demonstrates how little is known about sperm. Just what constitutes quality and what part sperm count plays in that concept is currently unclear.

Critique of semen analysis

How useful is the test as a diagnostic tool given such reservations? If it is to mean anything at all it needs to be performed by laboratories with expertise in semen analysis (Hudson *et al.*, 1987). Seminological work needs to be of a high standard and some say the test has been maligned precisely because it is the cinderella service in many pathology laboratories. Staff may not understand the physiology of seminal fluid and so end up giving wrong information to doctors (Jequier and Crich, 1986). There is another worry. A report saying 90 per cent of sperm are normal is suspect because the laboratory's microscopic facilities are probably deficient and unable to pick up deformities (Gregson, 1988).

In the 1970s, Eliasson also questioned whether a man's fertility could be evaluated on the basis of semen analysis. He said that most studies of semen samples had come from highly select groups such as men from barren marriages and those wanting vasectomies (1976). The inference is that far more information is needed about fertility in the general male population. (It is not clear that this information has been forthcoming in the intervening years.)

More recently Welford reports that some experts say the test is almost meaningless although most evaluations are based on it (1990). Researchers illustrate the predicament by saying that 3 per cent of fertile men have poor results whilst 25 per cent of infertile men have normal results (Aitken *et al.*, 1984).

Another difficulty is that the results are still for the most part based on subjective assessment. There are some developments which make objective assessment possible. There is an American computer that can analyse more than thirty subtle but crucial aspects of sperm movement (Welford, 1990), and a computer monitor originally developed for traffic control is being used to assess sperm movement (Mihill, 1991).

Generally results are still based on subjective evaluation. This is a real problem. For example, one research scientist said 'studies show that the same sample, given to different technicians, can produce a range of results of between 10 million and 120 million per ml.' (Welford, 1990). Interpretation of sperm shape similarly can vary. Forty-seven experts assessed 500 sperm but had differing opinions on half of the specimens (Barker, 1986).

The conclusion seems to be that there is no such thing as a normal sample only a range of normal semen values. Measures may be so misleading that a man with apparently normal semen may prove to be infertile (Pfeffer and Quick, 1988). A minimum of 20 million per ml. is the level often used to define a normal count, but one study found that 20 per cent of fertile men having vasectomies had counts of between 10 and 20 million. Another study showed that there were fourteen pregnancies in twenty-seven couples where the man had a count of less than 10 million per ml. Likewise the importance of sperm shape is not clear-cut; some researchers think 50 to 60 per cent abnormal-shaped sperm is not a problem whereas others do (Spark, 1988).

The mistake is to think that the test results yield anything more than descriptive information about the semen. The basic question is whether the test can measure the fertilising ability of sperm. Yet sperm have to be able to perform several functions to achieve fertilisation and the semen analysis does not measure whether sperm can perform these functions. The result is that it is impossible to be certain that an apparently normal sample is fertile (Hudson *et al.*, 1987). Further tests for instance revealed that two thirds of 137 men with normal test results had sperm unable to penetrate an egg (Sandmaier, 1991).

It is unclear how useful and what value should be placed on test results and there is no unanimous agreement on the exact way in which numbers, movement and shape should be judged. Apart from this, subjective assessment of samples means different technicians may well give differing results. The test can therefore yield little prognostic information according to Hargreave and Nillson (1983).

The semen analysis will also not answer why there seems to be an abnormality. About 75 per cent of men described as infertile have semen abnormalities, but no cause can be found for this (Hudson *et al.*, 1987).

Sperm function tests

The major advance in clinical assessment of the man has been the recognition that other tests are needed. Semen analysis on its own cannot predict male fertility because it fails to define the characteristics linked to fertilising ability

(Wardle, 1990). The functional approach dates back to the post-coital test developed by Sims in the nineteenth century. This test checks whether sperm survive after sexual intercourse in the woman's cervical mucus, but the test has fallen into disfavour in some clinics. Couples may find it distasteful and again results depend on criteria used. The test only shows that sperm can survive and move in cervical mucus and does not specifically measure other sperm functions. The wrong conclusions may be drawn when no sperm are found as they may have already moved upwards into the fallopian tubes (Spark, 1988).

The separate cervical mucus penetration test is more favoured. Developed in 1932 (Spark, 1988) and referred to in the 1950s (Schellen, 1957) many doctors think it is a good indicator of sperm fertility and say it should always be done as there may be a link between sperm transport and fertilising ability (Hull and Glazener, 1984). If sperm fail to penetrate fertile cervical mucus, a more sophisticated cross-over test can be done with donor sperm and mucus to determine whether it is the sperm or mucus that is the problem.

There are also other types of sperm penetration tests. Some infertility specialists believe ability to penetrate a hamster egg is predictive of fertilising ability. Others think that ability to penetrate a dead human egg is of more use.

The swim-up test is also a helpful measure of sperm fertility according to Winston. The semen is placed in special fluids to see how many sperm can swim properly. The normal ones separate from abnormal sperm giving an idea of sperm fertility (1989).

The acrosome reaction described at the beginning of the chapter is an essential prerequisite to fertilisation. There is a test which can measure whether sperm are able to do this (Mason, 1990).

At the moment there is no one definitive test of sperm fertility and some feel that functional tests have not lived up to their promise (Balerna and Piffaretti-Yanez, 1992). Specialists also seem to have preferences based on their own experiences and despite testing samples in a number of ways, one embryologist comments that fertilisation can fail at the IVF stage despite seemingly normal semen and sperm quality (Keith, 1991). Currently the ultimate test is to see how sperm perform during IVF.

Other checks

This is not an exhaustive list. I have listed those ones men most commonly come across. Doctors will talk to the man about his past to see if any reasons can be found for problems. The importance of physical examination has been stressed by doctors for many years (Reynolds and Macomber, 1924) through to the present. Emotional and sexual problems should also be checked out (Stanway, 1986).

Blood tests can reveal whether the man has any hormonal problems though these are rare according to Winston (1989). The measurement of follicle-stimulating hormone (FSH) can aid diagnosis because it gives information about the state of the man's sperm manufacturing ability. High FSH levels suggest this ability is severely damaged. Normal levels with very low sperm output would indicate the sperm are stuck inside the testicles because of a blockage inside them (Barker, 1986). Blood tests can also show whether the man has an acute infection which is damaging sperm and also whether he has sperm antibodies.

Testicular biopsy used to be done to find out what was happening to the sperm-making equipment in the testicles, but it is being increasingly replaced by the blood test. The biopsy should be reserved for men whose blood tests suggest a blockage in the ducts (Hudson *et al.*, 1987) though others may want a biopsy to confirm that they have little chance of becoming fathers.

The couple

Doctors have for a long time (Reynolds and Macomber, 1924) advised that couples should be jointly assessed. One partner, for example, may be far more fertile than the other. A man may not be that fertile but if his partner is very fertile, producing good eggs regularly, conception may result, but if she has fertility problems this is less likely (Bellina and Wilson, 1986).

DISCUSSION

Determining whether a man has a fertility problem, why he has one and what the implications are for his fertility is complicated. What comes across from this brief overview of diagnostic methods is that there is no way of knowing whether sperm are fertile or not. The semen analysis was based on the belief that there was a link between certain sperm characteristics and sperm fertility. Yet it is not certain what these sperm characteristics should be and too little is known about the fertility of men in the population at large. The result is that the measures used in semen analysis may be inappropriate because they have not been derived from statistically sound studies. The test has come in for heavy criticism and in a review of how to select men with the best fertility as sperm donors, researchers say that 'the relationship of traditional semen parameters to fertility is at best very poor' (Barratt *et al.*, 1990: 378).

Sperm thought to be normal may fail to fertilise eggs during IVF and vice versa. The test is also not done in a uniform way with two clinics judging the same sample differently. Obviously the test may be useful if results show over a period of time that the man has no sperm in his semen and blood tests suggest that his sperm manufacturing ability has been badly damaged. More commonly however, sperm are produced and the difficulty is then knowing how to interpret test results.

The problem still seems to be the same as the one identified some years back when a biochemist said 'it is obvious that there are enormous problems in the assessment of semen. We do not really know what a "normal" sperm looks like, and if we do not know what it looks like, how are we to look for it?' (Short, 1976: 161). Time and again there are references to definition problems being a major difficulty.

Hence the focus on sperm function tests. The cervical mucus test is a good predictor of fertility according to some doctors but there is no unanimous agreement that this is the best fertility indicator and other doctors favour other tests.

IVF has given more information about what is happening during fertilisation in the laboratory setting and allowed embryologists insights into questions of sperm fertility. Some have said to me that there is no adequate test of fertility other than seeing how sperm perform during IVF. One clinic sometimes uses natural-cycle IVF (where no drugs are used to collect eggs) as a way of seeing whether sperm can fertilise the egg (*Issue*, 1991b). IVF experience has highlighted the difficulties linked to a diagnosis of sperm fertility. Why do some normal sperm samples fail to fertilise the egg whereas poorer ones confound expectations by doing the opposite?

Ultimately the debate hinges round definitions of sperm fertility. Sperm have to be able to do several things in order to fertilise an egg depending on where they set out from. In unaided normal sexual intercourse, they have to get through various barriers in order to meet up with the egg. In addition, once the sperm is through the outer shell of the egg a variety of other tasks face it. As one embryologist explained to me, the whole process of fertilisation is extremely complex and the sperm have various hurdles to overcome. Exactly what the obstacles are and what abilities are needed to overcome them is uncertain. Sperm, for example, must become capacitated and go through the acrosome reaction, but there is still a lot more about the equation that needs to be known.

A plea for more fundamental research is made by some specialists. Further progress will only be made in understanding what is going wrong when it is realised that more research is needed into understanding male reproductive physiology (Cooke, 1988). Pfeffer also questions whether there is an inherent contradiction between defining sperm as independent individual actors and the 'sheer numbers of sperm found in many different shapes and sizes in a single ejaculate'. She says that the focus on individual sperm has led to the belief that minimum numbers are needed for fertilisation and meant that investigations into the molecular properties of sperm have been ignored (1985: 39).

Meanwhile, detection of sperm infertility increasingly centres round issues of quality not quantity, but the riddle of sperm fertility remains because it is not clear what quality means.

4 Causes and treatments

Why do problems occur and what treatments can men expect? The two questions are inextricably intertwined.

CAUSES

Certain consequences stem from the lack of research into sperm cell biology. The last chapter explored the problems of defining sperm fertility and the uncertainties surrounding the various diagnostic tests. Threaded into this picture is the fact that not a lot is known about why men have problems. The information provided by the semen analysis may be misunderstood. One research scientist explains for example, that the term oligozoospermia provides a description not a diagnosis. Far more basic research is needed into how sperm are produced in the testicles and sperm cell biology. Only then will it be possible to understand what is going wrong. Once this is known, therapies can be directed at specific defects (Mason, 1990).

Similarly sperm function test results do not fully reveal why there is a problem, though the findings may suggest ways round it (Sandmaier, 1991). It is not clear for example, why sperm fail to go through the acrosome reaction or become capacitated. To say that the cause of infertility has been found in such cases would be rash. More research is needed to get to the root of the problem.

Meanwhile it is not unusual to find gloomy comments made about why there are problems. Witness the comments made by doctors in the 1940s when they said that full investigation of a young healthy man would often fail to show why he was either sterile or infertile (Jackson *et al.*, 1948).

Some forty years on and the same thing is still being said. One report states it is difficult to prevent infertility because 'factors that contribute to abnormal or too few sperm, for example, are largely unknown' (Congress of the US, Office of Technology Assessment, 1988c: 4). Winston says that for those with low sperm counts 'most of the time the real cause cannot be established with any certainty' (1989: 97). Wardle continues in this vein saying that the majority of cases of male infertility are unexplained (1990), and finding a cause for defective sperm production is the exception rather than the rule (Hargreave, 1983).

However, Jequier takes a more optimistic view though she ends on a tentative note. She thinks that generally the cause of the problem can be diagnosed fairly easily even though there may be no treatment for some causes (1986).

Despite the general air of uncertainty, the reasons for some sperm transport and production problems are known.

Sexuality

Sexual causes play a part in male infertility though it is easy to forget them because they do not play a major role. There is also the temptation to sidestep discussion of them because of the possible embarrassment this may cause men. Impotence has for a long time been thought to be the only cause of male infertility and indeed has been thought to mean male infertility. Doctors are anxious to say the two are unrelated. Stanway says most impotent men are fertile (1986), and Winston comments 'there is no connection and a man's potency is in no way related to his ability to produce sperm' (1989: 95).

Though doctors rightly point out this confusion, sexuality and fertility are linked. A broad definition of male fertility includes sperm production, sperm quality and transport mechanisms. Men must be potent to impregnate their partners, and an absence of sexual activity may indirectly impair sperm production. MacLeod and Gold reported that longer periods of sexual inactivity led to a smaller number of active sperm (1952). Abstinence is therefore unlikely to enhance sperm quality because sperm movement is probably improved by more frequent ejaculation (Kaufman, 1969). 'Sexual activity gives a boost to testosterone levels, and hence to sperm production and maturation' explains Gregson (1988: 1266).

In the 1970s, urologists Dubin and Amelar said that the role of sexuality in human fertility was obvious but all too often overlooked by doctors. They reported that about 5 per cent of men with normal semen results had sexual problems. These ranged from impotence and lack of desire to premature or no ejaculation (1972). More recently, Bellina and Wilson say that impotence is normally transient in young men. If more prolonged the problem is usually psychological. Real impotence can start after the age of 50 and may be due to either psychological or biological reasons (1986).

Impotence can be caused by conditions such as diabetes or certain drugs and there may be problems of blood supply to the penis. A report on a French centre dealing with impotence estimated that it affects one in ten Frenchmen between the ages of 38 and 65 and that there is a physical cause for half of them (Gillie, 1986).

Psychological factors affect potency. Anxiety about a range of things such as work pressures can produce temporary impotence, and the stress of infertility investigations can result in passing impotence (Berger, 1980). Spark puts problems of sexual dysfunction between 9 to 18 per cent of fertile men (1988); 5 per cent is the figure quoted by Stanway (1986); less than 1 per cent by Winston (1989).

Ejaculation problems

Some men do not ejaculate properly. Retrograde ejaculation means that sperm end up in the man's bladder. The sign of this is that there is no ejaculate or very low semen volume with no sperm in it (Smolev and Forrest, 1984). There is also a rare anatomical condition known as hypospadias which means that sperm are not deposited in the woman's vagina.

Missing parts and blocks

A few men men have no vas deferens. Blockages inside the man's reproductive equipment can also cause problems. Normal sperm may be produced but are locked inside the ductal system in the testicles. A normal FSH level would indicate this was happening. Men can be born with blocks in parts of the ducts or these can occur as the result of infection (Stanway, 1986).

How common are these obstructions? They are rare, says Wardle (1990). Others say less than 10 per cent of men have them (Bellina and Wilson, 1986). Jequier, however, thinks that obstructive lesions are a common cause of infertility. A complete obstruction will mean no sperm can escape, but some may get out of the testicle if there is an incomplete obstruction (1986).

Vasectomies

Increasing numbers of men are having the vas deferens blocked off as a means of birth control. Vasectomies are becoming popular and Hodgkinson reports that 90,000 men a year are having the operation (1991) or one in 1,000 (Mosse and Heaton, 1990).

It is estimated that about 1,000 men a year will want the operation reversed and their fertility restored to them but that only about 40 per cent will achieve this (Bishop, 1991). A broader figure is given by Mosse and Heaton who say 35 to 91 per cent of men will regain sperm in their ejaculate (1990). The main reason for lack of successful reversals however, is that men start producing sperm antibodies after vasectomy. They impair sperm quality by affecting movement keeping the man infertile. Post-vasectomy infertility is becoming an increasing clinical problem according to Jequier. More men want reversal operations but the outlook is poor if the operation is done five years or more after the vasectomy (1986).

Other reasons

The testicles may fail to produce sperm because they have been damaged. An acute mumps infection for example, can harm sperm production, or a testicle may become twisted, damaging blood supply.

Hormonal disturbance accounts for about 15 per cent of male problems (Bellina and Wilson, 1986). A mix of hormones are involved in male reproduction. The pituitary gland is the body's hormonal control centre. It produces follicle-stimulating hormone (FSH) and luteinizing hormone (LH) which stimulate the testicles, which in turn produce testosterone. Any disturbance in these hormonal systems may cause problems.

Undescended testicles result in infertility. The testicles may fail to descend into the boy's scrotum after birth and so not develop properly. Higher abdominal temperatures seem to damage testicles with the result that no sperm may be produced or only small amounts. Apparently there is a well established link between male infertility and abnormality of testicular descent. In one study about 6 per cent of men had this problem (Hudson *et al.*, 1987) and a recent report mentioned a fourfold increase in cases (Connor, 1992).

Sperm antibodies also appear in men who have not had vasectomies. Affected sperm clump together and cannot move freely so affecting their fertilising ability. Estimates for numbers of men who have antibodies are low, around 6 per cent (Hudson *et al.*, 1987) and 8 per cent (Lilford and Dalton, 1987).

Speculation about causes

The main problem is that no cause can often be found for the majority of men who produce what is thought of as poor-quality sperm. This is also true sometimes for those who produce no sperm.

Are there psychological factors which affect male fertility? Could some men subconsciously be blocking their fertility? Abse referred to research which suggested a decline in sperm quality when the man was feeling anxious or guilty (1966). Basically this is an unresearched area. Little study has been done of men (the opposite is true for women) according to Christie and Pawson, but they refer to research which reported that sperm production stopped in men facing the death sentence. There is also evidence to show that semen quality is reduced in response to the stress of infertility investigations (1987).

Genetic factors may account for some types of male infertility. One press report said that a mutated gene might be responsible for lack of sperm production in some men (McKie, 1991).

Of course a cause may not be found if the man is not properly checked out. Yet causes may not be found even when all possible checks are done, or some factor may be wrongly seized on as the answer to the problem.

There is conjecture about the extent to which certain factors harm sperm quality. Infections may affect sperm production. They can produce inflammation which can result in scarring and consequent blockages in the ductal system. Sperm quality may also be affected by infection of the man's genital tract (Smolev and Forrest, 1984), but it is unclear whether non-specific bacterial infections in the genital tract do affect semen quality. Others conclude that this type of infection is not an important or common cause of male infertility (Hudson *et al.*, 1987).

Enlarged veins around the testicles called varicoceles are thought to result in sperm problems in a significant number of men. The theory is that warm blood pooling in these veins causes the testicles to overheat.

One article stated that varicoceles account for 35 per cent of male infertility making this the commonest reason for it (Conkling, 1991). Others are less certain. Apparently these veins were thought to be possible culprits back in 1952. According to Bellina and Wilson, elation greeted the discovery that a possible cause for male infertility had been found, but they say it is not clear what role, if any, varicoceles play. Though 35 per cent of infertile men have them, fertile men also have them (1986). The extent of varicoceles in fertile men is unknown but is probably not uncommon. A number of studies were reviewed by Hudson *et al.*, and they concluded 'we doubt the place of treating varicoceles in infertile men' (1987: 122). Similarly Jequier thinks that their role in infertility is uncertain (1986).

Age is an obvious factor in female fertility, but it may also play a part in male fertility in a number of ways. Hotchkiss referred to a study that found a significant relationship between stillbirth rate and the age of the father, but he said there was no sharp decline in reproductive capacity with age in men as there was in women (1945). Lately one doctor is reported as saying that though the influence of maternal age on birth defects is much greater, there is also evidence that the father's age can contribute to genetic diseases (Holder, 1992). More specifically, Winston says that as a man gets older there is a tendency for sperm quality to decline (1989).

Free radicals may also damage sperm. These oxygen molecules produced throughout the body by various cells may damage sperm. It seems they make the outer membrane of the sperm more rigid which makes fusion with the egg more difficult. Forty per cent of men with sperm problems may be affected by this phenomenon (Mason, 1990).

A variety of lifestyle and environmental factors can affect sperm production, but there is conflicting evidence about how important they are and exactly how they are implicated in male infertility. Some people may be more susceptible to some factors than others and Hotchkiss commented over forty years ago that the testicles are delicate mirrors of the individual's health. He speculated that highly robust people might be unaffected by factors such as stress, while others were (1945).

Mention of stress has cropped up in books and articles over the years as it has been blamed for reducing sperm quality. Reynolds and Macomber talked about the stress of modern life, and said that rest and country life could do wonders by improving the man's health and so his fertility (1924).

Why should stress affect sperm quality? It seems that anxiety may lessen the output of hormones produced by the vital pituitary gland, with sperm quality being affected. Jequier agrees that emotional and physical stress may affect fertility and points to changes in testosterone production in men undergoing physical training. She also comments that infertility can result in stress (1986).

Poor nutrition may also be implicated. Reynolds and Macomber (1924) said that diet should include all the necessary vitamins and proteins, a point also made by Hotchkiss (1945). Stanway says an adequate diet is essential for sperm formation but it is not known yet at what level of malnutrition sperm production ceases. Studies in this area have been poor and are difficult to assess according to him (1986).

Certain substances may cause mutation or genetic change in sperm cells and sperm defects may result in miscarriage rather than lack of fertilisation. This idea was talked about over sixty years ago. The father's genetic condition at the time of conception was at least as important to the developing baby as the mother's condition (Reynolds and Macomber, 1924). But Hotchkiss felt more evidence was needed to confirm the theory of male responsibility (1945). Currently the issue has been highlighted because of research which suggests sperm could be affected by radiation and so affect the health of future children (Gardner *et al.*, 1990). Other researchers believe abnormal sperm can cause miscarriage, reports Lazarides (1992).

Sperm production can be affected by a high alcohol intake. Heavy drinking can lead to men complaining of loss of libido and potency and they may develop shrinking of the testicles. About 40 per cent of sixty-seven patients were believed to have a problem related to alcohol with sperm problems improving once they gave up alcohol (Moncur, 1987). Excessive alcohol intake may result in reduced testosterone leading to impotence and sperm production failure.

Smoking is also thought by some to be linked to sperm problems. There was less sperm movement amongst heavy smokers than non-smokers in one study, but no statistical link was found between sperm numbers and smoking. The researchers wondered whether nicotine increases sperm movement initially, but then leads to a rapid decrease in it (Saaranen *et al.*, 1987). Jequier, however, says there is no real evidence to show that cigarette smoking is harmful to fertility (1986) whilst Winston says there can be no doubt smoking is bad (1989).

Other factors which may affect sperm production include obesity, certain medicinal drugs, marijuana and exposure to hazardous substances. This is by no means an exhaustive list and there are varying views as to the importance of each factor.

TREATMENTS

Most of them tend to be of a non-specific nature because it is unclear what is causing the problem, but there are ones designed for some problems. Sperm antibodies for example, can be treated by vigorously washing the sperm in a centrifuge to try and remove the antibodies. Alternatively cortisone may reduce antibody levels though doctors worry about the side effects associated with the drug (Mason, 1990).

It is clear what should be done about undescended testicles. They must be brought down into the scrotum as soon as possible once the child is old enough to withstand surgery safely. Hormonal treatments are sometimes used to bring the testicles down.

Blocks in the man's ductal system may be cleared through surgery though there can be doubt about which patients will best be helped by surgery and which techniques will result in enough viable sperm (Hudson *et al.*, 1987).

Another approach is to remove sperm from the epididymis. The man has to have a general anaesthetic and undergo surgery for this to be done. The sperm that are collected are immature and have to be put through various sperm preparation methods to mature them. They are then placed with the eggs in the IVF process to see if fertilisation happens. The birth of twins born as a result of this technique was reported by Ballantyne (1991).

Those doctors who are persuaded that varicoceles are the culprits, treat them by various methods and varying success rates are claimed for doing so.

There is no clinical data yet on the treatment of free radicals, but it makes sense according to one researcher to take vitamins E and C in order to prevent and limit damage done by the molecules (Mason, 1990).

Non-specific treatments

Because it is often not clear whether a man has a problem, why he has one, and what the implications are for his fertility, treatments tend to be vague and unspecific. Many are based on ideas about general sperm health. Mostly they are of unproven value at the moment and have not been evaluated in large-scale research trials.

Smolev and Forrest say that men whose infertility is of unknown origin represent the greatest challenge for effective treatment. Non-specific hormonal therapy may be used and sperm washed in various substances to improve movement (1984).

There is an air of scepticism about how helpful hormonal treatments are if there is no obvious hormonal problem. Pituitary hormones may be given in an attempt to improve sperm production. But the comment about this and other hormonal treatments is that they generally result only in greater sperm numbers not better sperm function.

New approaches are often in the news and are greeted with optimism. For example, a press item reported that a researcher had found that the amounts of the enzyme protein kinase C in sperm affects its movement and ability to enter the egg. Different levels of the protein had been found in human semen and by increasing its performance with drugs sperm function was improved (*The Times*, Update, 12 September 1991).

Lifestyle changes

This is a contentious area. General health measures are of value according to Gregson. Her comments are similar to those made by Hotchkiss in the 1940s. Sperm production is very sensitive to lifestyle and many men of marginal fertility can be helped by making some changes to their life (1988).

Yet the exact impact of environmental factors on male fertility is a subject of much debate and uncertainty. How critical such factors are to each man is unclear, but often where a man is thought to have sperm problems, he will be advised to stop smoking and drinking alcohol, wear baggy pants and avoid hot baths.

Though it is unclear how effective such measures are, they are advocated as part of a self-help programme. One report claims that about one in five men can reverse their infertility by making changes such as cutting down on alcohol and illicit drug use and losing weight. Obesity causes fertility problems because the testicles become encased in fatty tissue which increases testicular temperature, so affecting sperm production (*USA Today*, 1991).

Doctors vary in how effective they think particular measures are. Winston for example, thinks there is no proof that wearing baggy pants and bathing the testicles in cold water will help, but he concludes that there is no harm in wearing loose-fitting pants and avoiding very hot baths (1989). Neuberg, however, refers to 'one little gem of a treatment that I have found can produce significant benefit in about 50 per cent of the men who try it. It is called cold water treatment'. He advises men to spray the scrotum for two minutes morning and evening with cool water (1991: 133).

The conclusion to be drawn about non-specific treatments is that some doctors dismiss them as unproven whilst others advocate them because they seem to work for some of their patients. Hargreave says there is no evidence to suggest that general measures, such as wearing loose underwear, cutting drinking and so on, are of any use (1983). Taking vitamin C, operating on varicoceles and avoiding hot baths are unproven measures (Lilford and Dalton, 1987), but Spark says that vitamin C may improve sperm transport and that zinc may help in some way (1988). Basically the picture is confusing and uncertain.

Alternatives

Alternative therapies are being used by some men. For example, a letter in an infertility newsletter referred to Chinese medicine and its application to male infertility (*Issue*, 1989/1990). A holistic remedy may be sought because so little else seems to be on offer. Approaches that deal with lifestyle factors can seem attractive because the man may feel he has some control over his fertility.

Assisted conception techniques

Other treatments are based on the idea of helping the sperm (helping-hands approach) on their journey towards the egg. Artificial insemination of the husband's sperm (AIH) into the cervix or uterus has been used over the years but is dismissed as ineffective (Lilford and Dalton, 1987). It may be of use in a few cases of sexual or anatomical difficulty though it cannot help defective sperm to function (Gregson, 1988). Stanway refers to a 1976 study which found that when the method was used for 158 couples, only around one in ten women became pregnant (1986). Yovich and Matson however, say that it can be of use for those with low sperm counts provided there are no movement problems because sperm movement plays a vital part in ensuring successful fertilisation (1988). Basically AIH may be of value only where sperm quality seems reasonable.

The helping-hands approach has been developed further. Gamete intra-fallopian transfer (GIFT) has been used increasingly for the treatment of male infertility. In GIFT eggs taken from the woman's ovaries are mixed with the man's sperm and then replaced back in her fallopian tube before fertilisation occurs. Winston says GIFT is widely used for male infertility because the sperm can be placed next to the egg hopefully increasing the chances of fertilisation (1989). When GIFT is used it is not, however, possible to see whether fertilisation has happened. This is the reason why the Interim Licensing Authority (British) recommended that IVF rather than GIFT be used where there was a known sperm problem (1991).

IVF was originally developed to help women with blocked fallopian tubes become pregnant. Eggs are collected from the woman and placed with sperm in a dish in the laboratory. If any eggs are fertilised, then the developing embryos are placed back inside the woman's uterus. Increasingly IVF is being used to get round sperm problems. When used for men with problems, there was a 34 per cent success rate in achieving pregnancies in forty-one couples (Prentice, 1984).

There are various concerns about the use of IVF for sperm problems. It is an invasive procedure in the sense that the woman is normally given drugs to boost egg production. An instrument is inserted into her body to harvest the eggs and she can find the whole experience uncomfortable and painful. IVF success rates are also lower when the man has sperm problems. A recent report which claims higher success rates for IVF says these are achieved by excluding men with sperm dysfunction. Success rates are much lower in such cases (Hull *et al.*, 1992).

Others have attempted to determine fertilisation rates with different semen qualities. They report rates falling from 80 to 60 per cent where the man has one abnormality such as low sperm movement. If there are combined problems of numbers, movement and shape the rate falls to 10 per cent or less. They comment that though numbers are small, pregnancy rates following transfer of the embryo back to the woman's uterus are the same as for couples where semen quality is normal (Hudson *et al.*, 1987). Schirren, however, thinks that there is a higher rate of embryos failing to implant in the uterus when poor-quality sperm is used (1985).

Proponents of IVF argue that it can work provided sperm are carefully assessed beforehand. Sperm quality can be improved by selecting out the best sperm from the ejaculate by using various sperm preparation techniques (Mason, 1990). IVF also offers researchers the chance to find out more about human reproduction (Congress of the US, Office of Technology Assessment, 1988c) and as discussed under the detection section, it can be used as a direct test of sperm fertilising ability.

Various observations are made about the usefulness of IVF by Wardle. The procedure is attractive because relatively small numbers of sperm are needed as opposed to natural conception. Reasonable success rates have been claimed when it is used for male infertility as defined by semen analysis, but he says that fertilisation and pregnancy rates are disappointingly low when male infertility has been defined by sperm function tests. Still, he thinks it may offer an improvement on the chances of conception where the man has sperm problems and points to its diagnostic use as a function test particularly for men whose semen analysis results are normal (1990).

The debate about how successful IVF is for male infertility again turns on definitions of sperm fertility. Successes may be claimed where there is no major sperm problem, so confusing the picture. When sperm dysfunction is defined by failure to penetrate cervical mucus, there was a 17 per cent pregnancy rate per IVF cycle. This is much lower than the rate for normal sperm though it seems to be an improvement on past rates with defective sperm because of better sperm preparation techniques (Hull *et al.*, 1992).

Other modifications have been added to IVF when it is used for sperm problems to try and improve success rates. Claims are made that a drug designed to treat circulation difficulties, may improve sperm function. A news report said pentoxifylline makes sperm release enzymes which helps them penetrate the egg and the first British pregnancy was announced when sperm treated with pentoxifylline were placed with eggs in the IVF process (Kingman, 1991).

Yovich refers to his Australian research where five out of nine women became pregnant when sperm were treated with the drug. Previously fertilisation had not happened. In a larger study of 101 couples, IVF fertilisation rates improved for both severe and mild sperm problems. The drug acts in three ways. Movement is increased, in some cases the numbers of sperm that go through the acrosome reaction increases and the drug may suppress the formation of free radicals. It might also be of use in AIH (Yovich, 1991).

Others are cautious about the possible benefits of pentoxifylline. Further research and larger controlled studies are needed to show the increased pregnancy rate did not just occur by chance. Walker comments 'it may be that pentoxifylline will be a major contribution to reproductive medicine but at the moment the best that can be said of it is that it shows some promise which has yet to be realised' (1990: 18).

Micromanipulation during IVF is an extension of the helping-hands approach that justifies the use of IVF for sperm problems. Over 100 babies have been born worldwide using microsurgical techniques (Alikani and Cohen, 1992).

Holes are made in the egg's outer shell by various means such as drilling or cutting. The egg is then placed in amongst the sperm in the hope that some will move through these holes in the shell and that one will end up fertilising the egg. Various claims made for micromanipulation are qualified. For example, slitting the egg's shell can result in improved fertilisation rates but it seems sperm must be normally shaped (Simon *et al.*, 1991).

These methods mean that the sperm must be able to move reasonably well to get through the holes in the egg's shell. Sub-zonal insemination is a technique that has been developed for sperm unable to do this. One or several sperm are inserted through the shell into the space between it and the body of the egg. In an Italian study, nine out of 225 patients became pregnant resulting in twelve healthy babies (Mason, 1991).

There are reservations about micromanipulation. Neuberg says the news of such techniques will bring hope to men with sperm problems, but he warns that the techniques have a very low success rate, are expensive and sperm may be given an undesirable advantage (1991).

The Interim Licensing Authority (British) felt further research was needed to find out more about the best insemination procedure to use and which categories of male infertility would most benefit from micromanipulation. So far there is no evidence of a higher level of chromosomal abnormalities than in normal IVF (1991). The American government report wonders whether legal and ethical concerns will ultimately limit the use of certain micromanipulation techniques because of the possibility of selecting out one sperm (Congress of the US, Office of Technology Assessment, 1988: c).

Other researchers feel that micromanipulation is of use because there is so little else on offer (Mason, 1991), but one embryologist said to me that there might be no need for it if sperm preparation procedures were improved in ordinary IVF.

Donor insemination (DI)

DI has increasingly been used as a way of resolving male infertility. The woman is inseminated with sperm donated by another man. Artificial insemination has been practised for hundreds of years. It may have been used by Arabs for horse breeding in the fourteenth century and Spallanzani used it in the late eighteenth century to inseminate a dog (Austin, 1976). DI seems to have been first applied to people in the nineteenth century and was introduced into clinical practice as an infertility treatment in England in the late 1930s (Pfeffer, 1987).

It is 'undoubtedly one of the major treatments for male infertility', there were over 30,000 DI births in America in 1987 (Barratt *et al.*, 1990: 375) and demand for it is likely to increase (Hull *et al.*, 1985).

Others refer to it not as a treatment but a solution to the perplexing problem of male infertility. It is an alternative not a treatment (Winston, 1989) and bypasses the problem but may be the only way a couple can have a family (Wardle, 1990).

DISCUSSION

The increasing use of DI highlights the lack of effective treatments for many men. Reading books and articles on male infertility is a depressing business. Time and again there is reference to all the problems outlined. Various doctors say there is generally no effective treatment. Even excluding patients who produce no sperm, the chance of natural conception is about 20 per cent over two years. This is not improved by AIH and hopes about the usefulness of IVF have proved unfounded (Hull *et al.*, 1985) though the doctors seem a bit more hopeful in a later report (Hull *et al.*, 1992). Doctors may not want to work in the area. One report quoted a specialist as saying that male infertility was not a glamorous field and was one linked with failure (Prentice, 1984) and Barker observes that doctors may be discouraged from getting involved in it because it is under-researched (1986).

Many of the statements made by doctors many years ago still ring true today. The growing use of DI and the application of IVF and associated developments to male infertility show that not much has changed in some senses. Sperm problems are essentially bypassed rather than directly treated (though it could be argued that sperm preparation techniques constitute a treatment).

Other treatments are generally thought to be ineffective and have not been properly evaluated. In a discussion about the treatment of men with low sperm counts some years back, a urologist said that there had been very few good research trials into treatment regimes. He concluded that many apparently successful treatments were little better than placebos – dummy pills, when properly evaluated (Royal College of Obstetricians and Gynaecologists, 1976). It is unclear whether there have been substantial improvements in evaluation techniques since those remarks were made.

Lack of rigorous research is one of the main reasons why treatments are of a hit and miss nature. Lilford and Dalton conclude 'further improvements in managing male infertility will therefore depend on a deeper understanding of chromosome function and gene transcription in normal and defective sperm' (1987: 156).

The fact that there is no male contraceptive pill is also evidence of the lack of understanding about male reproductive physiology. Pfeffer argues that the lack of a non-mechanical means of controlling male fertility demonstrates the ignorance surrounding male reproduction (1985). There is a relationship between contraceptive and infertility research as previously discussed. The link was highlighted in the news item about the mutated gene which might be responsible for lack of sperm production. This discovery could result in a male contraceptive pill as well as a male infertility treatment according to the report (McKie, 1991).

The consequences of neglecting male reproduction have resulted in treatments designed largely to get round sperm problems. Both doctors and infertile couples are to blame for this, according to some. Heavy pressure from them has meant attention has been paid to searching for a cure rather than the cause of infertility (Balerna and Piffaretti-Yanez, 1992).

Treatments have concentrated on the woman rather than the man and she may end up going through what can be a traumatic experience as discussed. Such treatments are more often than not in the private sector, and are expensive. Having more treatment approaches to choose from may increase stress for some couples, according to one infertility counsellor (Ballantyne, 1991).

Despite the gloom, there may be some developments which are of use. More research has yet to be done into the role of free radicals and their effect on sperm health, but that may prove to be a way forward. Taking sperm out of the epididymis and maturing them, is another interesting development. Despite the reservations about IVF and micromanipulation, these techniques may help some men to become fathers, though it is not obvious which men might most benefit from them. One urologist said to me, it is unclear whether these methods will help those couples who might have conceived on their own eventually by bringing that date forward, or whether they can help men who might never have become fathers in the normal way.

Until more is known about whether there really is a problem and why there is one, treatments will be of limited value. As to the future, Barker comments 'it is difficult to contemplate that major advances in the treatment of male infertility will be made until after many fundamental questions about the subject have been answered more fully'. He continues by saying that manipulating the man's hormones in a random way meets with the success that any arbitrary form of treatment can achieve and says more understanding is needed about the underlying problems which need correction (1986: 69). This understanding concerns knowing more about the hormonal control of the developing sperm cell, more about the hormones produced by the testicles and how they interact with the pituitary ones. Until this happens, the clinical management of male infertility will remain in its present unsatisfactory state (Wu, 1983).

What can men hope for currently? Wardle says the best that can be offered is 'as reliable a definition of their degree of sperm dysfunction as current methods allow, and an attempt to give some estimate of their chance of conception'. The solution may turn out to be DI for many couples (1990: 130).

Part II

5   Discussions

Men's experiences are described in this part of the book. But how did I go about contacting willing interviewees, who were they and what were the issues I encountered during this stage of my research?

Early on I suspected that each man's story would be distinctive and would depend on a number of factors. In a fact sheet that I handed out to those interested in my project I explained:

> Each man's experience will be special, shaped by a wide range of issues, e.g. what his problem is thought to be; whether his partner is also infertile; what types of tests and treatments he may have been through; how medical staff have treated him; what it means for him if he is unable to have his own children; how his relationship with his partner has been affected. These are just a few of the issues that may be relevant.

I wanted to explore with men in an open way what they had been through and give them the opportunity to talk about their experiences in their own words.

My task was to search out people who were prepared to share their thoughts in detail with me. This was the main guideline I used. I was not seeking people at a specific stage of infertility, those with certain fertility problems or those who had opted for a particular solution.

THE SEARCH

Advertisements were placed in various British publications such as *Issue*, magazine of Issue, the national fertility association, *Childchat*, magazine of Child, another self-help group and 'Parent to Parent Information on Adoption Services' bulletin. Several infertility counsellors and clinics said they would distribute details about my research to their clients. A note was also put in the briefing section of the *Guardian* newspaper's Women's page. Men do read it and I hoped also that women might pass details to their partners. An advertisement was placed in *New Statesman & Society* which has a large male readership. Various friends and contacts passed the fact sheet to potential interviewees.

A niggling worry was at the back of my mind during this stage. How many men would contact me? Infertility and specifically male infertility are delicate, almost taboo subjects. General reactions to my research were mixed amongst friends and acquaintances. One person asked how I could write such a book since the subject merited only a few words. Some were undoubtedly embarrassed and I felt uncomfortable talking about the book. It was a subject to be passed over quickly in hushed silence. When people asked why I was doing the book I explained that I had a personal motive for doing so because of my partner's infertility. A couple of people intimated that the book must be very embarrassing for him and that I should have kept quiet about the subject.

One American study was not encouraging about the response I would get. MacNab reported the difficulties he had in trying to contact men for his study on men and infertility. He distributed 500 questionnaires through various networks but only fifteen completed ones were returned. He says his experience bears out the view that men are not keen to talk about infertility. Those who ended up taking part in the study came not from infertility clinics but from friends of friends. MacNab said that men feel unable to talk about the topic because of the pain it causes them (1984).

Apart from MacNab's account, I had received conflicting messages from all sorts of people involved in infertility about whether I would get a response. A few said I would have no problems, but the main message was that men would not contact me. One researcher pointed out that those who did speak to me would be highly unusual, in no way representative of the general population of men with fertility problems. Doctors told me stories about men who would only visit the clinic after dark or would not admit to any problem despite overwhelming evidence to the contrary.

MAKING CONTACT

In the end I talked to twenty-two men. Most of them approached me having seen articles in the self-help publications. Two men responded to the *Guardian* note about my research and one person got in touch after his counsellor gave him my fact sheet. It is worth also pointing out that at the end of each discussion I would ask the man whether he knew of others with fertility problems who might be interested in my project. Many said either that they had no close male friends or that they did not know if their friends had similar problems. One man, however, did have a friend in the same situation who contacted me.

This is in marked contrast to Pfeffer and Woollett's experience of contacting potential interviewees. They say that women put them in touch with other women (1983). Most of those I spoke to had not talked that much about their infertility to anyone else, an issue which emerges through the following pages.

INTERVIEW CONCERNS

I wanted discussions to take place in a setting in which interviewees felt comfortable. The last thing I wanted was for men to end up feeling threatened and, so, defensive. I was all too well aware this was a very sensitive and potentially difficult area for men to talk about. They are brought up to be strong, tough and emotionally unexpressive according to Rappaport. Discussions about sexuality or contraception can be very difficult for them he says. He talks about using special interview techniques when talking to men about family planning matters and infertility. These are designed to try and ensure that the man does not put up barriers which prevent him from exploring his needs and feelings. The techniques may sound manipulative but:

> the outpouring of feelings and emotions that frequently follows the use of this strategy is quite remarkable. Instead of the standard 'OK' or 'everything is fine' response, the men start talking about their nightmares about lost children, the sounds of 'little feet' in their daydreams, their fears that they will never be able to have children, their doubts about their partner's feelings toward them, and so on.
>
> (1984: 257)

The fear that men might become defensive followed me through the interviews. I tried not to appear threatening in any way and to be a neutral figure during conversations. I explained that men were making a positive contribution by sharing their experiences with me which I hoped reassured them. Inevitably I am sure that at times the process was intimidating despite my efforts to make sure it was not. I also stressed that identities would not be revealed in the book and this was very important to several people. Names used in later pages are pseudonyms.

There were other doubts. I wondered whether men would be more or less frank with me because I was a woman. Would they be more open about their feelings with a man and particularly one who had experience of male infertility? But I came across reassuring comments during preliminary reading. Hite for example, remarks of her own research that there was some controversy about a woman conducting a study into male sexuality, but she notes that one person said he had only answered her questionnaire because a woman was asking the questions. Later on she says that men commented that they found it easier to talk about their feelings to women rather than men (1981).

Men may be more guarded with their own sex because they find it difficult to admit problems to them, so they may well want to confide in a woman rather than a man (Heppner and Gonzales, 1987). As it turned out I felt my worry was unjustified though of course this is a subjective view. One interviewee emphasised that he had only agreed to talk to me because I was a woman.

THE SETTING

Discussions generally took place in the man's home which is probably where he felt most comfortable and secure. One person however, chose to write to me and another did so out of necessity. There were two phone interviews for reasons of convenience. Discussions were not rigidly structured as I envisaged an open interview which would be of mutual benefit. I was not looking for responses that could be standardised and had prepared an Issues Guide, a loose set of points which we talked around. The hope was that each man would feel able to talk about what was most important to him and not feel constrained by the Guide. But to an extent I clearly set the agenda for interviews with the Guide and this is mostly what was used (one person, however, said he would have preferred a more structured questionnaire).

There was another concern I agonised over for a period of time. During preliminary discussions, several men asked whether their partners should be involved in discussions. I felt uneasy about this because I thought the woman might dominate the discussion, being probably more used to talking about infertility. My main aim was to hear what the man had to say and I feared that his voice would be drowned by the woman's and that he would let his partner talk for him. In fact, this happened in a research study about new fathers. Women sat in on interviews though it had been made clear to them that interviews were with and about the father. Only one woman voluntarily withdrew:

> The rest, certainly to begin with, still reacted as if we were inquiring about motherhood, and it was not unusual for some of the women to answer the questions directed at the man, even to the extent of explaining what he felt. The man normally accepted this, and might act only as a spectator at his own interview. Later, when he did speak more fully, one sometimes felt the opposite dilemma: it was as if one was recording something very private.
>
> (Jackson, 1984: 6)

In the end most of my discussions were just with men, though one woman ended up getting involved in an interview because there was nowhere else for her to go in a tiny flat. In another session, the man and woman had agreed in advance that she would sit in on the discussion, observing it and making the occasional comment about her partner's experience. Another person said it was important that he talk to me without his wife so that he could have a chance of expressing his feelings and one man said he felt uncomfortable not having his wife with him.

However, I did want to speak to a few women in the belief that their thoughts might indirectly throw light on the male experience. Ultimately comments came across in those interviews in which women took part for one reason or another. I also had conversations with both the man and the woman in a couple of cases after I had talked to the man on his own and it was agreed that one woman talk to me on her own after her husband had finished speaking to me.

NATURE OF STUDY

The men make up a very special group. The one factor they have in common was their willingness to share their experiences with me in some detail. They were not reluctant interviewees and had reflected on their experiences and had opinions about what they had been through. So I spoke to a tiny number of self-selected men. The group was therefore highly biassed, but I was not attempting to draw statistical conclusions about the general population of infertile men from a representative sample. My main aim was to give men a chance to voice their own experiences, then to examine these and see what insights could be gained from them and whether there were any common strands in the various stories.

A SNAPSHOT OF THE MEN

What characteristics did interviewees have? I have selected out ones which I feel are relevant to this book's purpose. Firstly, all of them had known for at least two years that they had some sort of fertility problem. Possibly those at an earlier stage may find the whole business too painful to explore or may not have accepted the diagnosis and so not want to be tarred with the infertility brush. One urologist who spoke to MacNab explained that the shock of an infertility diagnosis was devastating for the men he dealt with. They were unable to make sense of it or talk early on about what it meant for them (1984).

Most were in their thirties though seven of them were in their forties. What sort of fertility problems did they have? They were not always certain about this, and were hazy about the exact details, all points discussed later on in the book. Still, it is possible to paint a rough picture. Ten had been told they had sperm problems and eleven that they produced no sperm. One man seemed to have normal semen, but had sexual problems. Many did not know why they had fertility problems, a point noted in part one of the book. Causes are often not found for male infertility.

Over half of them produced no sperm whereas statistics suggest this is a less common problem than I encountered.

I also checked whether the man's partner had fertility problems. There was no clear picture on this, according to most of those I spoke to. Four men said their partners had some sort of problem, but it was unclear for the others what the position was. No problems might have been found with the woman because she had not been extensively tested. Some reported their partners to be fertile whereas others wondered whether the woman might be found to have problems on further investigation.

What stage were interviewees at when I talked to them? One man's wife had become pregnant in the normal way just before our discussion. Four women had given birth to a child after donor sperm was used. Two women were trying to get pregnant by this method and two were pregnant. Four couples had adopted children, (two had done so at the start of the 1980s) and one was in the process of trying to do so. Five couples were still going through investigations and treatment. Women were mostly the focus of medical checks and several were going through various assisted conception techniques. Finally three couples were uncertain what to do. They did not have children, and were no longer undergoing medical checks or treatments. They were undecided about the future though one couple was probably going to accept a life without children.

The rest of this part of the book sets out what men talked to me about. The first part of each chapter is largely devoted to the men's voices. Then there is a discussion section in each chapter where I look at experiences and add in other information, comment and research which I think will help the reader understand more about the male experience. I continue to use the expressions 'sperm problems' and 'no sperm' to refer to diagnoses. They are vague inexact terms but the formal ones seem no better.

6 Coping with the medical experience

How did men deal with medical checks and tests? Often the woman rather than the man was the focus of investigations. How did men react to this? The medical management of male infertility forms the backdrop to what follows.

INITIATING MEDICAL CHECKS

Women tended to be the ones who started the ball rolling:

> My wife got things moving though I was a willing accomplice. She knew more about the health service so I left it to her. I had work worries and tended to expect that she would sort everything out, but I don't remember doing this consciously. I think it was grossly unfair for her to have to do this but that's what happened.

Bruce was the exception:

> I got things moving and went to see my doctor. I was more worried about the possibility of one of us being infertile probably because I tend to be more anxious by nature than she is. But I knew my anxiety could make matters worse and I wanted to get everything sorted out and not let things drift.

THOUGHTS ABOUT THE INVESTIGATIONS

Generally men did not talk in that much detail about tests and treatments. All of them for example, had given at least one semen sample, but mostly they did not say what they felt about the experience. Snippets of information were gleaned from a few people. One man who had been through a long period of impotence and lack of sexual desire said he had not managed to give a sample on one occasion. 'I told him I just couldn't manage it, especially with the little bottle. The doctor seemed rather disappointed in me even though he knew all about my problems.' Simon explained in more detail what he had been through:

> I had to give the first sample in the hospital toilet. After that I used to masturbate at home with my partner's help and then take the sample in. The hospital seemed surprised at us doing it this way. A special room with girlie magazines was provided at another clinic we then went to. I was always given clear instructions about how to give the sample though the bottles seemed a very odd shape to start with.

However, Andrew felt:

> The receptacle wasn't user-friendly. No instructions were given to me about giving the sample. I was just handed a bottle and a form. That was it. I used to worry that my sample would be overlooked and left lying around in the laboratory for days.

Trying to improve his sperm for various samples was important for Mike:

> I had been told that my sperm were pretty awful. The doctors said produce your specimen and we'll do what we can with it, so I tried to do my best to make sure the quality was as good as possible. I wouldn't ejaculate for several days before a sample was needed but I also made sure I masturbated regularly apart from those times to try and improve quality because we weren't making love that often.

Some men had been physically examined but again most did not dwell on this aspect of medical checks. Jeffrey, however, referred during our conversation to feelings of inadequacy after his testicles had been examined:

> The urologist said they were a bit small and soft. He said this in a detached sort of way, but he didn't realise how his words affected me. I had already taken a knock finding out I had no sperm, and then he said this. I was in my mid twenties at the time and he made me feel very inadequate. I was embarrassed about them. I suppose it's like a woman being told she has small breasts. Ten years on and I still feel bad about what he said and I quite often go to my doctor to try and get reassurance that I'm not abnormal.

Time had changed one person's attitude. 'I'd have been too embarrassed a few years ago to let a doctor examine my penis and testicles but now I think he should know what he is doing, after all he is a doctor.'

Fear of blood and needles affected Kevin. 'I felt funny about it all and giving the blood sample was a bit of a problem for me. There was no way I could have a biopsy done, in fact just talking about it made me faint.' Others were not frightened by operations. Ian was keen to have a biopsy. 'The urologist didn't seem to think there was much point in having one, but for me it was really important to find out why I had no sperm.' Peter had willingly had a varicocele operated on in the hope that his sperm quality would improve.

On the other hand, someone else remarked how little he had been involved in tests. 'I had several semen samples done and a couple of blood tests, but that was it. I was never physically examined and to be honest the doctors didn't seem that interested in me.'

Matthew had been told about a technique that might help him but discounted it:

> I'm producing no sperm in my semen because some tubes in my testicles are missing. The doctor said it was now possible to take the sperm from the epididymis, but I decided against the operation because the technique is still at an experimental stage. And it costs £5,000 a go.

THE STRESS OF INVESTIGATIONS

It was traumatic producing samples to order. 'Having to perform on certain days and have sex to order was difficult.' There was also another worry:

> I found it a strain having to give samples; it was very difficult producing one at home then having to get to the hospital within the hour. I also thought that my sperm must be suffering as a result of the stress. I felt I was getting poor test results because I was so agitated rather than anything else.

PRACTICAL DIFFICULTIES

A couple of men raised this though most were silent on the subject. Simon explained he had had no difficulties getting tests done when he had been unemployed. 'Since I've started working, I've had to take time off. This hasn't proved to be a problem in practice so far but I don't know whether there might be problems in the future.' Peter said he couldn't get time off from work to discuss his sperm problems and the treatments he had received. His wife went to the doctor on his behalf to discuss the outlook.

CONFUSION

There was talk of uncertainty and confusion about what was happening. For example, 'I didn't understand what my test results meant and I'm still not sure whether all of them have been totally negative or whether one or two of them showed up a few sperm'. Varying test results and concern about what had caused his infertility worried Simon:

> There was some question about whether a drug I had taken previously could have affected my fertility. Also the doctor said I had a slight varicocele. I tried to understand what was going on, but even though I have a scientific background, I found it difficult to get the right information and what the urologist told me didn't make sense. I wish my wife had been at that appointment with me so we could have puzzled it out between the two of us.

A similar thought was voiced:

> I couldn't understand the science of it. It was important for me to have as many checks as possible to find out why I had no sperm. Then I had to have all the tests repeated again at another centre I went to. That was difficult. I remember feeling very anxious because my appointment to see a specialist was pulled forward. I thought perhaps something sinister had been found in my blood test. But it turned out there were no problems, the centre was just trying to make amends for messing up a previous appointment.

TAKING CONTROL

John coped with his investigations by making a list of things that needed to be done:

> Not knowing why I had virtually no sperm was frustrating. I had to find out as much as I could, so we made a list of things that had to be done and ticked them off as we went through them. That narrowed down the options. It's like a maze you have to find your way through. I think deep down I knew I was the problem when the results of the first sample came back, but we had to see if there were other difficulties. We're lucky that we are an articulate and well-informed couple and determined and single-minded. For me my infertility became a project to be solved as quickly as possible and I was fortunate because I have medical insurance so I saw a private specialist early on.

Another man put it this way:

> I coped with it all by going from hospital to hospital for tests. I went through them all because I needed to know what was wrong with me. My priority was to get a proper diagnosis and get my wife pregnant somehow.

GUILT AND ISOLATION

Comments were also made about having to cope with uncomfortable feelings at times during investigations. Two men talked of guilt at not being able to give up smoking and drinking. They blamed themselves to an extent for their sperm problems. Mention of isolation cropped up in many interviews. 'I remember lurching from one option to the next, not knowing what to do and feeling there was nobody I could turn to about the tests.' Andrew remarked:

Because of my medical background I suppose I found it perhaps easier to cope with the various tests, but on reflection, it was tough even for me. I was given no support and had to work out for myself what the test results meant and what the outlook was for me.

COPING WITH THE WOMAN'S TREATMENT

There were mixed feelings about the tests and treatments that women underwent. Some of them had already been through IVF as a way of getting round sperm problems and other couples were contemplating this possibility. Several women had to have a small operation done to check their fallopian tubes were open before donor sperm were used.

Guilt was commonly experienced even if the couple ended up having joint infertility problems. Roger explained that because he had no sperm his wife had been through several DI attempts. These had been unsuccessful and eventually IVF with donor sperm had been tried. An ectopic pregnancy resulted and one of her fallopian tubes had to be removed:

I felt upset about my wife having to go through all this treatment which was inflicted on her. I couldn't do anything to help but somehow I had to cope with feelings of inadequacy on my part. The ectopic pregnancy alarmed and shocked me, I was desperately worried because of the threat to my wife's life. All through the tests and treatments, there had been ups and downs when she didn't get pregnant and I used to feel a sense of loss every time her period came round. Everything was much worse when she had to have the operation to remove her tube because of the pregnancy. We had come so close, but it still wasn't enough and my wife might have died.

Others spoke of feeling marginalised and uncertain about what role they should play during treatments:

My wife started off the investigations because she was more concerned about having a family than me. To start with she saw an incredibly unhelpful hospital doctor. That incensed me. Then I had some tests done and my sperm problems were confirmed. I felt helpless. Initially my sperm were used in several GIFT and IVF attempts, then the hospital started using donor sperm as well as mine during the procedures.

Nothing happened and I found it increasingly difficult coping with her feelings. Each month she approached her period with a sense of dread and anticipation and then crushing disappointment followed. GIFT was particularly painful for her and she hated having an anaesthetic. I just felt powerless through all this. In the end she got pregnant but lost the baby, yet somehow something had changed for her and she knew she could do it. She became pregnant again and gave birth to a healthy baby.

There can be a practical role to play but this can be traumatic:

My wife has been through IVF so that my sperm might have a chance of getting her pregnant. I had to give her injections for IVF and hated doing this because I knew they were painful and that I was hurting someone I love very deeply. I didn't find it easy having to coldly pick up the syringe and inject her. My wife has a medical background so she used to make the injection up and then suffer as I tried to inject it.

The whole business was incredibly difficult for me. I was anxious and frustrated about it but I felt I couldn't talk to her about my fears. She had enough to cope with. In the end things got so desperate that I had to talk to a very helpful female friend of hers. Basically I felt bad because my wife was having to go through all these indignities due to me.

Everything came to a head over the injections. It was like a volcano erupting and all the pain about my infertility came pouring out. Now I've got over the worst of it. After all, it's better for me to give her the injections sensitively because I have seen the insensitive way that some hospital staff give them.

Trying to cope with all the medical procedures has been very difficult. On one occasion I was so anxious that I masturbated to relieve the tension. My wife was furious because I was supposed to be saving my semen for one of the treatments. Maybe now it's getting easier though. I tend to think this is the pack of cards life has dealt me and it's not ideal but we've got to work through our options. I suppose I've come round to accepting that there is not a lot I can do about my sperm problems apart from wearing baggy pants and taking cold baths. The main way I can help now is by minimising the traumas my wife has to go through.

Alan was upset seeing his wife in pain:

She was told she would have to have her tubes checked before donor sperm could be used. It was an added pressure for me because she had to go through all that because of my lack of sperm. I remember seeing her in hospital after the operation looking pale and ill and I felt bad because it was all down to me that she had to go through the operation.

Feelings of exclusion came up repeatedly in conversations:

> I feel left out. She is going through GIFT and now IVF with donor sperm and suffering as a result yet there is nothing wrong with her. I'm the one with the problem but I'm not really involved in the treatments. I do my bit by giving her the drug injections and that helps but I'm not actually involved in the treatments and somehow everything feels unsatisfactory to me.

Lack of emotional support was mentioned:

> I felt so much on the sidelines once my wife started having DI and then IVF attempts with donor sperm. It was very unpleasant for her but I didn't feel guilty by that stage because we both had fertility problems. I remember holding her hand whilst she was having her eggs collected for IVF and trying to help her as best I could but we were on our own and had to cope as best we could.

Several people were uneasy about the use of assisted conception techniques:

> I'm just an adjunct, here to provide sperm, that's all. So far we haven't tried IVF but I'm worried about its intrusive nature and it's also treating the wrong person though I know my wife would be willing to try it. I suppose we might have a go if we think the clinic knows how to deal with my sperm problems.

John whose wife had a child after DI, talked to me about how he and his wife might try for a second child:

> I suppose we could consider the new micromanipulation techniques because I do produce a tiny number of sperm, but I think we'll probably go through DI again the next time. I think that all this talk of possible new treatments actually makes life more difficult for us rather than easier. Is it worth my wife having to go through a costly, painful, invasive procedure with a low success rate? Why should she go through so much pain and uncertainty? It just doesn't seem worth it.

This view was echoed:

> IVF might result in more pain and distress for her. I would feel dreadful, if my wife became pregnant as the result of my sperm being helped along by IVF, and then she lost the baby. My sperm might be defective in some way and that is why I can't get her pregnant in the normal way.

Coping with the process of DI could be very traumatic:

> Right from the start I felt mortified that we had lost control over what should be a natural event. The whole process seemed so cold, clinical and negative. My wife was laid out on the hospital bed and I was asked to leave the room when they inseminated her.

DISCUSSION

Men did not generally dwell that much on the tests and treatments they had been through and how they coped with them. Sometimes they were hazy about the exact details and asked me to check this with their partners. A lot of them had not been through many investigations although all had given at least one semen sample, some many more.

If anything they were more forthcoming about what they felt about the woman's treatment. For it was the woman more often than not who was the focus of medical help (a point discussed in the first part of the book). Many men felt unsure of what role they should play during the treatments, but one message was clear, they often felt marginal.

So how unusual were these experiences and can other information shed light on the male experience of medical investigations?

Firstly it is worth noting that though everyone I spoke to had been for medical help, this does not always happen. Not all couples seek treatment (Congress of the US, Office of Technology Assessment, 1988c). Doctors and researchers gave me anecdotes which suggested that many men are reluctant to go through tests. Possibly they are completely taken aback at the idea they could be infertile. One person recalled being shocked when asked to give a semen sample by the gynaecologist. He felt he must be fertile because his sex life was satisfying (Jones). Men may also find it difficult to get time off work for medical tests, a point raised by several of my interviewees.

Women do seem to initiate tests and Stanway says 'in more than two-thirds of couples it is the woman who starts the medical ball rolling'. The man and woman jointly consult the doctor in only about a quarter of cases. This is a reflection of the fact that children are seen as women's business and that most people assume the woman is at fault. Women also have far more tests than men (1986: 99).

The latter point is also made by Pfeffer and Woollett. Men are far less investigated and have less contact with hospitals and the man's experience of infertility checks is minimal regardless of outcome (1983). Services are geared towards the treatment of female rather than male infertility (Congress of the US, Office of Technology Assessment, 1988b).

All my interviewees had given at least one semen sample. This forms the basis of the male investigation as discussed in part one of the book. Samples were taken initially for diagnostic purposes but were often needed for later procedures such as IVF. There was little talk about the test other than in general terms or to comment that it was stressful producing samples to order. Simon talked about the uncomfortable room he had to produce a sample in when he was investigated in 1989. The lack of satisfactory facilities for men is now recognised at least in Britain. The Interim Licensing Authority (British) says this is an issue for concern and that there should be adequate facilities (1991). At the very least a lockable room should be available for men with their partners if they so wish and there should be no time pressure on the man to produce a sample (Pfeffer and Quick, 1988).

It is generally assumed men find it distasteful giving samples. None of my interviewees were that specific about this though some expressed reservations about the test. Parry says initial tests for women involve charts and blood samples whereas for men 'it is masturbation at 9am in a white tiled room with only girlie mags for company. Who can blame them for finding it hugely distasteful, (1991: 84)? Undoubtedly it is upsetting for some men. Blizzard writing about his experience some years back says he found the whole business subversive. The woman takes the man's sample to the doctor and they both act as conspirators, almost colluding against the man. He found the test alienating to say the least:

> he wanted to take a look at my semen – not me. I recollect that I felt no particular sentiments at this rather curious request. Later I felt insulted and trivialised by the peripheral position in which I found myself in respect of these investigations.
>
> (1977: 23)

Fort details the practical problems of having to produce a sample. On one occasion he had to produce it at work:

> I extracted a small plastic bottle and excused myself from the presentation. I went down to the men's lavatory on the first floor, locked myself in a cubicle and masturbated into the plastic container with as much gusto as I could manage.

Later in the article he writes about problems with the specimen bottles:

> This was the first of my love affairs with small plastic containers and, like a lot of first love affairs, it was a painful business. This was because there was a tiny plastic shard attached to the rim of the container, where the two halves joined. I did not notice this booby trap until I was trying to direct my ejaculation into the neck of the bottle. In my excitement the little shard nicked the end of my penis, causing a momentary halt in the proceedings.

> Have you ever gone to work with the end of your penis wrapped in cotton wool and elastoplast?
>
> (1990: 17)

Holman also writes about his experience of giving samples, during a time of great frustration and futility. He describes producing samples that his wife could be inseminated with. He would:

> masturbate into the plastic cup, later into two cups for the split-ejaculate method. This meant more self-control in the midst of depressing, mechanical orgasms. Then bring my pitiful borderline sperm to the nurse who helped me out by injecting it into my wife.
>
> (8)

During my discussions, there was passing mention of physical examinations. Again most did not say what they felt about this in any detail, though the memory of the examination had been painfully etched in Jeffrey's mind. Ten years on, he still fretted that his testicles were too small. Others made no comment because they had never been examined.

But it is important that men are examined according to Neuberg though he recognises they can be apprehensive about this. They need to be reassured that the physical will be done rapidly, will be painless and performed in private (1991). There may be another reason why physicals are not always carried out. One doctor I spoke to felt that some male doctors feel uncomfortable examining another man's genitals because of worries about homosexuality. In an article about men counselling men, the point is made that counsellors can fear giving physical support such as hugs to the client, because of worries about homosexuality (Heppner and Gonzales, 1987).

Testicular biopsies had been performed on several men I spoke to. Most did not express any fears or anxieties about the operation itself, apart from Kevin who said he would never have one, and Derek who had suffered terribly when a swab was accidentally left inside him after the operation.

Blizzard recounts his experience of having a biopsy done in Israel. It was traumatic. Looking back at what happened, he wondered whether he submitted to it as a form of penance because he felt he should have known or suspected that he was sterile. Apparently the operation was very painful because only a sedative was used and the blade cut across the unanaesthetized surface. His anger at the doctors who did the operation is understandable (1977).

One common experience was that of feeling marginal, on the sidelines looking on. Men felt uncomfortable seeing their partners often go through painful procedures. They could end up feeling guilty and tended to talk about the woman's treatment rather than their own which they often skipped over.

Of course one reason for this is that they might not have been through any treatments of note. (This may change if more treatments such as taking sperm from the man's epididymis become available.) MacNab made the same observation in his study. It was the women who went through all major surgical and medical procedures. 'The men described worrying about the side effects of fertility drugs, standing by while their wives underwent surgery, or watching with apprehension during artificial insemination procedures' (1984: 118).

Yet many do go through at least the experience of giving a semen sample and there may be other reasons why those I talked to did not generally dwell on their own experiences.

Perhaps they were reticent about this because of the expectation that they should somehow cope with the investigations and attend to the woman's needs. Sutkin and Good when talking about men's counselling needs in a health setting say that men are expected to accept illness and injury with stoicism and courage. Cries of pain, tears and fear are seen as unacceptable (1987).

It may also be that men's experiences of infertility investigations (despite often being minimal) are rather traumatic, because they have less general experience of doctors. Apparently it is not uncommon for the majority of a doctor's patients to be women (Jenkins, 1991). So fear of the unknown, ignorance of how services operate and a need to be able to cope may colour the male experience.

Getting advice and information about medical treatment was a practice adopted by quite a few of my interviewees. John and others like him tried to get advice from several doctors or researched the subject in libraries. There is now another source of help. A fertility helpline was set up in 1990 by ISSUE, the British infertility self-help group, but men generally may be reluctant to seek help this way. The helpline's first annual report says 89 per cent of calls were from women whereas only 11 per cent were from men (Dickson, 1991).

Despite this, the need for information was evident when I attended a workshop on male infertility at one of ISSUE's annual conferences. Men were very anxious to find out the latest news on research and treatment developments. Whether they want more information than women in a similar position is unclear. One infertility counsellor said to me that men cope with the medical experience by trying to take control of it and they do this by becoming knowledgeable about tests and treatments. But it may not just be men who do this. Woollett says both sexes can become infertility experts as a means of taking control (1985). However, one medical specialist I spoke to said in her experience men often wanted more detailed information than women about tests and treatment. She felt women more easily accepted their infertility problems whereas men were more questioning. Of course men may want more information because frequently little is available to them.

What other coping strategies were used to deal with the medical experience? There was limited scope for action. Those with sperm problems had sometimes been advised about giving up smoking and drinking and had tried these self-help measures. A minority mentioned alternative therapies. People like John said they tried to take control by being positive and making action plans and Brian had decided the most effective course of action was to do all he could to reduce his wife's stress.

Overall the experience may be particularly uncomfortable for men says Osherson, talking from his own and other men's experiences. There can be a deep fear of seeming foolish, silly or emotionally out of control and it can seem easier to compete with the medical staff and important to feel in control. Feelings of vulnerability, rage and sadness are not encouraged, but the result is that each partner in the couple can become constrained by stereotypes which are ultimately unhelpful. The man being invulnerable and unemotional and the woman emotional (1986).

Partners can become set apart from each other because they have different experiences during investigations. According to Menning, the woman may feel her husband cannot understand her hopes and worries and what it is like having a period when she wants to be pregnant. He in turn may find it impossible to 'share his anxiety over having to masturbate to produce a specimen of semen that is 'scored and counted' in a semen analysis, or performing for 'sex on demand'' (1980: 316). Certainly, making love to order was not something my interviewees relished, a point also noted in Woollett's study (1985).

Anxiety can figure in the male experience. Fifty-nine women going through IVF and DI were interviewed in one study and thirty-four men completed questionnaires. Both sexes experienced high anxiety levels generally (Cook *et al.*, 1989). Another study found that the longer the tests on the man the more he reported feelings of anger, guilt and diminished success (Connolly and Cooke, 1987).

Those of my interviewees who felt they had solved their problems relatively quickly, gave out an air of confidence and optimism, but others were still struggling with various options. No clear pattern emerged about how men coped with treatment dilemmas. I felt that perhaps those with sperm problems were struggling more with the medical experience as opposed to those with no sperm. Yet this was not always so and Jeffrey was still perplexed ten years on from his original diagnosis as to why he had no sperm. The lack of an explanation haunted him.

Finally certain emotions seemed to colour the medical experience. Men may feel peculiarly uncomfortable during the investigation phase. They have an uncertain role to play and can feel aimless, useless and unwanted. Guilt and inadequacy can surface because men feel they have inflicted suffering on their partners. These feelings coupled with a sense of powerlessness can make for a disturbing experience which men are unsure how to cope with.

7 The quality of medical services

There were wide-ranging views about how good medical services were. Remarks revolved round how men felt they had been treated and the quality of medical help and information received. A minority were basically pleased with the medical care they had received.

GOOD, WITH A FEW RESERVATIONS

John, in his early thirties, found out a couple of years ago that he had no sperm and had initially been with his wife to see their general practitioner (GP). They were worried because she was not pregnant after a year of trying for a baby:

> The doctor got the ball rolling. She was pleasant and helpful and relayed the results of the semen analysis to me. Basically I had very few sperm in my sample so she referred me to a hospital gynaecologist who specialised in infertility. Another test was done with the same results and I then went to see a private urologist. He gave me a physical examination and asked about my past to try and find out why I had problems. He concluded there was nothing that could be done and that I needed to go away and chew over the facts he had given me.
>
> Looking back over what's happened, I think the medical help was fine on balance. The GP was supportive, though the hospital doctor had to wade through our notes and had a bit of a struggle understanding what the problem was at first. As for the urologist, well he was very professional and unemotional and he presented me with the facts and courses of action open to us. But one thing I do feel we missed out on was counselling. We received none and I'm not sure what I feel about this gap in help.

There was much praise for the doctors who had helped Stephen. He had been told in 1980 that he had no sperm and that nothing could be done about his lack of sperm production.

I was pleased with the medical help I received. All along the various doctors I saw were helpful and sympathetic and the advice commonsensical. It turned out that the tubes in my testicles were far too tangled up, so that's why I couldn't have children.

Tim was also positive about his experience:

I was investigated before my wife when we went for help three years ago. When I was younger I had an operation for a twisted testicle, so I thought this might be the cause of our problems. The semen analysis showed a zero count and I then had a testicular biopsy which showed I had a congenital condition. A tube vital to sperm production was missing. I think the medical treatment was excellent all the way through. A correct diagnosis was made which saved time and anguish and any false hopes of being a father were quite rightly squashed.

But it was all very sudden and I felt stunned. In the space of three weeks I had gone from thinking I was going to be able to have my own children to finding out there was no chance of this. Nobody talked to me about what I might feel and the doctors didn't refer me to any counsellors. I had to deal with it all on my own.

EXCLUSION

Others were less happy about the medical investigations. Bruce was not allowed to see the hospital doctor at the first appointment:

We went to the GP after nothing happened. He said we were worrying unduly and to go away and keep trying. We did and still nothing happened, so we returned to the GP and this time were sent to the hospital gynaecologist.

We both went along together and had to wait in the antenatal clinic. My wife was eventually called in to see the doctor but he didn't want to see me even though I had taken time off work. I just had to wait outside. I was seething inside. The nurse went back to the consultant and explained I wanted to be involved in the interview with my wife but he again refused to see me. The upshot of that visit was that my wife had an operation done to see if her tubes were clear. I didn't have a semen analysis done.

So we went back to the GP who arranged a sperm test. The results came back and I had a low sperm count. Looking back I was just ignored at the beginning as all the attention was on my wife. Things did improve, however, when we were referred to a specialist centre. The doctors there were interested in me, did various tests and tried certain treatments to improve my sperm count. The quality seemed to improve but my wife still didn't get pregnant, but at least they tried to help me.

Jeffrey bitterly recalled being excluded from one appointment:

We both wanted to get checked out when my wife didn't get pregnant after a few months. The GP arranged for my wife to see a gynaecologist, so she went on her own and was told to bring my semen sample to that first appointment. They did various tests on her and she was told to return for a second appointment to get the results.

This is when the problems started. The gynaecologist only wanted to see my wife. I took her to the hospital and waited for her. When she came out of the doctor's office, she told me that the problem was with me rather than her. So I asked why the doctor hadn't discussed the diagnosis directly with me? She explained she had told him I was waiting outside and asked for me to be called in, but he refused and said she had to explain the results to me. That's why it was my wife who told me I had dead sperm in my semen. Apparently the doctor had started talking to her about adoption and DI solutions during that session. That whole experience made me very angry and I wince whenever I think of that man's name. After what happened I had no faith in him so I went back to my GP to discuss my problems and get proper help.

He arranged for me to have another semen analysis done. This time there were no sperm in the semen, so my doctor referred me to a urologist who did various other checks on me. He did a physical and a biopsy but it still wasn't clear why I had no sperm. But that was it in terms of medical help for me. I felt they hadn't got to the bottom of what was wrong, but the doctor said he couldn't do anything else for me. I felt abandoned.

Eventually we decided that the only way my wife would have a baby was by using donor sperm. The place we were referred to was miles away. It was a dreadful unit. I thought I would be involved in the whole process, but I was wrong. The man in charge was pompous and horrible, particularly to me. He said that I had to take a back seat because the procedure was nothing to do with me. My wife had several attempts at DI. We used to make a long journey to the unit, only to find out when we got there that I was shut out from the room when the insemination took place. I felt pretty useless. I started to lose my hair and felt as though I'd put on years as a result of all the tension.

ON THE SIDELINES

The feeling of being left out and on the sidelines was apparent in several interviews. Brian had given semen samples over a period of years for diagnostic purposes and then for use in various procedures. But the spotlight had never been on him:

> We've been through some years of investigations now and been to several infertility clinics, some supposedly specialising in male infertility. For example, we went to one that said it was interested in male infertility, but the way they actually worked with us showed they weren't interested. They tried to make out my wife had a problem instead of acknowledging that my infertility is the cause of our problems.
>
> Yet we still don't know after five years whether I can father a child. I feel helpless and powerless. With male infertility your partner is the one who is mainly treated and that makes you feel guilty. I go to work and return to find my wife with plasters on her after various tests and scans. She feels peeved and put out. I want to do something to help but don't know what to do so I just feel bad, but nobody wants to know or gives a damn about my feelings.
>
> I need people to recognise that the problem is mine, that I do exist and that I am important in the investigations, but my experience has made me feel that I'm useless, just a spare part in the wings.
>
> The doctors haven't acknowledged one of my main worries. I think stress affects sperm quality but no effort has been made to reduce my stress levels. At the very least, the tests should have been carried out as quickly and smoothly as possible to reduce my anxiety. Nobody has tried to comfort me, acknowledge my problems and talk honestly about what can be done. I've just been left out of it all.

There was a complaint about unsupportive doctors:

> Technically the medical help has been good, but I have never been given any emotional support. The emphasis is on getting the sperm and eggs to fertilise and no attempt has been made to involve me in a creative way in the investigations. There surely must be some sort of role for me?

Lack of information and feelings of being excluded from treatments also coloured reflections:

> I remember ringing the doctor to find out my test results but couldn't take in what he said. Then I was referred to a urologist who was very sympathetic. He did a physical examination, checked my hormones and did an operation on my testicles to see if there was a blockage somewhere, but no reason could be found for my problems.

> I think looking back that my GP was helpful and sympathetic but he didn't really give us any support or prepare us for the bad news. The urologist was helpful but once those checks were over, the attention shifted to my

wife. She had several DI attempts and then went through IVF with donor sperm. I wasn't involved in any of that and feel as though the doctors have finished with me now. If there is some breakthrough in male infertility I won't know about it.

Martin felt doctors had never been interested in him because they did not have any way of improving his sperm:

When they found out about my sperm problems, they immediately started talking about IVF for my wife. It was like someone saying your car is messed up but don't worry we've got something else for you in the car lot. I felt I was being told this is it, and there is nothing else on offer.

Nothing was said about why I had sperm problems and what I could do to improve matters. The specialists seemed more interested in showing off their technical wizardry than finding out why I had a problem and trying to cure it. They just weren't interested in me.

When my wife got pregnant by me without any medical help I felt a delicious sense of triumph over all those doctors who had said I would never father my own child and had offered me no help.

Lack of information about self-help measures was also commented on:

The doctor looked at me after the test results came through and said he was 90 per cent sure I was the problem because my sperm quality was poor. I had to then ask about what I could do to improve the quality. He said cutting out smoking and drinking might help, but he didn't volunteer this information. He was going on about putting my sperm directly into my wife's womb. He seemed quite uninterested in why I had sperm problems and what could be done about them.

Information about self-help measures was given to Luke but he felt this was not enough:

All they could tell me to do was to wear loose pants. The doctors didn't know why my previously high count was now low. The specialist examined me for a couple of minutes and then just suggested I take large doses of vitamins.

I ended up going to a herbalist and a homeopath for help. They seemed to have as much of a clue as to why I had a problem as the doctors did. I'm also upset that the doctors didn't check me out straightaway. Instead they wasted time examining my partner.

Mike had tried unsuccessfully to get his fertility assessed before he was aware there was a problem:

In the early days of my marriage before we had started trying for a family

I thought I would get my sperm checked out because of my medical history. I felt I might have sperm problems because of certain drugs I had been on, but my GP at that time was quite unreceptive to my request for a sperm test. He said I'd find out whether there were problems in the course of time.

My wife didn't get pregnant when we tried for a family and of course it turned out I was infertile and had a mix of problems. The consultant who gave me the news was incredibly insensitive and offhand, almost rude. He didn't seem aware that I might be in a fragile state and his bedside manner, if you can call it that, was deplorable. At least he could have sounded regretful, but there was not a hint of sympathy for me in his voice.

Overall looking back at my medical experience, it seems from that point on, the attention was on my wife. The doctors told me they needed to make her as receptive as possible to my sperm. I tried to do my bit by wearing baggy pants and having cold showers but there didn't seem much I could do.

NEGLECTED MEN

Peter assumed he was fertile because doctors did not check him out initially:

I thought I must be all right because they didn't do any tests on me. My wife was going through various investigations and I didn't really know what was going on. When they finally did a semen analysis they found I had sperm problems. I was pissed off, all that time wasted. Why didn't they test me at the beginning? But they do seem to be doing more now to get my sperm sorted out, so I'm not grumbling as much as I was.

Derek was upset about his medical treatment for a number of reasons:

One of the things I keep coming back to is why nothing was done about my undescended testicles until I was in my teens. Even then when the operation was done, the doctors said nothing about my sperm being affected, it was just about the need to bring the testicles down because I would be in great pain if this wasn't done as I got older.

Later on when I found out I had sperm problems, no real support was given to me. They did a biopsy and left a swab inside me. I was in agony and as a result was ill for some time after that. I then had a course of injections at a special unit to try and improve the sperm. That didn't help. Basically my treatment has been pretty awful and I have just had to get by on my own.

SPECIFIC THOUGHTS ABOUT DOCTORS

Several men said their GPs were helpful but felt let down by other doctors:

> Our GP has been sympathetic and helpful all along and has taken time to explain what my test results mean. I tend to think that if I rang her up now she'd fit me in somehow to make sure I get any support I need. However, the other help we've had from the medical profession has been disgusting. I was referred to a male infertility specialist who sat behind this desk in a coat looking cold and clinical. Then he started talking to me about biopsies and needles even though he had been told I have a phobia about needles. I keeled over and fainted. I was offered another appointment with him but declined it. There was no way I was going to see him again.

Simon likewise found things went well to start with but then changed for the worse:

> I got the news about my sperm problems from my GP. He took the time and effort to talk everything through with me. I felt he handled the interview well because he explained what the results meant and that one test result on its own was not enough to give an absolute diagnosis.
>
> So I had some more tests done and was then referred to a gynaecologist. She dismissed my sperm problems as unimportant and went on about inseminating my wife with a concentration of my sperm. She was in fact far more interested in finding out if my wife had some sort of a problem and wasn't really concerned about male infertility.
>
> Then I was sent to someone who specialises in male infertility. He said I had a slight varicocele but saw no point operating on it. We have now been to a centre which is going to look at how my sperm interact with my wife's eggs. The first appointment was a fiasco. We were kept waiting for hours and when we saw the doctor he didn't seem interested in my problems. It all seems such a waste of time. We've been going through the National Health Service at the moment but we may have to go private for help.

One man in his late forties was outraged because he had been told he was too old to treat:

> My GP has been good about the whole business. He arranged for a semen analysis to be done and then tried unsuccessfully to refer me to a specialist unit in a hospital. The doctors there felt there was no point seeing me because I was too old. They seemed to be saying a man of my age shouldn't want to have children. I was disgusted with their attitude but luckily for me another hospital agreed to see me.

There were some complaints, however, about GPs. Concerns often tended to be about the initial appointment with the doctor when test results were given. 'It was pathetic. He just blurted out that I had no sperm and that I stood no chance of being a father. That was the extent of medical help and support I received from him.'

One GP started talking about solutions immediately:

He asked me right away after he had given me the results whether I would think of adoption. That was absolutely the wrong thing to say. He also said he thought it would be quite easy for someone in my position (because of my medical background) to adopt. Of course that wasn't true and he should have checked his facts out first before saying that. What he should have done was to say something like 'go away and think things over and come back in a couple of days time so we can discuss it in more detail'. But he just left me in mid air and that was bad. Basically he gave me piecemeal rather than strategic advice and I had to take the initiative and find out more information.

Then I was referred to a urologist who it turns out had no interest in infertility at all. Again my GP should have taken the time and trouble to check this out before referring me to him. Instead I wasted time with this man and he offered me inappropriate hormone treatment which I decided against taking. Eventually I saw a consultant who did know what he was talking about and was helpful.

Matthew felt his GP had been very insensitive:

I was called in to see him to discuss my test results. He said I had no sperm and that I was only the second case of this sort he had come across in twenty-five years. There was absolutely nothing to be done he said. I thought, I don't want to leave it at that and so I had to ask to be referred to a specialist. I went to the local hospital where I saw a urologist who was fine I suppose. My blood tests were normal but he did a physical and said he thought some tubes were missing inside my testicles. Eventually I saw another specialist who confirmed everything the urologist had told me.

Basically the GP had nothing to offer me. He just said 'it's one of those things, I don't know why you have no sperm and you just have to get on with your life'. The urologist was more sensitive and didn't treat me like an idiot and the other specialist was straight with me and I appreciated that.

Alan saw two GPs. The first was unhelpful but the second was supportive:

My wife's GP gave me the bad news. He should have been more diplomatic but he just said that I had no sperm. I stood there and he didn't even ask me to sit down. I couldn't wait to get out of that interview, it was all so negative.

Then I went to see my own GP who was very supportive. I sat down and felt more relaxed with him and said I wanted to be properly checked out to find out why I had no sperm. He agreed this was a sensible thing to do, spent time chatting to me about my infertility and said I didn't have to rush off and start thinking about things like adoption. Later on I saw a urologist who did various tests on me. Everything seemed fine and he couldn't find out why I wasn't producing sperm but I felt I had been properly investigated. That was important to me.

Chris felt he had been let down by all the doctors he had seen. Delays and an abrupt consultation coloured his painful memories:

Our GP just told us to keep trying for another six months and not to worry. That turned out to be a waste of time. When I did find out I had sperm problems the local specialist was incredibly unhelpful. He told me one testicle was dead and the other one was no good and that our only options were to consider adoption or donor sperm. That was it and my case was closed. I was offered no more medical help.

Basically I think I was underinvestigated because only one semen test was done. The thing is that my previous partner got pregnant and she says I was the father. So it's difficult to square that with the information that I'm infertile. Also I was drinking a lot when I had that sperm test done and I've now read that alcohol can badly affect sperm. But I've never found out any more information about my infertility because no more tests were done.

DISCUSSION

Conversations were generally characterised by a sense of frustration and confusion. Evaluation of medical help was based on certain factors. How good was the medical information, how had the diagnosis been relayed and what support had been offered? Comments were also made about inadequate treatments and there were complaints about the lack of DI clinics in the National Health Service. Jeffrey, for example, drew attention to the paucity of such services in his area.

There was a general air of unhappiness about the quality of medical help. Martin's pleasure at getting his partner pregnant and so confounding medical opinion, illustrates the anger that many expressed. Put in a nutshell, men felt they had been left out and neglected, their problems glossed over or perhaps completely ignored. Valuable time had been lost for some because they had not been checked out early enough. According to others it was ironic that though they had the problem, they were not the ones being treated.

The loudest complaints tended to come from men with sperm problems. They were more critical of medical assistance because they felt if only they could get the right help they might be able to father a child and there was a suspicion they were not getting this help. Not everyone had been referred to male-infertility specialists and some had turned to or were thinking of going to private centres in the hope that more interest might be shown in their problems. These centres were also seen as the places to go for the latest high-tech approaches such as micromanipulation. A couple of men and their partners were thinking about these possibilities.

Alternative therapies had also been tried by a couple of men dissatisfied with what conventional medicine had to offer them.

The experiences tend to bear out the issues raised in part one of the book. Often the diagnosis was unclear and more importantly there was a sense that nothing much could be done.

Basically men with sperm problems were confused about their diagnoses. The semen analysis was sometimes the only diagnostic test done, despite the problems raised about it earlier on. Yet according to some specialists there is still a belief that this test alone will suffice (Glover *et al.*, 1990). Sperm function tests had also not been routinely used, to assess sperm quality. One interviewee knew about the swim-up test but was worried because two centres used different values to judge test results. This picture of uncertainty about how to evaluate men and hasty assessment of them is reinforced by one study which suggested that inadequate investigation may be common-place. The research found that 77 per cent of men reported as normal were found to be infertile on further investigation (Gregson, 1988).

The medical experiences described to me reflect the earlier discussion about the shortage of effective male treatments. Often not much was offered, though Peter had a varicocele operated on. Most of those with sperm problems had tried non-specific measures such as wearing baggy pants or taking more vitamins, all tactics discussed in part one, but often dismissed as of no value. Spark says the medical literature is full of reports about treatments which will improve sperm production and quality and so increase pregnancy rates, but though of dubious value, frustrated doctors grab them so as to get out of the 'quagmire of male infertility' (1988: 304). Interestingly some of my interviewees felt they had not even been offered this much.

There was also a widespread sense of being an onlooker, and feeling neglected and unwanted. This recurrent theme underlay the complaints about medical assistance and can lead to a strange situation. MacNab observed in his study that men had not been evaluated as thoroughly as women because there was less on offer in the way of effective treatments. This was a double-edged sword because though relieved of the anxieties of evaluation and treatments men became 'passive observers rather than participants in a process in which they were intimately involved' (1984: 20).

Out of all my interviewees few had received the sort of comprehensive care Menning says doctors can give. This includes the need to refer to specialists, to offer emotional support and to deal with the couple rather than the individuals and develop a treatment plan for them both (1980).

Doctors do talk theoretically about the importance of treating the couple so that joint fertility is measured, but in practice the woman is mainly assessed. In one article a gynaecologist explained how various basic tests could be performed to check the couple's fertility, yet most of those that were then listed were for the woman rather than the man (Doyle, 1991). Basically men are ignored when it comes to treatment and support and this is directed at women rather than men (Prentice, 1988).

My interviewees reported that they had been left out of investigations in a number of ways. Jeffrey and Bruce were actually excluded from consultations. This may not be a rare occurrence as, according to one study, in a majority of clinics partners were not seen together, though this is what they wanted. Men were also actively discouraged from some consultations (Bromham *et al.*, 1988). The organisation of medical services makes 'infertile men even more invisible; many hospitals do not encourage men to attend and, in most, the medical details of the male partner are kept in the case notes of the woman' according to Pfeffer and Quick (1988: 18).

Some of the men I spoke to would have felt more included in the whole process if they felt their needs had been taken into account. A note of anxiety was voiced about the stress of investigations because this might worsen sperm quality. There may be some justification for this alarm as seen in part one of the book though studies give contradictory results. One piece of research for example, found that semen quality did not worsen during infertility tests (Hammond *et al.*, 1990).

There was talk also not only about the lack of medical treatment but also about the absence of counselling support. Again this may be commonplace. Counselling is now acknowledged to be important for both men and women going through the infertility process. Doyal points out that 'most women (and men) undertake the very lengthy and complex process of infertility treatment without adequate information or experienced help in dealing with accompanying emotional problems' (1987: 184).

Counselling can help people come to terms with their predicament but this type of help is only now being more widely implemented. It has been left to doctors to discuss the emotional side of infertility whilst doing the physical investigations according to Pfeffer and Quick. Yet doctors do not have the time or training to counsel people. Perhaps this explains why 'all too often doctors ignore the social dimension of infertility and concentrate exclusively on medical investigations and treatment' (1988: 46).

Doctors could be particularly insensitive according to my interviewees when giving the diagnosis, yet this was a time when men could feel most vulnerable. Doctors sometimes blurted out the news and rushed into giving advice about adoption and DI, giving the man little time for reflection. Feelings of distress and anger stemmed from this. At the very least, men wanted the doctor to give them the news directly rather than through their partners and to be treated with respect and consideration by medical staff.

Dissatisfaction with doctors on this point was referred to by others. There is mention of research which found that husbands were unhappy with the way the news was given to them. There was criticism of how doctors handled the results and in some cases they evaded the issue by getting the wife to pass the news to the man. Doctors hid from the gravity of the situation (Snowden *et al.*, 1983).

One medical specialist I spoke to said it was important for a man to be given as much information as possible about his problems. This meant taking time to assess his sperm properly. She also felt stress could affect sperm quality, so discussed this with the man, and that the diagnosis should be given in the right way allowing the man time to think about the implications. His emotional reactions needed to also be recognised and worked through but she felt doctors sometimes delivered the diagnosis in a casual unsatisfactory way.

Male doctors may have particular difficulties dealing with male infertility. The physical examination can make them feel anxious because of homosexual worries as discussed in the previous chapter. There could be another reason. Male gynaecologists may feel embarrassed because they are not familiar dealing with reproductive abnormalities in their own sex (Glover *et al.*, 1990). Male doctors' reluctance in such matters is not a recent phenomenon and shared gender between doctor and patient did not help men earlier this century. They found it difficult to talk to male doctors about sexual problems and the doctors in turn failed to meet their patients' needs (Hall, 1991).

Shared gender may cause other tensions though these did not obviously emerge in my interviews. The male infertility specialist may particularly relish his job because he indirectly plays the role of father (Greer, 1984). If so this may encourage the doctor to exclude the man from treatments perhaps explaining why Jeffrey was ruthlessly kept out of his wife's insemination sessions. Separately the male doctor may share something in common with his male patient – an unease at admitting to and dealing with feelings of failure and – this may mean that certain issues are skirted round in the consultation.

To sum up, there are a number of things that may make the male medical experience unsatisfactory. The past still affects the present. Gynaecologists have dominated the treatment of male infertility with certain results. They do not have a burning interest in issues of sperm quality according to one embryologist who specialises in male infertility (Steven, 1991). Treatments are therefore not targeted at male problems hence the focus on IVF and DI approaches as a way round male infertility (Pfeffer and Quick, 1988).

The growth of andrology as discussed in part one perhaps suggests that more interest is now being shown in men's problems though one American andrologist said to me that male reproductive biology and andrology is still poorly taught in medical schools within the United States. In Britain instruction in medical schools is limited if it exists at all (Glover *et al.*, 1990).

Though there may be dissatisfaction generally with infertility services (Harman, 1990) male services are even worse and there are fewer of them. In America, less is spent on male as opposed to female infertility because of this fact (Congress of the US, Office of Technology Assessment, 1988b). Existing services may be seen as of poorer quality. Patient satisfaction with tests and treatment was evaluated in one study, but 'treatment for men was rated much less highly than treatment for women' (Owens and Read, 1984: 16).

It would be tempting to hope that medical services have improved in the intervening years since that study. This did not clearly emerge from those men I spoke to who had more recent experience of services on offer. One infertility counsellor I spoke to put it bluntly:

> There are few services for either sex, but when it comes to men they are just left out. Women are seen by the gynaecologist and the man may well not be seen. If he does have a problem his wife will give him the news so he ends up seeing no one. Men feel uncomfortable because they are often just observers in a process in which they need to be active participants.

Finally it is worth noting that men and their partners may want to consider DI because of the lack of other alternatives. The availability of DI on the health service in Britain is, however, limited and patchy (Mathieson, 1986). The outlook has worsened since then. The British Pregnancy Advisory Service, a charity which used to offer donor services, stopped doing so in 1991. Couples may have to increasingly go to private clinics for such help.

8   The diagnosis

How did men react to the news that they might have fertility problems? Firstly I asked them whether the news was a shock and whether they had anticipated difficulties.

NO SYMPTOMS

Generally most of them thought they were fertile. The ability to have sex was seen as proof of fertility. 'We made love regularly and I had no problems getting an erection, so I assumed I was fertile. A raw nerve was touched when I found out I wasn't.' Similarly:

> I thought my wife was infertile. I'm not impotent so I presumed I must be working properly. I suppose I felt that babies are a woman's business and that she must be at fault when things go wrong. It never really occurred to me that I could be to blame, but having said that I knew deep down that I wasn't impressively fertile because there had never been any accidental pregnancies with previous girlfriends.

> I'd only ever really thought about my fertility in terms of taking reasonable precautions to avoid getting someone pregnant. I thought I knew about biology and I remember thinking about donating sperm when I was fresh out of university. Basically I didn't think much about my reproductive potential and assumed I was all right and tried to make sure that I didn't damage vital equipment when I was playing sport.

John was at college when he first thought about his fertility:

> I remember a friend of mine at college got his wife pregnant and he said it was great to find out he wasn't shooting blanks. That was the first time I thought consciously about my ability to be a father. I didn't think much more about it until we started trying for a baby. I didn't know a lot about

sperm and I remember thinking my test results were quite good even though I had hardly any sperm.

The tendency was for men to see their bodies as straightforward and un-problematic and comments were made ranging from 'I assumed my body worked properly and that it must be my wife who was infertile' to 'in the woman the problems are greater but treatments are more effective'.

A minority were aware that all might not be well. Mike knew he might be infertile because of a previous operation to remove a twisted testicle. He also had other health problems he thought might have affected his fertility. Roger also suspected he might be infertile:

> I did have an inkling that all might not be well. I can't remember exactly when it happened but my semen volume suddenly became smaller. So this was at the back of my mind when I found out I was producing no sperm. I feel the drop in volume was a warning sign even though I have been told that this is unrelated to my infertility. Other than this symptom, I seemed normal so I thought it was probably my wife who was infertile. I guess I felt that my reproductive system was fairly simple. Of course I've since found out this isn't so and the doctors don't know why I'm infertile.

Several others had possible warnings but took no notice of them:

> I had mumps in my late teens but the doctor said I shouldn't have any long-lasting problems as a result. So there was nothing in my background to prepare me for the news that I had no sperm.

Two men had undescended testicles which were not operated on until they were in their early teens. However, neither of them had been warned of future fertility problems. As one of them put it, 'on reflection the only warning bell I ever had was that sometimes I had unprotected sex but no pregnancies ever resulted'.

REACTIONS TO THE DIAGNOSIS

What were immediate reactions to the news?

Strong feelings

Most had powerful reactions. Kevin was in his mid thirties. He and his wife had tried for nine months to have a child. When nothing happened he had a semen analysis done. He was told there were only a few sperm in the semen. No sperm showed up in a second sample and blood tests indicated that his sperm production had been damaged probably by a bad case of mumps in his early teens. He started crying as he remembered his feelings on receiving the news of the second test results back in 1989:

It was like a wave, you don't know what has hit you. That was really tough. I was devastated and emotionally torn up. I can't describe the feelings exactly, but I was standing when the results were given to me and I felt so weak that I had to sit down. The breath was knocked out of me, my head was spinning, my legs were like jelly and my stomach was churning. I can't really remember what the doctor said, I just wanted to go home. Perhaps the feelings were ones of sadness and anger all rolled into one. It's ironic but I suspect that the strength of my feelings must be rather like the ones you experience at the birth of your child. I went home and cried and cried but this helped me somehow. I went on like this for some weeks.

I remember having dreams. I was walking down the street where I grew up with a dead baby in a pram. People came up to me and asked what had happened and I explained this was my dead baby. I had that dream a couple of times. Another one was about having a cage round my body with spikes sticking into me, as I pulled them out I started feeling better. Maybe that was to do with me starting to talk about everything. I don't think I ever denied the diagnosis, it seemed so clear, but I searched around for reasons as to why I wasn't producing sperm, but I'm still not clear why this has happened to me. I went through months of sadness, depression and blaming myself.

Alan's experience was harrowing when he found out he was producing no sperm in 1989. No cause had been found for the diagnosis apart from a mild attack of mumps:

I felt odd. Why me went through my mind? To start with I thought the result must be wrong, but I know now I was clutching at straws. When I got the news I sat down and my whole body went into a state of physical shock for some hours. I felt small, and rejected and couldn't accept the news. I kept thinking a mistake had been made with the sample and that the results must have got mixed up.

Then I offered my wife a divorce because we had got married in order to have children and I felt I was letting her down. She didn't accept my offer, but I still felt bad, freakish, strange. Men don't have problems like this. It's an inbuilt right to have children and when you see men with their children you think they are fine healthy chaps. I started to think perhaps if I was really good, that would do the trick and the problem would go away. It didn't and I started to get very angry about all sorts of things, particularly men who abuse their children. My self-respect was battered.

Andrew refused to accept there was a problem to start with but changed his mind after a time:

> I started by blanking out the news that I had no sperm but I did start to feel less bad about it after a bit. I thought my infertility was like a malfunction, something beyond my control, so I started to accept it. It was like a part of me wasn't working properly and I felt as though I had a hidden disability.

Jeffrey's reactions were stronger because he couldn't make any sense of the diagnosis. He was in his early twenties; ten years ago when he found out he had no sperm:

> It was a dreadful experience. My two brothers had children so I just assumed I would be all right. It was pretty difficult dealing with the news at that age. I felt as though I had gone into a brick wall. There was just nothing to prepare me for it. I'm tall, hairy, masculine-looking and yet I had no sperm. It was a bombshell and there was no reason for it.

Knowing what caused the problem could help:

> I felt stunned and cheated for some time after I found out. After all, I had always thought I would have children, but finding out the reason for my infertility helped me accept it in the end. I was born with some vital tubes missing in my testicles so that explains why I've got no sperm in my semen.

Warning signs that all might not be well affected Roger's reactions:

> I wasn't totally shocked by the news because at the back of my mind I'd been wondering why my semen volume had changed. But I still felt pretty devastated when I found I had no sperm, enough to offer my wife a divorce because I couldn't give her a family. Then feelings of anger and failure started to well up inside me. Why me?

Julian had forgotten that his fertility might be harmed by cancer treatment he had received:

> It knocked me for six when the doctor said my chances of being a father were nil. I wasn't expecting the news even though I had been warned I might no longer produce sperm after the treatment. I thought I would be all right and I ignored the warning, it was hidden away at the back of my mind. These things always happen to other people but when it happened to me it seemed like the end of the world. I got home and cried. Even though my wife has a child from a former marriage I know she wanted our child. The one thing my wife wanted I couldn't give her and I knew

that no matter how much I made love to her we could never have a family. That was hard to accept.

A childless future and feelings of emptiness were recalled by Matthew:

I found out I was producing no sperm in 1987. For the first few days I think I was numb, going through the motions, going to work and somehow getting through the day. I worried about a future without children and felt anxious about what my wife would feel about my infertility. I was frightened of growing old without children and then I started to think DI might be forced on me. The next stage was going through wild swings of emotion. One minute I would be very positive thinking my infertility was a challenge I could overcome, then I would slump into depression. It was very important that nobody found out, I couldn't have coped with that.

Reactions could be less obvious or powerful for those who had a diagnosis of sperm problems. It took longer for some of them to realise they might be infertile. Brian recalls being let down gently over a period of time. Initial semen analysis results seemed normal in 1987 after six months of trying unsuccessfully to get his wife pregnant. In 1988 after moving house and going to a different infertility clinic for assessment, sample results started to suggest he had problems. After one particular test result showed he had a very low sperm count, he started to realise he might be infertile:

My wife says I was very quiet after finding out about that result. I don't remember exactly but I suspect that the news had gone in very deeply and very quickly. It was like an extremely sore wound which I didn't want touched. The hospital said that results could vary so I think I clung to that, denying that I really did have a problem.

I felt then as though I was in limbo in a curious way. Uncertain about what this news meant although I knew it was bad. I wondered whether playing a lot of sport when I was an adolescent might have harmed my developing sex organs in some way.

I suppose I was shocked by the news. It struck me forcibly that something I had always taken for granted, starting a family, wasn't going to be easy. There was a nasty angry wound left after that assumption had been torn away. It's taken about two years for it to start to heal. The feelings are less raw now though they are still there.

Initial semen analysis results were also fine for Luke. He had his semen analysed in 1986 because he wanted to see if it was good enough to donate to a lesbian friend who wanted a child. The results were fine. Though Luke donated his sperm to his friend for a couple of years, no pregnancy ever resulted.

When Luke and his partner had no luck trying for a child, they assumed she was the one with the fertility problem. She went through a series of tests and he was not investigated. But in 1988, he had a semen analysis done to see whether his sperm could be used for GIFT. The test results showed he had various sperm problems:

> It was a bombshell when the pendulum swung my way. There was this change of emphasis and I felt inadequate but didn't know exactly what was happening. I also didn't understand why there had been this change in my sperm. One reaction stands out. My partner was with me when the consultant told me I was infertile. At one point during the conversation, she turned to me and said something about my bad sperm. That really upset me and she later apologised for using the word 'bad'. I suppose she was feeling pretty upset and it just slipped out.
>
> I don't remember feeling particularly depressed or anything like that. Basically I was confused, why had my sperm quality changed? But I couldn't get any sensible information about this and I started to come up with my own theories about why I had a problem.
>
> Before I found out I was infertile, I had started developing various aches and pains whilst Katie was going through all the investigations. I felt these reflected the stress I was experiencing having to see her go through all sorts of tests. My feelings were all locked up inside me and the only way they could make themselves known was in this way. I then started to think that my sperm might have started to deteriorate because I was under so much stress. This theory seemed as good as any other, particularly since nobody had been able to explain why my semen quality changed.

Six years on from the original diagnosis Chris said he was only now becoming clearer about his reactions to his diagnosis of sperm problems:

> I wasn't distraught but somehow the shutters came down. There was a sense of opportunities being closed off. I wanted to have kids and this was being taken away from me. My reaction was to think about the infertility in terms of a problem to be solved, though I wondered whether I really wanted children and was perhaps too old for them. The point is that my wife and I never talked about all these worries of mine though I remember we had lots of rows and there were bad feelings around. We argued about donor sperm and related issues, but I don't seem to have had feelings about my own diagnosis. I suspect I did have ones but they were channelled into these other areas.

This point was also made by Martin:

The news wasn't a total shock, after all we had been trying for a baby for about twelve months without luck and I thought it could be me. I don't think I was angry or guilty when I got the news that my sperm weren't brilliant and I didn't spend a lot of time wondering why and searching around for clues. Having said that I did start to become angry because we began having problems. I started shutting off from my wife and felt she would be better off with someone else she could have children with.

Others found it difficult to understand what the implications were for their future fertility when they were diagnosed as having sperm problems. 'I've never really believed I couldn't father a child, after all I have got some sperm and it only takes one to fertilise an egg.'

Simon recalled a mix of reactions:

I think I was a bit of a hypochondriac for a time. I got the doctor to test me for a condition I thought might be linked to infertility but that tested negative. Then I remember rushing off to the library and reading all I could on sperm counts, trying to get as much information as possible, but I got depressed because my sperm count was lower than all the ones referred to in various books. I suppose with hindsight I latched onto all this research as a way of coping with what was happening.

Others recalled reactions of a different sort:

I wasn't totally surprised by my diagnosis of sperm problems because of my twisted-testicle operation, so I was alerted to possible difficulties. The way I reacted when I found out I was infertile was to see what could be done and do my best to achieve this. I'm a pragmatist and that helped me a great deal. In fact my wife was far more upset by the news than I was and it was her eventual depression, not my infertility, which started to affect me. I'm not very emotional and so was able to accept the news about my infertility without too much fuss.

John remembers:

I felt cool and detached when I found out I had virtually no sperm. It wasn't a major problem for me, though it was annoying not to have the family I thought I always would have. Basically it was a puzzle that had to be solved and I didn't blame myself for my infertility. It's a fact of life as far as I'm concerned like being tall or short and thinking of it that way has helped me.

DISCUSSION

Forewarning

Reactions to an extent were shaped by whether problems were expected. Yet on the whole most had no premonition of what was to come and were only vaguely aware of male infertility. Fathers, brothers and male friends were thought to be fertile and men assumed that because they were potent they were fertile. The complexities of male reproduction were unknown to them and most had not thought about questions of sperm quality.

Often they jumped to the conclusion that it must be the woman who was infertile. Basically they did not seem to have thought too much about their own reproductive systems and when they did it was along the lines of 'I seemed to be working all right so everything should have been fine'.

These views are not that unusual. Despite more being known nowadays about male reproduction, the view persists that potency is the only measure of fertility. In most societies men are assumed fertile unless they have been castrated (Greer, 1984). Children are seen as proof of male sexuality, says Bradbury. He quotes a man talking about the birth of his fourth child, 'at least it shows I can still get it up' (1985: 136). All sorts of men think this, including educated ones (Steven, 1991).

Ignorance about male reproduction is rife. An infertility specialist explained to me that men needed far more basic information than women about reproductive matters. Many of them, for example, did not know how long the sperm production process takes.

There are several reasons for this ignorance. One is that men are not continually reminded of their fertility in the way that women are. From puberty onwards, a woman becomes aware of her reproductive potential with the onset of her menstrual periods and changes in her normal cycle may alert her to problems. Men have no such cycle to remind them of their reproductive potential. According to Winston, they often have no warning signs, perhaps explaining why they can be resistant to being tested (1989). A few of those I talked to did have possible warnings but mostly had ignored or discounted them, so for most there may be no symptoms to suggest that something is amiss.

There was a dim awareness of the male reproductive system amongst those I spoke to and they tended to think of it as simple. Men pointed out that they had never been taught about their own bodies at school and any education they had received about sexual matters emphasised female rather than male reproduction and the complexities of the woman's menstrual cycle. Finding out then that men too had systems which could go wrong was upsetting and confusing. There was a sense of being particularly unprepared for the diagnosis.

The idea that women's bodies are the ones that go wrong emerged in a study on men and infertility, 'there was a widespread assumption that any problem was likely to lie with the wife as "there was more to go wrong" (Owens, 1982: 80). Parry puts it bluntly. 'The general attitude of the average man to his own fertility is that if it works, if it squirts and if it's in the right place at the right time, then he must be as capable as the next bloke of fathering a child.' The only types of male infertility that men seem to think about are impotence or physical blockages in the various tubes in the testicles, according to her (1991: 83).

So the complexities of male reproduction can pass men by. Luke explained to me that he used to think of his system as straightforward.

> I found out from the specialist that this was anything but the case. The doctor likened the woman's system to a store of eggs, the man's to a factory continually producing sperm. The store was easier to manipulate than the factory.

The reasons for the different perceptions of male and female reproduction are examined by Pfeffer. She says that men are seen as having 'systems which operate with mechanical ease and efficiency with few detrimental effects'. The man's system is thought of as simple and straightforward, rarely going wrong. In contrast, the female system is described as complex and more prone to all sorts of ailments because more can go wrong with it. Yet, as Pfeffer argues, the woman's system is thought of as complex because far more is known about it than the male system (1985: 30).

This may explain why men can be confident of their fertility. They are blissfully ignorant of what can go wrong. This all ties in with the discussion in the first part of the book about the lack of understanding of male reproductive physiology. This used to apply to female reproduction, but strides have been made in that area because of greater research into female contraception. Women are seen to be in charge of fertility matters generally and there have been virtually no family planning services for men until recently whereas services flourish for women (Rappaport, 1984). In my interviews, several men pointed out that children are more important to women than men. Most said their partners had initiated medical investigations and that women were more anxious about not having started a family yet than they were.

A lack of involvement in such matters may make men more unprepared for a later diagnosis of infertility. The link between sex and reproduction seems to be less obvious for them. In a study into men's views on menstruation, Laws notes 'on the whole these men seemed extraordinarily unconcerned with the reproductive aspects of their sex lives' (1990: 99). Sex is somehow separated from children. 'The significance of contraception commonly only occurs to a man when a pregnancy – or more particularly a birth – ensues. Often only at this point does the closeness of the tie between sex and reproduction impress itself on the male mind' (Smith, 1990: 6).

What this all boils down to is that men are on the fringes of reproductive matters. A number of historical, social and medical factors appear to have contributed to this. The result is that they are not expected to take responsibility for matters such as contraception and fathering.

The end result is that they may be ignorant about their own reproductive systems. The consequences of this are that when things go wrong for them, the experience can be devastating because it is totally unexpected and they are unprepared for it. Such feelings underpinned many of my interviews.

Reactions to the news

There were different responses and no such thing as a standard reaction. A variety of feelings, thoughts and short-term coping strategies emerged in conversations. Different messages came through at different points in discussions about the impact on their lives. One point everyone shared in common was that they all found out they had fertility problems at least two years ago. Several of them were still bound up with medical tests and treatments and this experience coloured reactions.

My interviewees were probably more prepared to talk to me at this stage because they were able to reflect on what had happened to them. (One man who contacted me had found out he was infertile more recently. He decided after a preliminary discussion not to take part in the interviews because he felt unclear about what was happening to him at an emotional level.) The worst was over and they could see a glimmer of light at the end of the tunnel in many cases. They could make some sense of the diagnosis and could describe their feelings. If they had spoken to me at any earlier stage, the whole business might have been too painful for them. As it was, Kevin was still powerfully affected by what had happened to him over two years previously and tears came into his eyes as he relived certain memories.

Strong reactions could last for weeks or months. The time varied with each person. But by the time I spoke to men, time had eased the pain of infertility and lessened feelings of inadequacy. James explained:

> To start with I thought I was defective when I found out I was infertile. I couldn't have my own child, something other men seem to do so easily. That made me feel even worse about the whole business. But I don't feel quite so bitter now and less angry with myself.

In contrast Chris was only realising now that he might have experienced more pain than he thought he had at the time. He talked about a year of rows with his partner after he found out he was infertile but did not recall during that time being upset about his infertility. Eventually his marriage split up.

Memories of reactions were generally fainter and feelings less powerful for those who had become parents in the intervening years since the diagnosis. Eight men had done so. Children had been adopted or babies conceived after donor sperm had been used. All of these men said they felt much better once they became parents as infertility was pushed into the background. John, for example, who had a young baby born as a result of donor sperm said 'my life is completely taken up with my baby, but it's wonderful being a father. Somehow my infertility feelings are less important now and my memory of them is blurred'.

This may explain why a couple of men recalled their reactions as being unproblematic. Time and parenthood might have dulled or changed the reactions they remembered, but for others memories were still tinged with a good deal of pain and anger. Emotions might be on the surface or perhaps in the background and powerful feelings of shock were most often described. The news was sudden and unexpected for most. There was a sense of missing out on an important experience for some and a sense of failure for others. A couple of men felt they had let their wives down and felt obliged to offer them a divorce. One man felt that his self image as a healthy fit man had been severely dented by the whole experience.

A common reaction was to search around for reasons for the diagnosis. Some men were also distressed because they thought their fertility might have altered and yet no reason could be found for the change. Roger was sad because he suspected that he had been fertile before his semen volume changed and had missed out on the chance to father children earlier on. Others were upset because 'what should be a natural event had been taken over by doctors'.

The various feelings of shock and sometimes anger that cropped up in conversations are to be expected. Infertility is a life crisis says Menning. There is an order of feelings that both men and women go through when they learn they have problems. Firstly shock and surprise that there is a problem having perhaps used contraception for a long while and taken their fertility for granted. Denial is often the next reaction, giving the mind and body time to adjust to the enormity of the news. Anger follows as a response to a loss of control over events once medical treatments are started, with feelings of isolation, guilt and grief following on (1980).

Denial was something that a couple of interviewees mentioned. With hindsight they felt they had rejected the news initially but had now come to accept it. Ultimately however, everyone now seemed to recognise they had fertility problems, though they might be unclear about the implications of such a diagnosis.

As discussed earlier, these reactions may not be typical because I spoke to a highly select group of men. One researcher said to me that his work supported the view that a more normal reaction was for men to evade and deny the diagnosis if possible and he illustrated his point by telling me about the man who had been told he had no sperm yet still believed he could father a child. Presumably this man protected himself from the news by not hearing it. Other writers also think that many men can never really accept the diagnosis and that those close to them try to shelter them from the news (Snowden *et al.*, 1983).

Reactions can be very painful for those who do eventually accept they have a problem. Other types of responses apart from those I have described are looked at in a study of couples' reactions to male infertility and donor insemination. Most men reported various symptoms. One started having an affair, and there were reports of impotence and depression. Some wives said their husbands seemed more withdrawn (Berger, 1980).

There are certain factors that may influence a man's reactions. Winston thinks guilt plays a part. 'Many men are much more distressed at being infertile than are their partners. Some become very disturbed or clinically depressed.' He reasons that men feel responsible and, so, full of guilt for what has happened. They are deeply ashamed (1989: 94). Possibly the diagnosis strikes a blow at their sexual identity though this was not the only issue for those I spoke to. Rather they worried about letting their partners down by not giving them children.

The type of diagnosis may influence reactions. Those of my interviewees who had no sperm said on the whole they had immediate powerful reactions of despair and hopelessness. They could not evade the diagnosis and harbour false hopes of fathering a child. Ultimately this helped them accept the news. The blow was somehow softened if they knew why they had no sperm and they seemed more resigned to the diagnosis. Jeffrey was unsettled because he was still searching around for reasons for his lack of sperm.

Those who had been told they had sperm problems tended to have less clear-cut responses to the news. Their experiences were often of a different nature. They were grappling with what the diagnosis meant and whether they could improve their sperm and so become fathers. The whole process of diagnosis was more drawn out. Brian, for example, had at least nine semen analyses over four years and his partner was still going through various assisted conception techniques to see if she could get pregnant.

Luke reacted strongly to being told he had poor-quality sperm (sperm problems). He found this a pejorative term which heightened feelings of inadequacy and made a point of referring to 'low quality' sperm which somehow seemed more neutral.

A diagnosis of sperm problems seems to cause more anxiety because of the uncertainty associated with it. Men also sometimes felt responsible for what had happened, fearing that their lifestyle might be to blame in some way. Drinking too much coffee and alcohol and smoking might have worsened sperm quality they reasoned. This all made for guilt. Those who discovered they had been born with, for example, a vital part missing felt blameless and less hampered by anxiety when it was clear nothing could be done about the situation.

Pain may have lingered more persistently for those of my interviewees who could not understand why they were infertile and were unclear as to what the outlook was for them. MacNab remarked also that uncertainty can cause more anguish. 'Having a definite diagnosis may provide an emotional watershed, a point at which some resolution of the effects of infertility can begin' (1984: 100).

Edelmann and Connolly also consider how diagnosis and prognosis can influence people and refer to a study which compared men with no sperm to those with sperm problems. 'Both groups reported feelings of depression, but the latter group showed evidence of poorer marital relationships, lower self-esteem and increased social isolation' (1986: 215). (In the future, feelings of uncertainty may become more pronounced for men with all types of diagnoses, if treatment options increase.)

The support the man receives from his partner may also affect his reactions. 'She was positive and started to make other plans for the future and wasn't distressed by it. I'm sure this made my acceptance of the diagnosis easier.' Those men who offered a divorce to their partners were relieved when the woman turned the offer down. Conversely Chris said he received no such support and he and his partner eventually separated.

Finally though there were some common strands in men's reactions, it is clear looking at the experiences, that they all varied. A number of factors may affect how a man reacts and these will differ for each person. Other factors may also affect reactions. For instance, Tim felt less anxious about his diagnosis because his partner was also infertile. Kevin felt his counselling background had helped him cope better with his reactions. It was important to let his emotions out and cry whilst for others it was important to be in control which meant not expressing feelings. Age may also influence reactions and Jeffrey said he was harder hit when he received his diagnosis because he was in his early twenties. It was a big blow to his sense of manliness. Mike said fatherhood was less of an urgent concern as he became older, as the romantic gloss of fatherhood had lost some of its shine.

A report sets out why experiences can differ.

Infertility in the male evokes a wide range of emotional reactions, depending upon the finality of the diagnosis, the investment of the male in
becoming a birth parent, the cause of his infertility, his partner's response,
and his readiness to confront the emotions that are evoked by the diagnosis
of infertility.

(Congress of the US, Office of Technology Assessment, 1988a: 16)

Reactions can be very powerful or less so depending on such factors. The
message that emerges from this discussion is that it would be unwise to
assume that men respond in a uniform way to a diagnosis of male infertility.

9 The consequences

Responses to the diagnosis were mixed and the news shocked some whilst others seemed less hard hit by it. What effects if any did men notice in their lives in the wake of the diagnosis?

IDENTITY

Does a man's sense of himself lessen as the result of finding out he is infertile and is his manhood called into question if he has problems fathering a child because 'the man who is seen not to have children is considered lacking in masculinity or virility' (Houghton and Houghton, 1987: 48)?

This was rejected categorically by several interviewees. Points were made along the following lines.

> Being able to father your own child doesn't make you more or less a man or human being. I don't think any the less of a female friend who has infertility problems so I don't see why a bloke should be any less of a bloke.

Others felt more perplexed. Andrew had no personal experience of people making jokes about infertile men but he still felt there was a link in people's minds between infertility and virility. 'To be a man you need to show that you can father children and it's a sign of failure if you can't.' Matthew had worried people would ridicule him ever since finding out he had no sperm in his semen in 1987:

> I was worried then and now about other people finding out about my infertility. I feel I just couldn't cope with people knowing. I was in the pub once with some friends and there was talk about a male friend getting his wife pregnant and having proved himself. That remark still haunts me. I thought, what are they going to think about me if they find out I have no sperm? What will they say behind my back? I'm not a macho man but I

work in an all-male environment where there are lots of crude jokes about sex and related things and I don't want to be the butt of those jokes about a seedless Jaffa. I don't know what I would have done if someone had said that about me because social reaction bothers me though I know it shouldn't. I'm a married man, but we couldn't have a family because of something I couldn't do and that hurts. I have had to keep quiet about my infertility to protect my self-respect.

The importance of self-respect was also stressed by Alan:

One of your basic instincts is to have children to carry on the race. I can't do that and my machismo has been affected.

It goes against the grain when you find you can't do your bit. Perhaps it's not so important to me now but it is to the outside world and I have to put on a brave face with my male friends. We all share a sort of bravado when we are together though I guess most of them are softies underneath it all. I suppose I've changed my views a bit since I found out I was infertile, but before this happened, I used to think part of being a man was being a father. I don't think less now of men who aren't fathers because I'm in that position myself, but the public's view of infertile men is that they are effeminate and impotent. Deep down most men know this and that's why they are frightened of talking about their infertility.

Others were less sure whether their manhood had been affected:

She has her instinct to have a child which I think men have less strongly, but I feel that men have to live up to this virility image because of all this confusion in people's minds. They think if you make love a lot you will be fertile. Even though I don't feel downgraded by my infertility, I was worried to start with that people might think I was impotent because I was infertile.

Mike began by saying there were no issues for him:

I don't feel less of a man. It's not what comes out of your loins that makes you a man it's what you do with your life. I get very upset when I see men who have lots of children they can't look after properly. But I did find it insensitive when a friend remarked to me how he had proved himself by getting someone pregnant. Yet I thought less of him than myself for saying that though I did feel a twinge of pain because he meant that comment to reflect on me.

For others there had perhaps been a change but it was to do with not achieving goals. Luke put it this way:

Generally I still reject all this stuff about a man having to prove himself by getting his partner pregnant. In the past I was quite clear about this and wouldn't have admitted or recognised such a link. I've shifted a bit on this because of what has happened. There does seem to be some sort of a link between how I view myself and my ability to father children. I can't deny that now, but I think it's more to do with not being able to accomplish something as a person rather than thinking I'm less of a man.

SEX LIFE WITH PARTNER

The strain of having to perform at the right time and for various medical tests and treatments took its toll in the short term. Mike explained:

I wasn't a performing seal but I felt like one when my wife was doing her ovulation checks. Sometimes she would wake me in the early hours of the morning when her temperature peaked and we had to make love. It got to the point when we didn't do it any more because it was all so cold and clinical and I was there just to get her pregnant. Our sex life hadn't been brilliant previously but it was almost non-existent for some months when we were going through all the medical treatments.

Others talked about the pointlessness of making love since they had found out they were infertile:

It was like reproductive sex. Having sex when you don't want it but you've got to do it because it's the right time of the month. There were times when I felt what is the point of doing this, I've got lousy sperm. It wasn't a pleasant experience.

Peter was puzzled:

Our sex life isn't brilliant, I don't know why. I just go to bed and want to go to sleep. Before we started trying for a family things were better and we were quite active but everything became mechanical from the time that my wife started taking her temperature charts. I found that really difficult. Then I found out I had sperm problems.

Sometimes I think my lack of interest is to do with my age [thirty-six years] but I guess it's more likely connected to my infertility. Why this should be I don't know. The pleasure has gone from sex and it's just to do with having children. Sometimes I think it might help if she put on sexy clothes, if I want a family then I have got to get turned on somehow.

Kevin's circumstances were different:

I wanted to make love more often and craved physical and emotional reassurance once I found out I had no sperm. I needed to know my wife still loved me. The problem was we both reacted in different ways to start with. My wife almost didn't see any point making love, but I wanted to. The result was that our sex life suffered for a time.

Brian had fantasies:

I have sperm so I wondered what my chances would be if I went for a wife who was super-fertile and much younger than me. Or if I had a string of floozies something might be just right with one of them. All these thoughts crossed my mind fleetingly but they would return when I felt low. It was all to do with trying to reassert my confidence.

One of the infertility tests had long-lasting effects. Jeffrey's sex life had been affected ever since he was told he had small testicles ten years ago:

It's at the back of my mind, even all these years on. When I make love to my wife, I feel a bit self-conscious about it. I think about it during foreplay and then intercourse and worry about this even though my wife says she isn't bothered.

Others said their sex lives were unaffected. 'It's fine, just the same, we make love just like we used to.' A couple of men also said their sex lives had improved since contraception had been abandoned, as sex was more spontaneous.

RELATIONSHIP WITH PARTNER

There was a sense of regret and sadness amongst some men when it came to discussions about their relationships. 'I feel I've let her down, reduced her chances of having children. She doesn't agree with me, but it's something we have to talk about from time to time and I feel bad about it.'

Relationships had gone through rough patches as a result of the diagnosis: 'The strain was incredible at times. I felt it would be better if we split up, then at least my wife could have children with someone else. Perhaps I could find a woman who didn't want children.' And:

We screamed at each other a bit. I became quiet and uncommunicative, busy with other things and I shut my wife out. There was no other outlet for my tensions and they came out in the marriage. I made life pretty hellish for her for a time whilst still trying to keep the marriage together. Part of me was trying to be reasonable and keep things going and be supportive whilst underneath there were destructive parts looking for other ways out.

Bruce had talked to his wife about the future of their marriage:

We talked seriously about splitting up. Children were very important to us both and so we started thinking about separating some months after my diagnosis. My wife concluded that I was more important to her than children. I think children were less important for her whereas for me it was vital to have a family. I was obsessed with the idea.

Derek did separate for a time from his wife:

We were apart for just under two years. It was due to a combination of things. We just hadn't been talking about our feelings. I was trying to cope with awful remarks at work about me not being a father and was wrapped up in my own painful world. I was so distressed that I tried to shut out all the upset, but my wife felt I was shutting her out too. The stress at work together with the business of having to produce samples just overloaded me. In the end our marriage broke down for a time. Things had got pretty bad and we had been going at each other hammer and tongs for a while, but we missed each other dreadfully and eventually got back together and started talking.

Rows also figured in other experiences:

My wife doesn't hold anything against me because of my infertility, but when we argue it sometimes comes out about me not having established myself, not having a proper home, not having a family. I get blamed. It blows over the next day but I feel bad about it.

Chris explained:

It was the tension produced by powerlessness that sparked off all the arguments. The decision to have children was no longer in our hands. I also think that my wife resented me because of my infertility, that was another part of it. The whole business was bruising.

The result of the various stresses meant you had to protect yourself, according to Alan. The result was a stronger relationship. 'You become more self-centred and insular as a couple. It's an either make or break situation because the pressure is tremendous, but we were lucky and the bond between us became stronger.' Jeffrey said his wife had stood by him though the going had got rough at one point. 'We hit rock bottom and she said she couldn't cope anymore, but we went to a see a more sympathetic person about donor sperm. Things then started to improve.'

FAMILY, FRIENDS AND SOCIAL LIFE

The effects on these areas varied. Family relationships were very important to some men and thoughts about how these were affected are looked at in the 'Dealing with people' chapter. It is worth noting here that a few relationships went through a period of strain. That increased for example, when a brother or sister had another child. Andrew's poignant words illustrate this. He is the eldest in his family: 'When we started trying for a baby, my three other sisters hadn't produced children, but they've all had children now, and one has had her third child. Somehow each new baby is an extra indignity for me.' Derek felt cut off from his family:

> My brother has two children now. He is a family man and makes me feel bad because I'm not. He doesn't seem to understand what we've been through. It's sad because we used to be close but we've grown apart. He just doesn't want to know what's happened to me.

Isolation was also raised. Robert had been trying to have children for a long time:

> You really feel left behind when other people start having children. The biggest thing is the awful loneliness it causes. You see more and more friends get pregnant and have children. Their lifestyles change and they mix with people who have children. I think they also feel guilty and uncomfortable when they are with you because they know you want children so much, so there's a barrier between you. They avoid you because they don't want to hurt you and they disappear into the woodwork not because they don't care, but because they can't cope with your distress.

WORK

The impact on jobs varied. Several interviewees mentioned a loss of drive and ambition. 'Everything seemed pointless for a time. I didn't look for promotion and in fact a job was pushed at me.'

Job satisfaction was lowered for a time:

> I've always liked my job but I didn't enjoy it so much in the months after I found out I was infertile. I think infertility was responsible in some way for this though there were other factors at play. At the time I saw no connection between my job and the diagnosis but ended up moving jobs which helped because the new one was not linked to the time I received the infertility diagnosis.

James felt isolated:

> I just felt what's the point of working hard, who am I supposed to provide for? I felt set apart from the other men in the office because most of them have children. I felt incredibly lonely at one point.

Two men said their jobs had definitely been affected. 'I started a course at work but my performance took a dive. I was very anxious at the time and became very insular and self-centred as a result.' And:

> Infertility took up too much of our life at the beginning. We were always talking about it and I'm sure looking back that my work suffered. I was doing well in my particular speciality and suddenly everything went wrong. I took some exams which I failed, so I had to turn my career round. Several job changes resulted and I'm now doing something which probably suits me far better than the original job. Perhaps it's been a blessing in disguise.

CONFIDENCE AND FAILURE

Personal confidence could be shaken:

> I had to try and regain my confidence. Before this happened I felt I could do anything and never questioned my ability. I'm not so assured now as I used to be, though this may be to do with getting older as well as infertility. For example, I used to take it for granted that I could manage hiring a car and find my way round in a foreign country. Now since finding out about the infertility, I worry, will I get lost, will I cope? I can't talk to my wife about this as she expects me to be good at travel arrangements. She relies on me.

Matthew said he had to work to keep his self-respect:

> I had to do this to stop losing my morale. I kept saying it's not my fault. It was like I had to get over this hurdle somehow and I kept reminding myself that there were other opportunities in life.

Feelings of failure were a step on from loss of confidence. A sense of it had spread into every part of one man's life and was still there several years on from the diagnosis. Another point was made:

> I felt like an outcast, a failure. All round me there were pictures of happy families, so I felt incomplete. There was an awful feeling of being different to everyone else because I wasn't like all the smiling men you see with their children.

GUILT

This emotion was mentioned regularly as discussed in the previous chapter. This could be an immediate reaction that was finished with relatively quickly, but it clung to some men and they continued feeling bad.

DEPRESSION

A couple of people said they had considered suicide but not seriously. Bruce was the only man who said he had taken medication to deal with severe depression:

> I got very low. I was involved then in work with children but found the cases difficult to handle because of my infertility. Powerful feelings kept surfacing all the time and I wallowed in self-pity because things weren't going my way. I was the eldest in my family and wanted to be the first to have a child. Then this happened.
>
> Later on, things were set back when we were trying to adopt a child. The whole business hit me hard and I became very tearful. I went onto medication for a bit to help me. It was Christmas and there were various family gatherings which people came to with their children. I had none. Because of all this I started to try and avoid people with children, it was all too painful and I didn't want to impose my depression on others. The end result was a feeling of desolation.

OTHER EFFECTS

Uncertainty had spread through Simon's life. Certain decisions about jobs and home had to be postponed until his infertility had been sorted out.

Positive effects were reported. Sex lives had improved and the experience had enriched some relationships:

> There were good things about what happened and it wasn't all bad. It was a problem we worked on together and this brought us closer together. Our relationship became stronger because we found out more about each other and our different needs. We had to become much better at communicating with each other.

DISCUSSION

The effects of male infertility can be severe for the man, according to one article. Failure haunts him, marriages crack and there is much bitterness. Many men feel castrated (Prentice, 1984).

Those I spoke to painted a less dramatic picture. The range of reported effects was wide and varied over time. Mostly interviewees presented their lives as continuing much as before, though Bruce became extremely depressed about eighteen months after receiving his diagnosis. One marriage eventually split up and another couple separated on a temporary basis. Jobs could be affected. It was difficult to tease out what the effects really were and easy to jump to the wrong conclusion, according to some men. Lack of confidence, for example, as Roger observed might have been more to do with his age rather than infertility. The diagnosis might or might not be implicated in work worries, according to someone else.

The effects were not necessarily obvious and could take time to appear. Isolation insidiously crept up on men as contacts with friends and family were lost or weakened. Sex lives were altered for a number of reasons. Making love to order provoked anxiety. Peter talked of wanting to go to sleep rather than make love. Possibly it was easier not to have sex rather than face up to what he saw as failure if his wife did not become pregnant after making love. Kevin wanted his wife to reassure him she loved him by more love making and Brian dreamed of regaining his confidence through other women.

Having an affair may be one way of restoring sex as a pleasurable activity unlinked to fertility, and boosting confidence. None of my interviewees said they had actually had affairs though some thought about this as with Brian and his 'floozies'. Blizzard says he turned to another woman for a time to get away from the reality and pain of what he was going through with his wife. 'Ann was fixed firmly in a reality in which I was nothing. Margrethe could fly with me into any dream.' He could reclaim lost illusions with her as his lover restored his torn sense of masculinity to health (1977: 100).

Time clearly plays a part in how infertility affects lives. Effects may be short- or long-lived and some may arise sooner than others. Positive ones may appear in the longer term. MacNab refers to studies that suggest that people deny the effects of infertility for a year and concludes from his own research that this period is much longer for men, around three years. Many changes were reported by those still struggling with infertility past this point, particularly those with an uncertain diagnosis (1984).

The effects of the diagnosis can ripple through someone's life though most of my interviewees did not mention this. Elsewhere one man wrote how he slipped into a severe depression. 'Several factors brought this on but infertility fears were the major catalyst. I withdrew from my wife out of guilt. I was too embarrassed to consult my male friends.' He goes on to say that he avoided people who had children, found himself distracted at work, felt events were beyond his control and went through fits of uncontrollable crying (Jones).

What reasons could account for such distress? Male infertility can hit a man at a time when he is trying to establish himself at work, says Winston. The sense of failure the man experiences can reach into other parts of his life, affecting professional ambition (1989). Guilt, which several people talked to me about, can be all-pervasive, according to Menning. She thinks it can spread into every part of a person's life. The result can be feelings of worthlessness and self-destructive behaviour such as drug abuse and alcoholism. Guilt feelings are resolved by realising that not all aspects of life can be controlled and that fertility and worthiness are not related (1980).

Another explanation for the ripple effect is that the goal of parenthood is linked to other ones such as being a worthwhile member of society. Failure to become a father may mean the other goals seem unattainable and the person starts to feel worthless (Clark *et al.*, 1991). This may explain why confidence can be shattered by a diagnosis of infertility. As someone explained to me, 'your life plan dissolves and everything is called into question'.

Blizzard's blunt analysis of his own predicament shows how traumatic the experience can be and why in his own case his life was markedly affected by his diagnosis. His marriage, work and mental health suffered at various times. 'Sterility is a disorder, it is not an illness. It may, however, by a continuing intrusion into a person's thoughts generate an illness'. Then 'in consciousness however, it casts new perspectives on inheritance and on destiny and these are formidable issues' (1977: 170).

The question of how hard men are hit by the diagnosis and how much lives are affected by it was difficult to gauge from my discussions. (I wondered whether they downplayed any possible changes because of wanting to appear in control, or were unaware of any.) Research studies on the male response to infertility are minimal compared to female studies (Bents, 1985). Those studies that have looked at men point to certain effects. Infertile men may for instance be more anxious and less confident than fertile men (Kedem *et al.*, 1990). Other researchers report that men complained people 'took advantage of them and did not give them proper credit for their achievements' (Berg and Wilson, 1990: 659). Only three out of sixteen men in Berger's study reported no symptoms in response to the diagnosis (1980). Male infertility may be more stigmatising (Miall, 1985) perhaps explaining why men want to hide their diagnosis. Owens says 'there is considerable evidence that the diagnosis of infertility has a greater impact on the man than on the woman' (1982: 80). Men and also women reported greater emotional and marital turmoil when male infertility was the cause of childlessness (Connolly and Cooke, 1987).

Why should this be so? Some possible explanations have been put forward. There are others. According to one psychologist a man's sexual identity is threatened by infertility. 'A man can cope with having a straggly beard or his head being bald, but his definition of himself as male belongs primarily to his sexual functioning' (Cozens, 1992: 60). Neuberg says:

> Initially, men certainly seem to be hit much harder than their partners and less able to cope with the knowledge that they themselves are actually infertile. It's the age-old confusion between virility and sterility, the

feeling that a man is lacking in something essentially male in being unable to prove his masculinity to society by getting his partner pregnant.

(1991: 126)

Another study reported that infertility was seen to be linked to sexual as well as reproductive failure, but the failure was greater for men because 'their ability to have sexual relations and their fertility are usually considered to be closely linked' (Woollett, 1985: 478).

These explanations may be incomplete. One piece of research reported that men did not see their masculinity as threatened (*Issue*, 1991a) and Owens found in his study that the threat to virility was not the real worry. Men felt concerned that they could not be proper husbands because they could not give their wives children. It was not so much personal or psychological inadequacy that was the problem as the failure to meet marital expectations (1982).

There were mixed thoughts about masculinity amongst my interviewees. Clearly the term means different things to different people. Some were upset because they felt they had failed to prove themselves. In their world, masculinity essentially meant getting a woman pregnant, but that was not the case for everyone. Peter felt he had failed in his husbandly duty towards his wife. For others feelings of inadequacy were more to do with the need to achieve and succeed. Failing to do this was what hurt, said Luke.

There was a pervasive sense of impotence in a general rather than sexual sense in some of my discussions. Men felt powerless, unable to achieve something they thought would be easy to do. The anguish came from finding out they could not fulfil expectations they had always taken for granted.

The way men are brought up may also make it harder for them to deal with life when it does not go the way they planned, a point that cropped up in my interviews. Men can be vulnerable to major life changes, lose a sense of worth and feel incompetent because they are brought up to achieve and be in control. Fear of failure is terrifying for them (Carlson, 1987) and they are driven by the need to be potent, to compete and win. Impotence is seen as feminine, undesirable behaviour, something to be avoided at all costs (Dubois and Marino, 1987).

Difficulties in expressing feelings and admitting the need for support may also play a part in how men's lives are affected:

Any psychological attachment to the dreamchild he hoped to conceive with his partner will be dramatically altered with the accompanying feelings of emptiness and sadness. For males who have been socialised not to express emotions associated with grief, there is likely to be more comfort in expressing the anger felt at being deprived of the role of being a birth parent.

(Congress of the US, Office of Technology Assessment, 1988a: 3)

Isolation was the main feeling shared by my interviewees. This stems from the veil of secrecy that surrounds infertility. People do not talk about it openly possibly because of its link to sexual behaviour (Dunkel-Schetter and Stanton, 1991). Men may feel peculiarly isolated and shut off from all sorts of people they have previously been close to and may become closer to their partner as a result, a point made to me by some men. Woollett explains this can happen to both infertile men and women as 'they become each others main buffers against the shock of discovering they are infertile and they share the depression, anguish and sense of failure'. Relationships were not always strengthened in her research. Anger and grief could be directed at the partner seen as responsible for childlessness (1985: 480), something Chris spoke to me about.

The sense of loneliness may increase for men because they feel cut off from other people. They can be out of step with friends and work colleagues and feel the problem is unacknowledged. They may also not know of other men with fertility problems and so can feel unique and marked off from other men (Snowden and Snowden, 1984).

Not being able to talk to another man about the problem may make matters worse. Osherson believes feelings of isolation are intensified in times of difficulty because men cannot talk their problems over with members of their own sex. When he and his wife were experiencing problems he wanted to talk to male friends but all too often let opportunities slip by. Men may be embarrassed because of the link between infertility and sexuality and may find it hard to talk to men because of wanting to appear invulnerable. Yet people need to have the problem recognised by their own sex (1986).

The effects on men's lives may be harrowing for the sorts of reasons outlined, but lives are affected in different ways. Factors that may influence effects include how well the man and woman communicate with each other, the importance of children for the man and his partner, and the support and understanding received from family, friends and medical staff (Mahlstedt, 1985).

There is no practical evidence to show that specific reactions are common amongst infertile people say Dunkel-Schetter and Lobel. 'If anything the effects of infertility on the marriage appear to be positive as often as negative, as measured by self-report.' But they note that infertility may affect views of one's self as potent and they point out that such findings may well depend on the stage at which research is done. For example, people are most commonly interviewed during the treatment stage when they may be more hopeful (1991: 50). Possibly men are unaware of or downplay what they see as more threatening changes in their lives. The other problem with research evidence is that men's responses to infertility generally and to male infertility specifically have been neglected.

10 The desire to be a father

The way a man reacts to the news that he is infertile must surely depend in part on how much value he places on fatherhood. It is important to understand what price men and women place on the goal of parenting and to see what part it plays in their sense of identity (Dunkel-Schetter and Stanton, 1991).

How significant is fatherhood for men? In the early 1980s Jackson wrote in his study of first-time fathers, that little was known about them. He spoke of the 'invisible man' who seemed remote and distant from the child. In autobiographies 'frequently father is dutifully there in the opening chapter, possibly overshadowed by mother, and then fading from the narrative at a very early stage' (1984: 3).

My interviewees had a mix of reasons for wanting to be fathers.

MOTIVES

Childhood

There was a desire to improve on upbringing as Bruce told me:

> It was more selfish than wanting to get my wife pregnant. It was more to do with my own upbringing. I was the eldest of four children and I remember my childhood as being happy, but I also remember feeling that I wasn't that close to my father. Apart from family holidays, I had little to do with him and that's always something I wanted to put right. I felt I had missed out in a way because as time passed by my father became more involved with the younger children in our family. I think I needed to recreate my own childhood and improve on it.

Matthew recalled a childhood tinged with greyness and wanted to be a father so that his children could have fun.

Pride

Others wanted to prove themselves. 'I wanted to be seen with my pregnant wife and have that sense of pride and excitement of being involved in the pregnancy.' Brian had a fantasy of founding a dynasty. 'The idea that I could start off generations from good stock and produce people capable of great achievements was very attractive.' Someone else wanted to recreate himself, 'I know it's vanity but that is one of the things I wanted and I've missed out on'.

No obvious reason

Often it was unclear why fatherhood was an attractive notion. 'It's not to do with proving myself in any way or doing my duty towards my wife. It's just that we both want children.' For others it was the normal thing to do. Kevin explained that he did not get married to have children but had come round to the idea.

Jeffrey did get married to have children:

I was always good with children, mix with them well and love playing with them. I married expecting and wanting us to have children. We got engaged, had the wedding, moved to a lovely home. Everything was going smoothly and we waited for the first pregnancy but nothing happened and the natural progression of events stopped.

HOW IMPORTANT WAS FATHERHOOD?

Another way of exploring what men felt about fatherhood was to get them to talk about this related issue. What weight did they attach to fatherhood? Most were uncertain about this, but Bruce said he had an obsessional drive for children. Jeffrey talked about female as opposed to male desire for children:

It was vital for me too. A woman has a biological push to have children, but I also think men have an equivalent drive. If we were still wild animals I would have been allowed to hang around my wife for a bit and then driven off. I think that's why I feel so bad sometimes. I don't want to but my instincts make me feel like that.

There was an opposing viewpoint. 'Right from the start my wife wanted children more than I did. I felt if it happens that is fine and if it doesn't that is fine.' Uncertainty was also expressed. 'She was much keener to start with but because I love and wanted to stay with her I began to change my mind.'

Death had an effect:

> When I got married I thought we would have children at some point, but my wife was keen to start as soon as possible. She idolised her mother who had died recently so I think my wife was keen to start up her own family.

The passage of time played a part in certain ways:

> As soon as I found out I might have problems my desire became more urgent. Time suddenly seemed to weigh on me very heavily and I felt my chances slipping away. There seemed to be a direct link between wanting it and it not happening. It became an acute yearning.

Peter was worried he would be too old. It was very important for him to become a father without delay.

> I think you need to be able to play with your children so you need plenty of energy. I almost feel too old now I'm in my mid thirties. I'm worried I won't be able to play football with my children because I will be in a wheelchair.

LOSS

Discussions ranged round whether men sensed any loss when they found out there was a question mark over their fertility. I wondered whether anyone would talk about 'genetic death' (Prentice, 1988).

Only Kevin told me about dreams that symbolised loss. He had recurrent ones of pushing round a dead baby in a pram after he found out he was producing no sperm. Nobody else recalled such dreams. Others felt they had lost an intangible thing and tried to describe this to me. Robert had been struggling with infertility for some years and his wife was still attempting to get pregnant with medical help. He was explicit about how his vision of the future had changed:

> My stake in the future was gone somehow when I found out I was infertile. There was suddenly a big hole in front of me. Having a family was one of the key elements of my life so my future had gone. My career and other things in my life just didn't matter anymore. My desire to be a father was enormous and I'd always assumed I would be one, so my identity was shaken up. I'd also lost out on the chance to create something with my partner.

Fantasies were lost for Luke:

> The grief I went through was not about feeling inadequate but to do with

the many fantasies and images I've had of being a father with my child. As a man I thought about what would happen once my baby was born rather than thinking about pregnancy and childbirth which is what I'm sure women do. I know my partner said she used to think about this and seeing pregnant women would upset her.

I would visualise playing with my child and would conjure up images of what I thought fathers do with their children. These fantasies would be sharpened by seeing fathers in real life playing with their kids. That really upset me.

It's strange because in my mind I had created a child which didn't exist. I wasn't upset about the thought that I was infertile but I did feel sad thinking about this child of mine who had only ever existed in my mind. I suppose this was my way of dealing with what had happened and I used to imagine taking my child to my parents and saying here is my child, your grandchild. I would hold the baby out to my father.

There is also something else I think I'm losing out on though I hate saying it and it goes against the grain. I want to be able to say to other people 'this is my baby, our child'. There is a sense of possession, of the baby being my property because it is a part of me. I regret not being able to do this even though a part of me is horrified at the thought of thinking of a baby as my property, but it's the way I feel.

Now that my partner is pregnant, probably as a result of donor sperm being used, I still daydream about taking the baby to my father, but there's a difference. There is a question mark in the background about whether I'm the biological father.

Jeffrey had a vision:

The child I haven't had has been with me these past ten years. I've had a vision when I've been out gardening in particular, of a child running round, playing in the garden. I used to think if things had worked out properly, I would have this child. As the years passed, my child grew older. The feelings of loss were very hard to bear.

I used to also get very upset seeing babies and families with children. I felt so sad because I thought we could give a child a happy home and yet other people produced children without difficulty and yet didn't seem to care for them. Seeing other children was always a reminder of what I was missing out on. I remember one Christmas leaving a big store because I was so choked up seeing all the children there.

Now that my wife is finally pregnant after donor insemination, I still have images of my child sometimes, but they are not so strong. I don't feel the same way. There's a real baby to think about now.

James spoke about not being able to pass on his experiences to his children. He felt bitter about his infertility:

When I found out I was infertile, I felt disappointed. Part of myself was lost. I'd built up all this experience and suddenly realised how much I wanted to pass it on to the next generation. I hadn't thought about this before. All my experience of life seemed such a waste, what was I to do with it? If you have children you can pass on your knowledge and help them understand the world, hopefully help them avoid some of the mistakes you made. I could see how much fun and pleasure other men seemed to get playing with their children and teaching them. I realised that children provide an exciting challenge and stimulus which is handed to you on a plate. People with children don't see this and just take it for granted. Yet for me I was going to miss out on these things, and every-thing, including myself, seemed pointless.

It's not the loss of caring, after all you can look after a pet. Having a child would make sense of my existence, justify it in some way. I'm not bound up with any images but I wanted the chance of being with my child from birth to adulthood and beyond. What I've lost is this relationship with a child I've created which grows and develops. I'm missing out on a unique experience and I don't know what to put in its place. When I see other people with their children I get pangs of jealousy.

The loss of potential was identified:

I hadn't bothered a great deal about fatherhood and I didn't think I had any great desire to pass on my genes, but when I was told about my infertility, that all changed. I felt a sense of protest inside me because I've come to an evolutionary full stop. It's a philosophical thought rather than a gut feeling. My brothers and sisters can carry on the family name because they've had children, but there is nothing for me, just an emptiness.

Not being able to pass on family characteristics saddened Kevin who came from a family of two girls and one boy:

Sometimes I feel a bit nostalgic. I look at my sister's little boy and girl to see whether they have any of my father's mannerisms. I really like my dad and I think it's a shame there isn't going to be any more of him. It's not that I feel there won't be any more of me, rather I feel sad because in some strange way I want to reproduce my parents and I won't be able to do this because I have no sperm.

I look at my feet which are horrid and despite this I think nobody else will have these and I feel sad about that. It's in some way the loss of my past. There won't be any more of my parents, we've come to the end of the line. This is what weighs most heavily on me. It's the personalities that I've grown up with and love and respect who will come to an end. I don't want to see that happen whereas the idea of carrying on the family name doesn't mean anything to me.

It was important to pass on something for others:

My brother has two children so the name will go on. That isn't the problem, but I feel sad that I can't carry my side forward. This loss together with losing out on the pleasures of family life, make me sad. Nieces and nephews can help but there's still something missing.

And,

I don't know why I've picked up this idea but I'm sad because the family line will run out with me. When I see a strong likeness between fathers and sons I feel miserable because this will never happen for me.

Others were uncertain if they had lost anything. Alan's wife had given birth to a baby after going through DI:

Genetic death doesn't mean anything to me, after all it's only a few cells that you are passing on, but I do accept that when I go that's the end of me. Now we have our child, the family name can go on and I can pass on the values and attitudes that I think are important. My daughter is mine in that sense and if she had been mine naturally I'm not certain whether anything would have been different.

You see, the loss I felt bad about when I found out I had no sperm was to do with the thought that I would never be a parent. I wanted to prove to myself and to the world that I could be a good dad. Now I can do that.

SUBSTITUTES

The importance of parenting as opposed to fatherhood was a point that continually came up. Any sense of loss was washed away some said, because their main goal was parenting and they could achieve this. John emphatically rejected the notion of genetic death. His wife gave birth after DI was used. Nurture not nature was what counted:

I think the environment plays a big part in shaping the future adult. So the fact that the baby is not biologically mine is irrelevant. All my experience in the teaching world, points to the influence of surroundings rather than inbuilt characteristics.

I feel very strongly about this. My wife is adopted and yet you can see that she is part of her family not set apart in any way, but she is not biologically connected to her parents.

Bruce felt the same and added:

> It's how you bring the child up that matters rather than the raw material you start with. Maybe I'm protecting myself with this view and rationalising away uncomfortable thoughts, but I genuinely believe this.
>
> If I'm honest about it, there are things I'm glad I can't pass on to anyone else. We've both got bad eyesight whereas our two adopted children have excellent vision. Of course there is the thought that when I go that's it there will be nothing to remember me by. Maybe that's why I got so depressed all those years ago, but I can't clearly remember now how I felt then.

Tim and his wife were in the process of adopting a child when I spoke to him. He said there were certain advantages in becoming a parent this way:

> The idea of being the father of a newborn baby was unimportant to me. In some ways the best thing about adoption is that we won't get a baby but will be dealing with an older child. I've never liked babies so the fantasy of visiting my wife in hospital with a baby at her side wasn't attractive to me. What I would have really missed was the chance to be a parent and help and guide children through those years.

DISCUSSION

Do men yearn for fatherhood? In the play *The Pool of Bethesda* by Allan Cubitt a young doctor dying of a brain tumour mourns the fact that he will never have his own child. Fatherhood is portrayed as an important concept for him. Clearly the issue of loss for this character faced with death was more clear-cut than for my interviewees. They had a variety of options still in front of them or felt they had resolved their infertility in some way. I wanted to find out what loss if any they felt. Was the idea of being infertile in itself upsetting or were men sad because they could not reproduce themselves? Or did they see themselves as losing out on something else?

The messages I received were hazy. It was often unclear why men wanted children. An air of ambivalence hung over conversations on this point but could be coloured by powerful longings. Bruce was clear why he wanted children. He needed to redress the wrongs of his own childhood. One person's future had crumbled away, and another started to see that he was missing out on a rich unique experience that was irreplaceable. Others longed for what they saw as the pleasures of fatherhood and some felt it would confirm their masculine status. Desire for children could also be heightened by the need to compete with brothers and sisters who had produced offspring. Passing the family name on was important to some and not others as was the idea of genetic death. Bruce talked about feeling remote from his father but generally men did not say much about their fathers.

I wondered whether men mourned the actual or possible loss of the ability to have their own offspring, but this was far too narrow a definition. Conversations continually turned to the subject of parenthood rather than fatherhood. The chance to care for a child should be grasped and it was immaterial who the father was. Those men who now had families stressed the delights of being a parent and said or implied that they had nothing to grieve over. John insisted that getting a family either through adoption or DI did not seem strange. It was all a question of what you were used to. After listening to these opinions I often came away feeling that biology was irrelevant.

Yet the possibility of being a biological father was still on the agenda for some of those with sperm problems. They were mostly still striving for this goal whilst downplaying the need to have their own children. The idea of biology was not totally discounted by interviewees generally because several of them wanted the woman to have the chance to have her own biological child if possible.

The reasons for wanting children are explored by Owens in his study of working-class men who might be infertile. Children were seen as fun and men looked forward to the pleasures of being with them. Having a family was important because the man could have the status of father and the woman that of mother. Men talked of the importance of fulfilling the role of husband by giving their wives children. Owens speculates that the failure to give his wife children can provoke as much anxiety in a man as any threat to his virility (1982).

Husbandly duty was mentioned to me. Roger and Alan had offered their wives a divorce because they felt they had let them down, though the notion was alien to others. Brian had never considered this though his wife felt he should have as it would have been a thoughtful gesture for him to have made.

Romantic reasons may explain why some men want children though this was not something that obviously came up in my discussions. The desire to have children as proof of a romantic bond may play its part for some men, 'if we have a child, somehow we will be joined forever' (Jones, 1991: 10). The British media personality Jonathan Ross made this point plus others in a magazine interview when asked why he wanted children. His wife was pregnant with their first child. He replied: 'because I can, I suppose. Just showing off, basic ego. I really like children and it's a special thing to create something with the one you love' (Smith, 1991: 45).

Asking anyone why they want children may well result in rather vague, possibly trite replies. Owens says of his research, 'men had little idea of what fatherhood would entail and ideas of how it would affect them were extremely hazy' (1982: 78). One reason for this may be that it is difficult to know exactly what you feel about something until you have experienced it. There are other possible explanations.

Infertile men and women were often unable to be very specific about why they wanted children, according to Woollett. She wonders whether this may be because they are unwilling to accept the finality of infertility and also may not think that much about taken for granted events such as parenting (1985). Having children may be an inherited goal which people automatically assume they can achieve, so they may not analyse why they want children (Clark *et al.*, 1991).

There may be particular issues for men which make it more difficult for them to know what they feel about fatherhood. Woollett says of the forty-two women and eight men who took part in her study, that the women were more willing than the men to discuss infertility. This reflects assumptions that children are less important to men she says (1985).

Two infertility counsellors I spoke to about this issue expressed conflicting ideas. One felt that having children was of crucial importance. Men had a strong need to reproduce themselves but did not recognise this desire in themselves.

The other one made the point that men valued the concept of their fertility more than anything else.

> If I could say to all men with fertility problems that by some secret means I had made them fertile, then they would be happy. Children aren't vital to them, but it wouldn't be enough to say this to a woman. She would actually want children.

This uncertainty about the value of fatherhood was evident during my conversations. There are practical reasons for this as Richman points out:

> both medically and sociologically the father's relationship with the foetus has been considered a 'second' one, mainly on the commonsense ground that fathers do not carry the child, undergo no hormonal or physical change, do not abandon their work patterns, and do not enter directly into clientship with medical agencies.
>
> (1982: 94)

The view that children are more important for women than men may ignore the need men have for power and status and a sense of place in society. There are various theories which essentially stress the power aspects of fatherhood. Becoming a father may be part of the man's rite of passage into adulthood. As one man put it in Hite's study of sexuality:

A man should have a family and be its rightful head. When my wife told me that we were going to have a baby it gave me a feeling of satisfaction as somehow it made me feel justified. Now I could take my rightful place in society.

(Hite, 1981: 62)

From a historical viewpoint, Bradbury argues that fatherhood is a public statement of private power. Biological fatherhood is important in this view. By becoming fathers men become potent, that is powerful (Bradbury, 1985). Another theory is that men have a child because this 'is to do as their father has done'. Biological fatherhood provides a clear link between the man and his children. Yet he maintains a distance from his children rather than developing close relationships with them (Richards, 1982: 70).

These ideas seem dated in today's world. More appropriate perhaps is the idea of fathers wanting fun with their children that Owens referred to (1982). In the study of new fathers men were anxious to express the pleasures, joys and delights of fatherhood. The 'tap-roots of fatherhood run deep' but Jackson says men are less practised in talking about gentler feelings. 'To release the full force of fatherhood will mean breaking the masculine taboo on tenderness' (1984: 135). Richman's analysis of men's experiences of pregnancy and childbirth is that they are interested in such matters, and break the rule that men should not show feelings by crying (1982).

Fatherhood and the thought of it may mean a lot to men because it can provide them with a chance to care for children and experience feelings they might otherwise not have. They may be able to understand more about their own childhood, relive and put it to rights if need be and get a sense of the passing generations.

Yet they may feel uneasy about admitting to such longings because of their upbringing. Male conditioning means that work and power are emphasised. Men are defined by work outside the home and family life takes second place to this (Richards, 1982).

These contradictions may explain why I received ambiguous messages from interviewees about what fatherhood meant to them. They more clearly expressed sorrow about the woman's loss at perhaps not having children than their own. Interviewees could resolve any qualms they might have by becoming social rather than biological fathers. That route could provide them with most of the things they wanted. Some did express regret at not having their own children but in a muted fashion, though Robert and James were more explicit about the pain they felt.

Biology still lurked in the background. James was unusual because he only wanted his own children and would not consider other ways to parenthood. Generally men wanted the woman to go through DI so that she could at least have a child that 'was half hers'. Elsewhere Colin Tracy wrote about why he regretted having a vasectomy. He had made the decision with his head not his heart and made a huge mistake. He realised too late he did want his own children (1991) and Smith agonises about the importance of biological fatherhood:

> From my own experience I know that I have more emotional attachments to 'my' child – the child of my 'seed' – than to the children of other female friends. Yet I feel uneasy about this. Why shouldn't I love all children equally?
>
> (1990: 6)

He goes onto say that this worries him because as a man he is not tied to a child in the same way that a woman is. Smith suspects that the attachment to biological fatherhood has more to do with property rights than with anything else – a point that Luke made to me.

The drive for a biological link is, however, powerful according to Stephen Lottridge, who has known about his infertility for twenty years. Having adopted a son he still says 'I and my father and brother are one flesh. But I cannot give that to anyone. My son will never see me in his body, or know himself in a brother's limb. The biological flow runs dry in me. Sometimes that knowledge aches and gnaws like an amputation. I long for my cut-off children' (39). Being unable to father children made his life seem senseless and he felt he could not 'join successfully the ranks of men' (1988: 41).

Such regrets did not plague most of my interviewees. Biological father-hood was not a necessity and they were amenable to the idea of being a parent to another man's child. In fact social rather than biological fatherhood dates back to primitive people when the male role in reproduction was misunder-stood (Johnston, 1963). Letting go of 'biology' may be sensible and deciding that children are not vital or that social parenting is sufficient may make sense (Clark *et al.*, 1991). Retaining the belief that biological fatherhood is the only option may keep men trapped in a very painful situation if they have little prospect of achieving this.

This may explain why the idea of loss did not come across that strongly in many of the interviews. I felt it was skipped over or dealt with almost too quickly at times and was aware of the theory that says infertility is a process to be worked through. Grief and so recovery may fail if loss is not recognised or there is uncertainty about what that loss is. Resolution of the crisis means working through various feelings (Menning, 1980).

Researchers talk of men denying their infertility by stressing the nurturing rather than genetic role (Snowden *et al.*, 1983). I wondered whether men were stuck because they had bypassed the grieving process.

But perhaps men were coping and adapting well to their infertility rather than evading or denying it. Theories which say people must all go through the same experience are too rigid and do not take account of the different circumstances of each person's life.

Men were ambivalent, perhaps with good reason, about what fatherhood meant to them. Ideas about fatherhood may be changing as time passes by but men may well still be confused about what they are supposed to be missing out on by not having their own children. They may sense they are losing out on a role which could give them some status in society, but their upbringing and the importance of work in their lives may lessen a sense of loss. The importance of job and other types of satisfaction was something several men raised as they felt they had other interesting roles to play in life. Given this, they may not have acute feelings of sorrow and feel able to think more easily of other ways to parenthood.

Others may, however, find themselves peculiarly isolated. Lottridge (1988) is able to describe a sense of loss that others newer to the experience may find harder to articulate. They may sense their fertility is important to them but not know why this should be so. All around are messages that say fertility is more important to women than men so though they may want to grieve the loss of their fertility they may feel they have no right to do so.

11 Creating a family

Everyone I spoke to had considered what they would do if they could not have their own children. Adoption and DI were on most men's agendas. There were those who had become parents by pursuing these options, others were trying to become parents by these methods and a few were just thinking about them.

DI

This was a significant part of most men's experiences of infertility. As one man explained:

> Most men will have to look at this option once they get over the emotional trauma of finding out they are infertile. They will have to think about how they are going to deal with the absolute or partial knowledge that they are not the biological father.

DI as s possibility

A majority of men said they had no real qualms about DI. Some had been resistant to the idea at first but had then come round to it. For Martin it had just been a hypothetical consideration. 'I was neutral about semen donation. It wasn't something to be embarrassed about.' His wife had later become pregnant by him without any medical help.

Kevin explained he needed time to think it over:

> My wife seemed to be rushing ahead of me. When we found out I had no sperm she started talking about DI but she seemed to be glossing over certain things. However, I felt I needed time to digest what had happened. You see I wasn't clear what I felt about my infertility, but I've gradually changed my mind. My wife could have children as far as we know so why

should I deny her that possibility? We've made the decision to have children and there is no point backtracking on that.

Adoption worries me, I don't think I would want to go through with it. Because of our ages we would need to adopt an older child, perhaps one with some sort of a handicap and we don't have the resources to deal with that.

We could have a baby by DI and I would then have the chance to be a parent. If we do decide to go down that path I can see there will be hard times for me and it won't all be plain sailing. For example, if we're successful I'm sure I might have moments of thinking this isn't my child. I would be thrown back to all the thoughts about my infertility, but I would have to think of the child and its needs. I know some people might say we are selfish to have a baby in this way but I think we've thought far more than most about the implications of having children.

DI seemed a positive option for someone whose wife had been through four DI attempts:

The main reason for deciding on this was that it seemed a good idea at the time. Up till that point everything had been so negative and this seemed a positive thing to do. We knew the success rate wasn't high but decided to have a go. Other people didn't need to know donor sperm had been used so it was the obvious direction to go in.

It was also important for there to be at least one natural parent:

I came round to the idea of donor sperm fairly quickly. I could have a family this way and I think that the person who brings up and cares for the child is the most important one in a child's life. But my wife and I also felt DI would be a good idea because she would be the natural parent.

Practicalities dominated Andrew's agenda: 'This seemed the right solution to the problem. I do have a mechanistic attitude and I felt if I couldn't provide the sperm we could get some from elsewhere. The point is that nobody need know what has happened.'

Brian unlike his wife was prepared to consider DI at a later date:

She feels uncomfortable about it because it seems like adultery to her. There are deep moral issues for her and she also dislikes the clinical side of insemination. For my part I don't have any particular grumbles about donor sperm. This may be because I've already considered what it would be like to bring up another man's child. A few years back before I met my wife, I was thinking about ways and means of settling down and having a family. I thought that perhaps because of my age (mid thirties) I might have to think of marrying a widow who already had children. It was an abstract idea but I did think a bit about what it would be like to care for another man's child. Perhaps I started to come to terms then with the idea. I also increasingly feel that the only way I will get a family is by someone else's contribution.

DI seemed less invasive to Simon:

We're still trying to find out whether I have got any chance of fathering my own child, but I think we both feel that ultimately DI may be the answer for us. It's safer and my wife won't have to suffer in the same way that she would if she went through IVF. We both feel comfortable with the idea and if after we've explored other avenues DI seems the most sensible option then we'll go for it. It's a private matter between us and the clinic and not for the world at large.

Against it

Three interviewees were unhappy about DI. Peter felt faint-hearted at the prospect of DI:

I hope my wife is going to get pregnant in the normal way now that my sperm have improved. DI is not on the cards yet and I'm not keen on it. If it comes down to it perhaps I would think about it, but I don't like the thought of my wife getting pregnant with another man's sperm. It would be a last resort.

James explained that his feelings about donor sperm had not greatly altered since he found out he was infertile three years ago:

I don't want a child at any cost. I want to be a parent but the most important thing is that the child is mine, a part of me. I would see my child as a continuation of myself so a donor baby could never fulfil these aspirations. It may sound selfish and irrational but the need for a blood tie is strong in me. I would also worry about the baby's background and that it might have various handicaps. Having said all this, if my partner really wanted to go through pregnancy and childbirth and put a lot of pressure on me, then I might come round to the idea.

Matthew felt a powerful gut reaction against DI. He and his wife had adopted two children:

I was always frightened pressure would be put on me to agree to it once I found out I had no sperm. Basically I didn't want my wife to become pregnant by another man. This was the strongest feeling I had and I didn't want to see her getting bigger and bigger each day thinking someone else was responsible for her condition. If there was one issue that could threaten our marriage it was this one.

My relatives seemed to think I should agree to DI if my wife wanted it, but I didn't want to talk about it. It was like saying I was no good so we will find someone who is.

I'm not against DI but what upsets me is the assumption that as an infertile man I will automatically be in favour of it for my wife. I felt I wouldn't be able to accept a child born under those circumstances and I think that my wife and I were in agreement on this, though perhaps my feelings were stronger.

Even though we've adopted children I still feel as strongly as I did four years ago. I would have been prepared not to have a family even if that had been the only way of becoming a parent, but maybe I can now afford to say that because I have a family.

Openness or secrecy?

Who should be told about DI? This plagued men from the outset even when they were just thinking about the idea. Jeffrey put the idea to his father. 'He didn't like it because he belongs to that generation that felt you were blessed with children and if you couldn't have them that was it, but he didn't put us off the idea.' Kevin had talked to his parents about the possibility:

They say a child is a child, no matter where it comes from, so they seem all right about the idea. I don't think they would treat the child any differently, but it is difficult for them because of their age to really understand what it means. I don't think they can grasp the wider issues.

It is strange in a sense asking for permission to do what most people do without thinking. My wife has told her family that we're thinking about DI and we've also talked to a couple of good friends about the possibility.

I think we would tell the child because research on this area seems to show it is better to be open rather than secretive. The reason I haven't been totally open about what has happened is because we need to act in the best interests of any future child. Telling everyone would serve no purpose, in fact people might shun the child if they knew, that would be very hurtful.

Andrew suspected he would keep quiet:

I would definitely not tell relatives. There is always the possibility that any child born as the result of DI would be excluded or rejected in some way and I wouldn't want to take that risk with my family. If we did have children I have a strong suspicion that I wouldn't tell them about their origins. I know this goes against the child's rights but then how many children know who their biological father is?

Parents

Four men had children and two men's partners were pregnant. I asked them about their various experiences of DI. They all picked out different aspects. Alan had a year-old baby. He recollects that DI was first mentioned after his doctor told him he had no sperm:

> I was totally against it then because I was so upset, but over a period of about six months I started to change my mind for a range of reasons. I did want to be a father and I wanted my wife to go through pregnancy and childbirth. We didn't rush into DI and I went through various medical checks to try and find out why I was infertile. We also thought about adoption, but I wasn't keen on it because I don't find other people's children that appealing.
>
> I had very mixed feelings for a time about everything. We wanted to keep our options open and read everything we could on DI and knew the success rates weren't too good. We also decided to go through the adoption process despite my reservations about it and thought we would try DI meanwhile. The whole situation was pretty complicated and we worried that because of my age we might not be considered for adoption.
>
> I had to start thinking about what to say to other people about what was going on. I ended up saying there was something not right with me but that the treatment I was going through should put matters right. I worried that if people knew about sperm donation they might treat our baby differently. It was not that I was ashamed of being infertile, but I didn't want our baby seen as an oddity or rejected by people like my parents.
>
> Big pressures built up before the first attempt. We wondered whether it would work and had been warned it was unlikely to do so first time round. My wife also had to have a small operation done to check her tubes were open before the clinic would agree to DI and I felt guilty about her having to go through that.
>
> I decided to take a day off work when she had the insemination done. We both thought we would make a nice day out of it and celebrate afterwards with a good meal. Amazingly she got pregnant after that first time. I was thrilled but then started to worry, would I love the baby enough, those sorts of fears. The pregnancy went well, but I had additional anxieties. I worried that the baby might have some handicap due to the donor sperm. Despite all these gnawing thoughts, everything was fine.

Labour went quite well and when the baby popped out, all my worries melted away. The baby was ours.

Looking back, I've a mix of feelings about DI. It's a clinical procedure but through this mechanical intervention you create another human being. I've had to put any uncomfortable thoughts about DI to the back of my mind and get on with loving our child.

Mike's experience of DI was coloured by his wife's desire for children. Mixed sperm (his and donor sperm) had been used for the inseminations. They now have two young children but he did not want them to know he was not their natural father as this might needlessly hurt them:

Also deep down my wife would prefer to believe the children are mine and I suppose I would too. I could go for a blood test to see whether I am the father but I have no intention of doing that voluntarily. The important thing is that they have a loving stable home environment.

We do worry about appearances and are glad that they look like my wife. We don't want other people thinking they might not be my children. Our relatives, for example, don't know and I'm not certain how they would have reacted.

Mixed sperm had also been used for John's wife:

We were lucky first time round. I liked the idea of mixed sperm. It seemed like you were giving the weaklings a sporting chance and then sending the cavalry in afterwards.

I think DI was our first choice rather than adoption. We wanted to be as near to normal as possible, just like everyone else. Of course the way it was done makes me think there is always the chance it could be my child. I feel at some level that I could be the father. People in fact look at me and the baby and say how much we resemble each other.

Chris explained why he felt vulnerable when his wife started going through DI:

Three months after I found I had sperm problems my wife started trying to get pregnant with donor sperm. I just accepted this, I guess I never really looked at the situation from my viewpoint. At the time it seemed there was this problem and the solution was to get a baby.

I was upset when I found out I was infertile but not because of the family line dying out or things like that. I wanted to be a parent, that was my main desire. We both wanted children but my wife had this over-whelming drive for them. Everything was subordinated to that need and I went along with her I suppose without really examining my own feelings in depth. What I needed was reassurance that the children would be ours and not hers. I also believe in principle that children should be told what has happened, but for myself I didn't want this to happen. I was concerned the children might reject me if they found out I wasn't their real father.

These issues have been around ever since our first child was born. They developed into arguments because my wife wasn't prepared to give me the security I craved. It was strange because we seemed to be like two people locked together in some weird fight not knowing what the rules were. We just weren't prepared for the things that came up.

When our child was born we shared care but under the surface something was bubbling away. The question was whether we were joint parents or whether I had fewer rights because I wasn't the natural father. When it came down to it my wife acted as though our daughter was hers and not mine. My position as a parent felt very weak and we never managed to resolve this fundamental issue. Our marriage has now broken down.

On top of this my wife now says that she hated going through the inseminations and felt violated by them. She went through it all because she wanted children and to stay with me. Now we've split up all she says she remembers is how alienating and raw the whole experience was and feels very bitter about it.

Then there were the prospective parents. Luke's partner was pregnant after having been through several DI attempts:

One part of me thinks the baby is not mine. After all, she never got pregnant before this happened and I now know that I've got sperm problems. There is another part of me which thinks maybe this was the lucky moment when one of my good sperm did manage to get through and that it was a coincidence this happened at the same time as DI. After all, we've still been making love through all the inseminations, so I'd like to think I'm the biological father though I have my doubts. Currently this thought isn't a big worry. I'm very excited about the pregnancy and looking forward to the baby's birth. Maybe there will come a time when I do want to know, when curiosity gets the better of me. Obviously the child will have a right to know details about the biological parent later on but at the moment these issues are in the background though they do crop up from time to time.

When my partner put forward the idea of DI I felt if this is what we have to do, so be it. I had doubts about it though the desire to be a parent by then outweighed any reservations I had. I felt inadequate when the subject came up, my sperm were no good and good sperm were going to be used. I started to compare myself to other men and felt surprised I was having these feelings. After all, the whole thing about your genes and biological fatherhood is highly charged and sensationalised. From a political viewpoint I felt unhappy about the importance attached to being a biological father, yet I do have a longing for my own child though I don't quite know why.

At one point we thought about asking a male friend whether he would consider donating sperm. He agreed to help us, but in the end I went off the idea. Somehow it was too close having sperm from someone I knew. I wondered what he would feel about the child, would he want the child and I wondered what I would feel about the child knowing he was the father.

I realised how uncomfortable I felt about using a known donor and I wanted an anonymous one. It was to do with the immediacy of it, I felt in a way more inadequate being measured against this other man who I knew, more vulnerable. I do feel there is some sort of a difference in not being the natural father. Ten years ago I would have said it didn't matter, but I've changed. There is some sort of a difference but I'm not quite sure what it is.

Jeffrey's wife was also pregnant when I spoke to him:

Adoption was never on our agenda. It's making the best of a bad situation but it's hardly ideal. Yet I was horrified by the thought of DI to begin with, but had dreadful feelings about my wife not being able to go through pregnancy.

For a few months I was in a state, then I accepted it. I was having one of my frequent chats with my doctor about my infertility and he said that I shouldn't discount DI because it was the next best thing. Yes, it would be someone else's sperm but it would be my wife's baby. It dawned on me within hours that this was the solution though I can't explain why I changed my mind so quickly.

My wife had also been against it until that point, but I think the doctor stopped us acting irrationally. To start with I think we were just misinformed about DI and thought any old sperm might be used, without the need to go to a hospital. It sounded a bit dirty somehow. Then we read an article about it and started gradually to think along different lines. I suppose my doctor's advice just pushed me further down a road I had already started along though I wasn't aware of it.

We went through several awful DI attempts at the clinic we eventually found but I was barred from them. The experience was so dreadful that I lost some of my hair. In the end we changed to a much better clinic where I wasn't shut out of the inseminations. Now she's pregnant I'm thrilled.

ADOPTION

Adoption was seen as more fraught generally. There weren't enough babies to adopt and some men feared they might be thought too old to adopt. They were also nervous about being vetted by the authorities. Because of all this, several of them said that their partners were trying DI at the same time as going through adoption attempts.

However, Stephen preferred adoption. 'The most important point was we wanted to share the children equally. My wife also said she wasn't particularly keen on going through pregnancy.' Matthew chose adoption because he couldn't bear the idea of DI. Bruce had no choice over the matter. He had adopted two children at the beginning of the 1980s and was never told about DI services.

DISCUSSION

DI was the preferred route to parenthood for most men.

Yet there were qualms about DI to begin with. Often it was rejected at the outset but then accepted when it seemed the most sensible way of resolving childlessness. Only a minority continued to feel unhappy about it.

Various advantages were stressed. The one most commonly mentioned was that the woman would have a chance to go through pregnancy and childbirth and the baby would be half hers. This biological connection was important.

Other points were raised. The family would look normal to the outside world, nobody else need know what had happened. A couple of men said it was the easiest way to get a family and partners would not have to suffer painful medical treatments. Any anxieties that it might be a 'dirty business' went for Jeffrey when he found out that insemination would be done in a clinic.

Underlying these comments was a sense that men felt they and their partners would be more in control of what was happening. The adoption process was seen as more rigorous because of its vetting procedures whereas it was easier to get accepted for DI. On balance DI seemed a more promising option.

There was another big plus. Three out of the six men whose partners had given birth to babies or were pregnant after DI, had some sperm. They harboured the belief that they might be the child's father and two men's sperm had been used in DI, strengthening this feeling. Even though this had not happened in Luke's case, he said that he and his partner continued to make love throughout the inseminations, so he too felt his sperm might have been lucky. Seeking confirmation of paternity through a blood test was a possibility raised by a couple of men. Mike rejected the idea though it was possibly on the cards for Luke.

Biology seemed to be a vexed subject for most despite assertions to the contrary. Luke revealed uncertainties in his feelings, once the issues were no longer theoretical but for real. Though Chris was quite happy with the idea of donor sperm and said biology was unimportant to him, he feared his child might reject him precisely because of the missing link.

Chris also raised another point. His marriage had been plagued by uncertainty ever since his wife gave birth to a baby in the mid 1980s. He felt his wife was the dominant parent and that he was in an unequal position because he was not the biological father. Eventually his marriage disintegrated under the strain of arguments about this point.

There were other uneasy thoughts to contend with. Luke felt feelings of inadequacy were heightened by the use of another man's sperm. Most men at times worried about how they would react to the new baby. Though DI was generally seen as uninvasive for the woman, the circumstances surrounding it could be disturbing. There had been times when men felt brutally excluded from the inseminations and even when this had not happened, the memory of the clinical nature of the event was something Alan had tried to blot out. (It may also be an unpleasant, traumatic event for the woman as Chris explained. Having to go through DI in order to conceive a child made his wife perhaps more resentful of him.)

The other problem with DI was the secrecy surrounding it. Those who had children generally gave the impression they would not tell the child. Mainly this was to protect the child from potentially painful information which was seen as probably unnecessary. It was a difficult dilemma and men were uneasy about it. The theory of what should be done conflicted with actual experience. Chris believed in the child's right to know but did not in practice want his child to know for fear of rejection. Kevin theoretically thought the child should be told but his partner had not yet started going through DI.

Despite reservations, men generally felt DI was the best solution. These experiences do not seem to be unusual but reflect a move away from adoption that has been going on for several years. One study in the mid 1970s reported that both husbands and wives unanimously favoured DI over adoption (David and Avidan, 1976). In the mid 1980s an article reported that DI was more popular than adoption. A consultant involved in the area said from his experience, that in 1970 only one or two couples in ten would have opted for DI. Now at least eight in ten would go for it (Moorehead, 1984).

DI also seems to give couples a better chance of becoming parents. Over 17 per cent of couples had become parents by DI as opposed to over 13 per cent by adoption (*Issue*, 1991a).

This solution has not always been so popular. It became the subject of a public outcry in 1945. Various groups including the Catholic church were against it. The latter because it 'involves masturbation, a practice it condemns, and because it intervenes in the holy sacrament of marriage'. Others also disliked it because of its use in animal husbandry. People were not animals (Pfeffer, 1987: 92). Despite all this, in 1970 a panel of inquiry recommended it should be available within the Health Service (Snowden and Snowden, 1984).

It became more popular as adoption became more difficult. There are obstacles to adoption in its traditional form, according to Humphrey and Humphrey. The decline in adoptions from 1968 was due to a falling birth rate, easier abortion and more widespread social acceptance of single parenthood. The long wait for adoption and uncertain outcome encourages couples to look at DI (1988).

The advantages of DI mentioned by the men, plus others, come up in various studies. People feel a stronger bond towards the child and there is no past to deal with as for the adopted child (Snowden and Snowden, 1984). There were five reasons given as to why husbands would agree to DI. It would satisfy the wife's maternal instincts, husbands feared the marriage breaking up if the wife's childlessness was unresolved, the child would be 50 per cent theirs, the family would appear normal and the man would have his desired heir (Snowden and Mitchell, 1981).

Men may also minimise the importance of donor semen. One study reported 'they regarded the semen of the donor as a mere fertilising agent whose product in conception, imparted nothing alien to the marriage' (David and Avidan, 1976: 531). This may explain why Luke disliked the idea of a known donor because it is then less easy to view the semen in an impartial fashion.

The downside of DI is also stressed. It is not unusual for men to worry about what their feelings will be towards the new baby (Congress of the US, Office of Technology Assessment, 1988a). A news report said that infertile men found it difficult coming to terms with their wives having a child by DI and men became confused about their relationship to the child (Prentice, 1988). Blizzard says DI made him feel superfluous and he is uncertain whether he would recommend it (1977).

Questions of biology come up in other studies:

> Rather more husbands in our series have been found on semen analysis to be producing some sperm than none at all, which gave them the option of clinging to the belief that a child born after DI could be genetically their own after all.
>
> (Humphrey and Humphrey, 1988: 140)

This may work against the man coming to terms with his infertility (Snowden and Snowden, 1984).

There is an argument that DI hides a welter of feelings whilst appearing to solve the problem of male infertility (Humphrey, 1986). The presence of the child born as a result of DI can be a constant reminder to a man of an inadequacy to which he might otherwise have come to terms with (Christie and Pawson, 1987) and marriages can break up as a result (Snowden and Mitchell, 1981).

As for secrecy, one study found that 86 per cent of couples had not and would not tell the child about its origins and 81 per cent of those who had told at least one other person about DI would not do so again. In retrospect many seemed to feel telling others was detrimental or unnecessary (Klock and Maier, 1991). Total secrecy, however, stops people working through the various conflicts that lie underneath the surface, according to Berger (1980).

Rushing into DI may cause problems. Kevin felt he needed time to come to terms with his infertility before thinking about DI, but felt his wife was rushing headlong into it. Two studies on this point report different results. One asserts that it makes sense not to rush into DI. The couple will be better adjusted (Berger, 1980). A more recent one found no such link (Klock and Maier, 1991).

The infertile husband may also need particular emotional support from his wife and the marriage should be assessed before DI is started (Humphrey and Humphrey, 1988).

To conclude, most of my discussions on other ways to fatherhood revolved round DI. Adoption took a back seat for most though a couple of men were anxious to talk to me about traumatic adoption vetting processes they had been through.

Clearly DI is not a straightforward solution. It is attractive in some ways but problematic in others. Some studies particularly earlier ones, suggest it is a short-cut solution fraught with danger, but though Chris had a bad experience, others seemed reasonably optimistic about it. Various observations were made because everyone was at different stages. For example, a man with a seven-year-old child is likely to have different views from someone whose partner has just given birth and indeed Blizzard's story shows him going through a mix of feelings as the years pass by.

Though I felt men were perhaps glossing over too quickly what they really thought about the loss of their own biology, this is in part a reflection of my own feelings on the subject. It would be silly to think that everyone has the same attachment to this idea and that all men are denying and hiding away from the issue. A pragmatic point is made by researchers:

Couples who opt for artificial insemination using a donor must face the realisation that the child will not have the genetic makeup of the father. For some, acceptance of these losses comes more easily than to others, depending upon the meaning of achieving such goals in parenting and how invested the partners were in achieving these particular goals

(Clark *et al.*, 1991: 171)

Looking at existing goals and giving up some in order to become a parent may make sense. The loss of a particular goal will depend on how important it was to the person in the first place and cultural and psychological factors will determine this.

On the plus side there is the possibility of sharing in the birth process and bringing up a child. What can perhaps cause problems is if the man is at a different stage to his partner when reassessing goals. The result may be conflict.

Meanwhile changes have taken place at least in Britain which will affect men's experiences. The Human Fertilisation and Embryology Act 1990 means that mixed sperm can no longer be used in DI. Also clinics offering DI will have to keep a register of information on donors. A child born as a result of DI will be able to find out details (currently non-identifying) of the genetic parent.

12 Dealing with people

Decisions had to be made about whether to tell people about fertility problems. This was a particular concern for those thinking about DI, as discussed, for if the use of donor sperm was to be kept secret, then others must not know the full extent of the man's problems. That aside, men were still faced with the question of whether to tell certain people about their infertility. Families tended to top the list of those who might be told, with friends, work colleagues and casual acquaintances further down it.

FAMILIES

Parents

Parents' reactions were important for most, but the news of infertility was greeted with mixed reactions. Brian recalled with some bitterness and sadness how his mother and father had responded:

> My parents reacted with disbelief, they just couldn't believe it. They saw me as someone who had always been very fit and powerful and because of that they thought I must be fertile.
>
> I suppose they were being protective towards me but they started by accusing my wife of having an obsessive desire to have children. They can't accept that I also want them and that I am the one with the problem. They don't ask how things are going and never raise the subject at all. If we bring it up, they push it aside.
>
> I think my mother feels particularly hurt by my infertility. She produced this big strong healthy son and she can't understand why I'm infertile. She hasn't said this to me openly so I'm guessing at these reasons, but it helps explain why they have reacted like this.
>
> There is also another issue. We borrowed some money from them for a house purchase and want to delay repayment because of some expensive

IVF treatment my wife is going through. My father was happy for us not to repay the money straightaway but my mother was not. Possibly she feels this way because she thinks I'm being forced into having children.

I've had to cope with these reactions by effectively separating further away from them. We've been through some very difficult times and they haven't been there for us. I have my own life to lead and I've got to the stage where I don't give a damn about them though at a deeper level I still care about them. The way I see it now is that I have my own life to live and occasionally my parents are a part of it. I won't go out of my way to be more than dutiful towards them. I did want to involve them and talk about what has happened but their response has been very negative. The result is that I see them far less than I used to.

We also haven't told my wife's mother as she'd go round saying that her daughter had made a mess of her life by marrying someone who can't father children. She would just cause unnecessary aggravation, so we've told her we have joint fertility problems.

Unsupportive responses were reported by Bruce:

My family knew about my sperm problems, but I wasn't looking for particular help from them and didn't get any. My mother said there's more to life than having children (she has four boys), and my father said nothing. My mother basically couldn't recognise we might be suffering. The same is also true for my wife's mother (who has six children). I think both mums felt they had missed out on things because of having children so they just couldn't understand why we were upset.

Lack of sensitivity was brought up:

I've told my parents but they just don't seem to understand. I think my mother secretly hopes there will be some sort of a miracle and my wife will get pregnant. I can't live up to her expectations. She won't talk about it and I feel she thinks I should just keep on trying and somehow everything will work out.

I get upset because they don't seem to sense what I'm going through. For example, we had tea with them and my mother produced lots of old family photos. She asked me what she should do with them and I had this dreadful feeling of total failure. I had let her down because this was the end of the family. I didn't say anything to her about how I felt and maybe she didn't realise the effect the photographs were having on me. My wife's parents know but I haven't had much of a response from them apart from her father thinking I'm impotent.

Jeffrey reported negative reactions from his parents:

I'm very close to my parents so I told them about my infertility. My father's English isn't too good so it took him time to grasp the problem but he didn't acknowledge it once he understood. My mum knew what I was saying but I got the impression she didn't want to think about it because it was too horrible to be true.

My mum was very upset early on. She asked whether she had done something wrong when I was little which could have caused the infertility, so I reassured her there wasn't. Later on she was a bit poorly because of several problems and it came out in one talk I had with her that she was worried about us not having children. She burst into tears about it all, so I told her that we were happy and not to worry. I didn't want to impose my problems on her.

My mum also didn't understand what was wrong. She asked me quietly one afternoon in an embarrasssed sort of way whether I was 'doing it properly'. She obviously thought I might be impotent. I think she thought that if that was the case my marriage might be at risk.

Parents could be bewildered by the subject:

I told my parents that I had sperm problems because of my undescended testicles (they were operated on in my teens) but my dad's comment was 'why do you want children?' I guess he found life pretty hard when he was bringing us lot up, but he made no attempt to put himself in my position and see how incomplete I felt without children. I felt pretty cut up by his insensitivity and wanted to ask what he would have felt like if he hadn't had children, but I bit my lip and said nothing.

Kevin's father was quite sympathetic:

He reacted fairly well because he comes from a community where sons are supposed to carry on the family line, so I could have been a big let-down to him. He said 'I'm very sorry for you if you can't have children' and that was it. He wasn't as blunt as I thought he might be so that was good, yet he could have been more sympathetic but he thinks you just have to get on with life.

Peter's mother felt responsible for his infertility so paid for his varicocele operation. Tim's mother was less involved:

I always used to share confidences with my father but he is dead. I was closer to him than my mother but I told her about my infertility because I didn't want her to blame my wife for our childlessness. She knows about it but we haven't talked about it in detail and she doesn't know what my feelings are on the subject.

I've never talked to her about intimate things. When I was at boarding school I was taught to have a stiff upper lip, so I couldn't really open up to her about my feelings because it would have been too much of a shock for her and that wouldn't have helped me. Basically she sees my infertility as a physical problem like flat feet. She is concerned about it but because she has never had to face infertility herself doesn't really understand what it feels like.

John said it seemed sensible to be unspecific about the problem:

I wanted to protect my parents from being hurt. They knew we were having problems generally but not that I was infertile. I don't want to say to them you created me yet I have this genetic problem which means I can't have children. That would have hurt them and they might have blamed themselves. If they really wanted to know they could ask me for the details but they haven't. There were times when I would have liked to ask my father whether he ever had problems but it's too late for that now.

We've told my wife's parents everything because they had fertility problems. They've been great but I sometimes wonder whether they are disappointed. Their fertile adopted daughter married someone who isn't so repeating the infertility cycle.

Alan had also been vague about his infertility:

They know we had problems but not that I have no sperm. I suppose my family is a fairly typical-working class one. We're quite close but don't discuss certain things such as sex. I told them I was having treatments and these had worked when my wife became pregnant.

My parents have no idea what it feels like to be told you are infertile. If I talked to them about my feelings they would probably be supportive but they don't really believe in men needing psychological support.

Simon explained his wife's mother knew about his infertility but his parents didn't:

She knows what we've been going through and has been very supportive. She says she loves us whether or not we have children.

But I decided not to tell my parents because I felt they would fret and worry over the whole business. I'm sure they would come up with pointless advice all the time and keep asking me what was happening. I was uneasy about the way my mother might handle the news. She may in fact suspect we're having problems but she won't ask us directly about our intentions. She tends to fish around for information and is the sort of person who doesn't openly voice her concerns but for example, would say that her sister thinks we're selfish for not having children.

I also think the news would hit my father very badly if he thought his genes were going to die out. He drops hints about how much he wants a family. For example, he said recently, 'I'm making up this family album and I suppose I'll have to give it to my nephew's son'. When we first got married I was asked questions about when we intended starting a family. I remember saying we'll wait five years before trying for one. My father said that was too long. Now we're eight years on so I don't know what he must be feeling about the lack of grandchildren.

The situation is pretty difficult for me. My sister has no children and there is nobody else to take the heat off me. My mother's sister has four children and all of them have offspring. I know my parents are jealous about this. I think they feel that my aunt is trying to score points off them. They have reacted by withdrawing from her when in fact they could spend time with their nieces and nephews.

The pressure has been hard on us both. My parents have been rude towards my wife because I think they subconsciously blame her for our childlessness. Basically I don't talk to people generally about my infertility and my parents are just two more people.

Andrew tried to tell his father:

I wanted to tell him but he was very ill and frail at the time and I could see it was a painful matter for him and that he couldn't cope with what I was trying to say. Now he's dead that opportunity has gone forever. I also haven't told my mother. If we get anywhere near the subject of my childlessness she changes the subject, so I can't unload anything onto her.

Brothers and sisters

Other family members were mentioned less often, but they could be helpful. Andrew for example, said that though he had been unable to talk to his mother, he had told his youngest sister about his infertility and she was sympathetic.

Jeffrey confided in one other family member:

I haven't told most of my brothers and sisters because we want to keep it private. I was close to one brother but he has never asked about anything, he's just not interested. One sister who I've always been close to has been kind. I think she understood more about what I have been through because she has had some rough times, so we have that in common.

John worried about whether to tell his brother:

From time to time I think about telling him. He is younger than me and not married yet but he might have the same problem as me, so I don't want him to waste time thinking things will happen. It doesn't matter too much at the moment as far as I know. He has a girlfriend but I don't think they've started trying for a family. If I can find the right moment to speak to him I might bring the subject up because I don't want him to go through the frustrations I have been through.

Alan said his brothers had been unhelpful:

When our daughter arrived after DI they said 'good lad'. Before that they used to joke about me being in my late thirties with no children. They haven't been very understanding really despite knowing we had some sort of a problem. I had a talk one day with one of them and said we were having difficulties and might not be able to have children. I tried to be not too specific and didn't tell him I had no sperm because he might have thought I was less of a man. Anyway, his reaction was to go on about how tiring children are. Then he made a joke about how he could get a friend to come round and sort my wife out. I know my brother was trying to lighten the situation when he said that, but he ended up making me feel awful.

FRIENDS

Decisions had to be made about whether or not to tell friends about the diagnosis:

They used to ask me why I had stopped drinking and smoking, so I told them I was infertile and was trying to do something that would improve my sperm. People, particularly men, seemed to almost ignore what I said and pass over it quickly. In the end I tried to avoid saying anything because I felt uncomfortable about the whole subject and so did my friends.

Mike made no secret of his infertility:

There was no point hiding it because I'd always been open about the operation on my twisted testicle which was removed. One woman friend at the time said I was half a man as a result. I wasn't too upset about her remark as it said something about her, but it did sting a bit.

Once we started having problems, friends knew it was down to me. Generally they were sympathetic, with some exceptions. One friend offered his services to my wife in jest, that was pretty insensitive. We also used to be good friends with a couple who had children. They just couldn't understand our problem and thought the solution was simple. We should adopt. They just didn't have a clue because I guess they had never had their own infertility problems.

Male friends could be insensitive. Luke explained:

> One friend wrote to me saying he now had a child. He enclosed a picture of his baby. That made me very angry because he knew about my problems but seemed totally insensitive to how I might react to his news. I was pretty upset but there was nothing I could do about it.

There was also a wry remark about why male friends were not told. 'I don't have any, it's as simple as that.' There was in addition a fear about how male friends would react. They might be cruel. Jeffrey explained why he had to be careful:

> I can't be that open about it and have had to be careful who I talk to about my infertility. The lads I play darts with would just laugh and make jokes if they knew I had no sperm. They wouldn't realise how upsetting those jokes are to me. On the other hand I've got a good friend who is a bit older than me. He knows about everything and has been an ally.

Sharing the news with sympathetic friends or those who had similar experiences seemed the best course of action for John:

> I don't normally go into specific details. There is also another male friend who has a similar problem so I've talked to him. There's no point talking to people who aren't going to understand what has happened and I don't want to bore people. It's also a taboo, so we've only mentioned it to close friends who we think will be sympathetic. It turns out that some of them have also had difficulties.

Simon said the subject came up at supper with friends:

> When the topic came up one evening, my wife said I should explain to them what was going on. There was a slightly stunned silence. I then said something but not much about what had happened and that was the end of it. They didn't seem to want to discuss it, but I guess not all our friends are like this. Some will discuss it but they tend to have had problems themselves.

WORK COLLEAGUES

People at work had generally not been told about the diagnosis. Simon would have liked to be more open in order to find out why other work colleagues were childless. 'I'm dying to know but I feel I just can't ask them.' Two men however, had unpleasant experiences etched in their minds. Jeffrey recalled:

> I was feeling a bit low a few months back when my wife was still trying to get pregnant through DI. A lad at work, five years younger than me,

announced his wife was pregnant. He is a bit of a joker and I normally get on well with him, but this time he directed a remark at me saying 'at least I haven't been firing blanks all these years'.

I laughed if off and went away. That was in the morning. It was on my mind all day and I got home feeling awful. I had a shower and then just sat down and cried. That seemed to clear the air but his remark had really got under my skin. To put it in perspective, this man meant no harm. It's a fairly typical joke that men make but it knocked me sideways because he seemed to be rubbing my nose in it. It was a dreadful reminder of my infertility.

Derek had to put up with several jokes at his expense:

I didn't exactly tell people at work about my infertility but they put two and two together when I had to go for hospital tests and the like. They put notes in my locker making jokes about a pencil without lead, that sort of thing. They poked fun at me and made me feel very down. They were guessing at what my problem was and trying to get a reaction, but I didn't tell them anything. I just had to bottle my feelings up. In the end they stopped making fun of me but I'm not certain why.

ACQUAINTANCES

One person said he had been open about his infertility with no bad consequences. Most, however, expressed reservations about broaching the subject with casual friends and acquaintances.

Bruce felt too embarrassed:

I felt cut off from other people and ashamed of the infertility label. I knew of no other men in the same boat as me so there was nobody for me to talk to. On reflection I think all these messages were inside me and not coming from people round me. When I did tell people they were generally sympathetic.

Luke decided to be more open about his infertility because he was fed up with the secrecy surrounding male infertility:

I wanted to open it up because it is such a closed subject. I wasn't on a crusade but I was sick of it being hushed up. I remember making a point of asking loudly for my semen analysis reports when I went to the clinic, I didn't hide my infertility from the receptionist. She said to me on one occasion that she didn't realise men also had problems, so I suppose I was getting the message across.

DISCUSSION

Parents' reactions were generally important to men, yet the understanding and support that some craved was not forthcoming. Parents could not understand the issues and choices facing their sons. They shied away from the subject of male infertility. At the very least, there was a hope that parents would acknowledge their son's distress. There was disappointment when this did not happen. Brian had harsh words for his parents and felt badly treated by them. Others expected little from their parents and so were not upset at the apparent lack of concern.

The main explanation for the lack of parental sympathy was that parents had no experience of infertility themselves. They were from a different generation, unable to understand present attitudes to infertility. Decisions also had to be made about when to give the news to parents and whether to reveal full or partial details of the diagnosis. Simon for instance felt his father would be dreadfully upset if he knew about his son's infertility. The 'family line' was very important to his father and this was one of the reasons why Simon said nothing to his parents. He did not want to have to cope with his father's distress.

There was also a sense of wanting to protect parents from pain, as in John's case, perhaps with good reason. Peter said his mother felt responsible and, so, guilty for his situation.

More often than not families did not seem to provide much comfort, though there were exceptions. The decision whether to tell friends was tricky. Most interviewees felt they would only confide in those they trusted, probably those who had been through similar experiences. Men were also wary of telling male friends for fear of being made fun of by them.

Work colleagues were not generally told about the problem. Most men had no pressing need to do so from a practical viewpoint, because they were not having to take lots of time off work for tests and treatments, though some were trying to go to clinic appointments in order to support the woman.

Throughout the interviews, I was struck by a sense of loneliness. Men did quite often share the news of their infertility with their families, but the response was one of incomprehension. Men also felt they could not afford to be too open. Fear of ridicule haunted some. Derek and Jeffrey had been deeply hurt by the remarks made by work mates. Interviewees tended to say they had to be discreet about their infertility in order to protect themselves from possible hurt, and those men whose partners were going through DI had an added burden of secrecy to bear. They were uneasy about disclosing what was going on to anyone else in case people found out about the inseminations and took against any children born as a result of DI.

It is perhaps not surprising that there was this worry about who to confide in. Infertility for both sexes is stigmatising. It is not well understood by the public and myths abound such as the one about virility and fertility. There is little education on the subject (Dunkel-Schetter and Stanton, 1991) and male infertility is even more stigmatising because its causes are not clear. This makes it seem more threatening (Snowden *et al.*, 1983).

Cultural ideas, about how men should cope, perhaps also explain the rather flat parental responses. Parents sometimes seemed to be saying their son should not moan about his infertility and should just get on with life as best he could. A few of them appeared not to want their son to find a remedy to his problem. Perhaps this was to protect him from the pain of possible failure or a throwback to the time when people just accepted their infertility.

Another possible explanation is that parents found the search for medical solutions shameful. Many approaches to male infertility now involve assisted conception techniques. These are often not available on the health service so people have to pay for them privately, but by doing this Pfeffer says 'the infertile are seen to place a monetary value on an experience which, for many, ought to be a 'gift from providence'. Their very seeking after parenthood becomes the mark of their degradation' (1987: 97). This may partly explain why Brian's mother did not want to help him with the financial costs of his wife's treatment.

Yet whilst parents might feel unhappy about their son and his partner seeking such help, they could also feel sad. Several men felt bad because they thought their parents yearned for grandchildren whilst giving out mixed messages about how their sons should go about getting a family. Parents sometimes seemed to want the problem to be waved away and for grandchildren to magically appear.

Perhaps in the future, mothers and fathers may be more sensitive about the subject because they are better educated about infertility. They may also have experienced it themselves and so understand it better. Of course, parents may have seemed flat and unresponsive not because they did not understand their son's predicament but because they just found it all too painful. They were powerless to solve their child's grief.

13 Survival strategies

Certain aspects of coping have already been looked at in terms of dealing with medical investigations and other people's reactions to the diagnosis. But how did men cope overall with the experience of infertility and what did they think they were coping with?

STRATEGIES

Partners

One method was to cope with the woman's needs. This could be at the man's expense according to Luke:

> I helped her cope with all her investigations. Then when I found out I was infertile, she seemed to be saying this was another problem for her rather than me. I felt I couldn't talk about my feelings when the spotlight was on her though I was affected by what she was going through. She had enough on her plate. I thought my infertility would give me an excuse to say more about what I was feeling, but I still couldn't do this.
>
> Her need for support seemed so obvious that I spent all my time coping with her feelings. She used to be very upset every time her period arrived when she realised she wasn't pregnant. Her need for a child seemed stronger than mine so I inevitably attended to her rather than myself and didn't get to grips with my own feelings. When Katie discovered she was pregnant after DI we were incredibly excited as we'd been waiting for this for six years. But that night I cried my eyes out when she reached over to caress my face. I suddenly felt as though I'd been missing that attention from her over the past years. I was so knotted up trying to deal with what was almost an obsession for her. Infertility had taken over and there wasn't any time for anything else. I felt as though I had given her masses of

support but received very little in return though I know the woman suffers more and has to cope with monthly reminders of failed conception.

There seemed to be an imbalance somewhere and a sense of not getting what I needed from her over the years. It was a strange feeling to have at such a happy time and it was probably very difficult for Katie to understand why I was so upset. Two days later, the same thing happened again and feelings poured out of me. Then I started to feel better.

Matthew echoed these thoughts:

My main way of coping with everything that was going on was by giving my wife as much support as I could. She is far more open and emotional than I am and I could always see when she was upset. When she had problems trying to cope I knew I had to help her. This meant putting my own feelings to one side and I don't know what happened to them. I suppose it was easier for me to support her because I'm a good listener whereas she isn't. If I tried to talk about my own problems we ended up talking about her needs. Mine remained buried deep inside me.

Mike's experience was different because he felt he didn't have that many of his own needs to deal with:

It was devastating for her to think she might not be able to have children, but my position was different. Looking back, all the difficulties I had from a mental viewpoint were not insurmountable. I think men can manage better than women and I could compensate for the lack of children by throwing myself into activities and clubs. Women can't do this so easily.

There were partners who did help:

When I found out I had no sperm I felt very angry and frustrated. I felt cheated rather than having a sense of grief or loss. Someone had been unfair handing out the cards to me. There was nothing specific to get upset about, no child to cry over, just this sense of unfairness.

There was a period of perhaps a year when my wife helped me get all my feelings out into the open. Basically I thought someone had a grudge against me, but this was an undefined feeling and I couldn't get hold of something or someone to shout at. There was just a sense of frustration washing around inside me with no place to go.

My wife said direct it at her and used to encourage me to shout at her. This was a device she used because she knew something about counselling. The anger inside me was like an unlanced boil and directing it at her helped me cope with my feelings. She was able to sit there and take all my shouting without thinking she was to blame in some way or that I was furious with her. If she had taken offence I think we would have been in trouble, but she was secure enough to take everything I screamed at her. Eventually, after all this shouting, the whole business became less important.

The rage I had was to do with feeling impotent not in a sexual way but in a general sense. I could do nothing about my infertility and that's what made it so difficult. All I could do was endlessly talk about my feelings and try to reconcile myself to the fact of infertility. I wanted a plan of campaign but it wasn't possible to have one, all we could do was move along step by step.

Talking about emotions in the early stages helped Alan:

To start with I felt infertility was just my problem. I had all these raw feelings and became very selfish and bitter trying to cope with them, particularly in the first six weeks after the diagnosis. It helped when I talked to my wife, but the feelings of loss didn't come out until about six months later. I remember lying on the bed, saying I really wanted to be a dad.

Everything seemed so unfair, I just broke down and cried. That was a release. These softer feelings of grief had been pushed to the back of my mind because I was so cross about my infertility. When the feelings came out I started to feel better though the problems were still there. I started to think about getting on with my life and if kids came along that would be fine but the chances were they would not. There were different parts of me. One was saying try the treatments and see what happens but another part said just put everything behind you.

Kevin found there was a time early on when he wanted his partner's help:

I was pretty upset when I found out I had no sperm. I'd be driving along then suddenly find myself during term time going past a school. I'd see parents taking their children into the playground and a lump would come to my throat. But my wife was very matter of fact about it, in fact she thought the reason we couldn't have children might be something to do with her. Perhaps this was her way of coping with me. Then she seemed to withdraw towards her family, sorting out their problems instead of ours. Though we've always both been close to our families I wanted her to concentrate on me rather than her parents.

Everything came to a head when we were driving along a motorway one time. I suddenly burst into tears and told her how neglected I felt. I know we had other things crowding into our lives then but though these thing were a worry they weren't of the greatest importance. Yet she put her energy into them rather than me and I felt cut off from her. It was almost as though she was saying 'you're infertile so not worth bothering about'. I felt redundant and her silence seemed like a rejection. Life seemed pretty grim then though I wasn't suicidal. I couldn't have kids and my wife seemed not to want me. Eventually we did start talking and it probably took about eighteen months to start to come to terms with it.

Action

Problem solving was used. John explained:

To start with there was a black hole in front of us. I knew that because of me we were going to have problems having a family in the normal way, but once we started to tackle the problem it started to shrink. I knew it was going to be hard work to achieve what we wanted but it was a major project which had to be solved.

The feelings I had at times were difficult. There were all the worries about the various treatment options. Thoughts can go round and round in your head though this doesn't happen all the time. There were these feelings which I felt I needed to sit down and examine to see what they were all about. I felt frustrated, basically because I like to get things done and be in control and it was awful for me thinking we weren't progressing. We were just stagnating at times.

I'm not a great one for sitting around. I feel if you have a problem you read about it and sort it out yourself. I never remember feeling really gutted by the experience but I was sad and resentful and needed to work out why I felt like this. Each time you hit an unknown you go round in circles and imagine the worst and then you have to look at all your feelings again and take control.

Jeffrey felt he was coping with a missing part:

I suppose you start by looking here and there for an answer. I'm practical in some ways and once you find for example, that a finger is missing and you won't get it back you have to live without it.

Alan organised an agenda:

I set myself various tasks so I had something to occupy my time. Infertility is then kept at bay and isn't a monster sitting on your shoulder the whole time. There are all the tests to concentrate on, then I looked for causes. After that I went through a time of denial and decided that all the tests must be wrong. I worried that perhaps my fitness training had harmed me in some way. After that I thought my sperm would improve if I was really good. I guess I was just going on from one stage to the next. What helped was time. As it went by, things got easier for me. But it was difficult to start with and I brooded despite my agenda because I felt so alone.

Exploring childlessness

Looking at what was lost could be helpful. Roger's partner was still going through medical treatments:

> The feelings I've had to cope with haven't got easier during the past three years, despite what other people tell you about time healing and so on. In the last few months I've noticed a little boy in the opposite house and he makes me think about what I'm missing out on. Recently I did a family tree, something I never bothered with before. I talked to my mum about it to find out who was who. Doing this somehow helped me see what I might be losing. It was a way of looking at who had gone before.

Martin looked at his desire for children:

> As time went by I began to question whether I really wanted a child. I thought we were both getting on, and wondered how a child would fit into our busy active lives. We had an arrangement whereby we looked after a friend's child on a regular basis and I felt perhaps this might be enough. Then I used to think that there were too many children in the world. It's important to say that my desire for a child varied over time, it wasn't with me constantly and I'm sure this is true for a lot of people. You don't have to cope with it all the time.

The home

Work on the house helped Mike:

> It wasn't a conscious feeling but when we moved to this house (we were still childless then) it was a wreck and I thought we'll have this as a project. I suspect I was saying subconsciously 'we'll take this on for me to have something to do'. It would have been very selfish if I had consciously thought that. In a way it was a child substitute. It was great because it took up all my time and energy. I used to get home early in the evening and then work on the house doing various things till midnight or so. This went on for some months.

Sport

Tim used this to get away from unsettling thoughts:

I felt stunned for about two months after receiving the diagnosis. It was a case of getting on very hard with things that couldn't possibly be connected to infertility. Tennis was excellent. I knew it was a safe area where I could be as certain as you can be that people aren't going to mention male infertility.

Brian lamented the fact that he couldn't play sport:

I needed to try and prove myself and restore my self-confidence. The way I've done this in the past was through sporting activities, but I couldn't do this because I had a debilitating illness at the time.

Work

This was also used as a way of boosting confidence. Brian turned to work when he found he was too weak to get involved in a sporting activity:

I tried working harder but this also failed. The illness tired me out and I just didn't have the stamina, so I started thinking of other ways of coping and regaining my confidence. Alternatives to staying with my wife. Of course these thoughts didn't help my marriage.

Tim eventually found work was a safe refuge:

My job was something I could throw myself into, a way of getting away from infertility thoughts. But I became unhappy in it, perhaps the infertility contributed to this though there were other things as well. I started to feel frustrated and put upon generally. Then I got a new job and that was good. In my previous one I was worried that people might notice a change in me because the job seemed very much linked to the infertility business. My new job helped me because in my mind it was in no way connected to the time I received the diagnosis, so I could put it in a box and say to myself these two things, work and infertility, have nothing to do with each other.

Other interests

Matthew used this as a deliberate coping strategy:

I did go through some rough times in the two years up to the adoption and coped by putting my effort into work, but this was only one thing. It was important to find other things to do. We booked a holiday a few days after my biopsy so that we could get away and relax. We were determined to enjoy ourselves and found we could. I wanted to know that we could cope if the worst happened and we didn't have children. Neither of us wanted to sit around with long faces.

Our social life was quite active. I also used to do a lot of amateur dramatics and then started to play the guitar and joined a group. There was plenty to do without getting stuck into destructive behaviour such as heavy drinking.

I think all these things helped by broadening my outlook and keeping things in perspective. I remember we also thought after a good night out that we wouldn't be able to do this if we had children. It was a way of keeping a sense of balance.

Jeffrey remembers:

Chasing company. We used to drag people round here and want to have a good time. I suppose it was a way of filling the gap. I think men and women have a basic instinct to create a family and if something stops that problems result. I used to search friends out in perhaps an excessive way, reaching out for others to fill the hole. They were the family I didn't have. Now my wife is pregnant I no longer feel I need to see people so much.

Luke had other creative areas of his life to turn to:

Being a father wasn't the ultimate aim of my life. We weren't one of those couples who set up a home and then wait for the children to arrive. There were many other satisfying interests in my life before I was diagnosed as infertile. They were fertile parts of my life so I knew I could seek fulfilment elsewhere and get it. I think this helped me cope with knowing I might never be a father.

Children

Other people's children could help. Jeffrey looked after a child. 'Our friends had a little girl, who sometimes used to stay with us at weekends. We treated her like our own and in a way she helped fill the gap.' One person ended up managing a football team. 'I started taking boys for football training and things developed from there. It helps.'

Helpful thoughts

Certain ideas proved useful at particular times. The chance to be a parent rather than a father was a comforting thought. Also, 'I've had a full life and been very lucky' helped. Another common one cut down isolation:

It does help to find out you're not the only one and that there are loads of others in the same boat. To start with everyone else seemed to be normal but finding out that lots of men have problems eased my feelings of distress.

John felt that: 'It helped when the doctor said he was 95 per cent certain it was genetic. That was reassuring somehow because nothing could be done about it. I didn't endlessly have to fret about why I had no sperm.'

Kevin took comfort from his relationship. 'We didn't get married in order to have children, that idea came along later, so it helps to remember that we have each other.'

Others found it easier to cope because their partners were also infertile. 'I think I would probably have felt more guilt if I was the sole reason why we couldn't have children.' Also, 'it did help once we found out we were both in the same boat. We could listen to a programme about contraception and laugh about our good fortune on that score'.

Previous coping experience

Several people said they were thrown and shocked by their infertility because they had suffered no previous set backs. This was the first time anything had gone badly wrong.

Julian had been through a traumatic experience previously:

When I was ill I found out that you have to take life day by day and not look too far ahead. I had to make the most of my friends and relationships and not get too worried about less important things like money. You get things in perspective and that's made me get my priorities right. It's also helped me make sure I'm not dragged down. There is another way of looking at this. I could have had children before the cancer developed and if I had died then my children would be fatherless. That's a sobering thought.

Other types of support

A couple of men saw counsellors to help them cope. Their experiences and other support issues are explored in the next chapter.

THE DIFFICULTIES OF COPING

The problems of coping were highlighted. 'I have to put a brave face on it and cope on my own. There is nobody to help me. Articles all focus on the woman and the medical profession isn't much help.' Not being able to get things done made some men feel they weren't coping. 'I so wanted to have an action plan but that wasn't possible.' Feelings posed difficulties for some but not all. Comments were passed about having to 'bottle them up' and 'clamming up'. Matthew said he had been brought up to think men who showed their feelings were 'milk sops'.

Bruce felt angry that men were taught to contain rather than show their emotions. This could cause pain:

> I became depressed because of a number of things. Being male was part of it. Everything was shut up inside me and I just wallowed in self-pity.
>
> I also had no previous experience of coping with failure. I'd done well at school, then at university and expected everything to go my way. Nobody warned me about how to deal with the feelings. I think at the very least it would have helped to know they were acceptable. I suppose this all contributed to the depression that I eventually had. There was this idea inside my head that I should be able to cope. In a curious way my job as a welfare worker didn't help because I thought I should be able to manage and assumed I was doing so. I felt that I needed to be seen to cope otherwise other people at work might question my decisions and judgements. Something positive has, however, come out of all this. I don't try to cope on my own now if problems come along. I am more prepared to ask for help whereas in the past I didn't.

James found it painful adapting to infertility:

> Part of the problem is coping with changes in how you see yourself. I think women are perhaps more able to do this because they get used to dealing with the physical changes that they experience. Men are more able to ignore changes and are lost if they do have to confront difficult or uncertain ones.
>
> To start with I wasn't that aware of my reactions to my infertility then I started to notice them but didn't know what to do about them. I felt jealous of people with children, and babies made me sad. I felt anger and then despair at not being able to do what seems so easy for most men. My work was affected. I realised that the life plan I had taken for granted for years had gone. The potential for children couldn't be realised. I gradually saw that if this part of my life plan had been changed other parts might also be.
>
> I expected to be able to cope. In the past I would have drunk more to blot out worrying thoughts but I couldn't do that because I'd stopped drinking in order to improve my sperm. So I wasn't able to hide away from feelings of inadequacy, something I think men normally do. I couldn't ignore the fact that I wasn't able to do something I thought I had the potential to do.

I started to look at all the expectations I had of myself, rearranging them and asking whether they were too high and I questioned everything which was very painful. Now I'm back to accepting things a bit more. I'm probably less afraid of my feelings now and more prepared to talk to my partner about them. I feel more comfortable about saying that I feel sad at times because she thinks it's better for me to acknowledge the feelings rather than ignore them. I think the hardest thing is to accept myself the way I am and to understand that there are some things I'll never be able to do. Being a father is one of them. So this is what I'm coping with at the moment. I've also thought about the fantasies I had of fatherhood and realised I'd painted too rosy a picture. It's not all wonderful. I'm looking now for other ways of making my life satisfying.

Brian wanted to escape:

For at least three years I needed to try and keep away from reminders of my infertility. I had this awful feeling of being trapped with no way out. In my mind I would go through various escape routes, climbing mountains just to get away, but I couldn't do this. Now the feelings are less vivid though they still bounce around in the background.

After my diagnosis I couldn't have spoken like this. I made out that I was handling my infertility quite well and that it really wasn't a problem for me. I would have said then that we were doing something about it, looking at the various options.

With hindsight I know now that there was a lot going on under the surface which I wasn't prepared to admit to for some years. At one point I could hide away from it all at work and get immersed in my job which was a diversion, but in the end I was forced to look at my feelings and learn how to cope with them because of the help my wife gave me. She dragged them out of me and I started to understand what they were. I guess I was deflecting all my uneasy thoughts into other areas where they bubbled under the surface, but I've done this for a lifetime so why change these habits? I'd been trained not to show my feelings though I had started to change a bit. When I was a teacher I found at one point that I was getting very angry with the children so I had to look at why this was happening. That might have been a preparation for what happened with the infertility.

Isolation marked Derek's coping experience:

I did my best but I wanted some understanding and support to help me through and got totally the opposite. No support at work and none at home at first. I found it difficult accepting that I couldn't do something that men are supposed to do and to be honest I don't think I've ever really come to terms with that. In the end I coped just by getting through each day. As time passes and the chances of becoming a father fade, I keep a stiff upper lip. I feel I need to do this for my wife because it won't help her if I go to pieces. She's having a hard enough time as it is. I'm only the man and the loss is less I think for me than for her, so I need to keep quiet about the whole thing. I try to keep my head above water to keep my sanity.

BECOMING A PARENT

Life was better once children came along. Bruce's remarks were echoed by other parents:

It made a big difference to me when we adopted our first child. Before that I was depressed but I changed once our child arrived. Now we've got two children, a lot of the original pain has gone. I feel more secure though feelings of regret will probably always be in the background.

DISCUSSION

Partners' views of how men coped

The purpose of this book is to give men a chance to voice their experiences, but a few women gave me their views about the man's coping experience. I have set out some of the woman's contributions because I think they shed light on the subject.

One woman whose husband had a diagnosis of sperm problems had the following thoughts on how he had coped so far. She was hoping she would get pregnant now that his varicocele had been operated on:

It was a big shock for both of us finding out he had problems. Initally his test had seemed fine and the spotlight was on me, but then he had three further tests and all the sperm were dead. He was told not to smoke or drink alcohol for six months.

To start with I worried about how he was going to cope with the news, but he didn't say anything. He was good about trying to give up smoking and drinking but found it difficult having to explain to his friends why he needed to do this. I ended up getting very cross on one occasion when they kept buying him drinks and told them what was happening. He did go back to drinking after a bit though he has cut down his alcohol consumption, but I think he was pretty upset when he found out his semen tests were no better. Then the doctor suggested the varicocele operation which he agreed to have.

Basically his way of coping as far as I'm concerned is to keep very quiet about it. He thinks it's his problem, keeps it to himself and shuts off from me completely. That makes it hard for me to talk about it. I think he hopes the problem will just go away. From my standpoint he likes the easy options, that is his way of coping and it makes me cross. It's easier, for example, for him to have the operation than to make long-term changes to his smoking and drinking habits. Yet I've had to give up a lot of things and go through all sorts of tests. We've had some rows because of all of this. I feel that I've put in more than he has in trying to get this sorted out. But I guess it has been hard for him coping with male friends who smoke and drink heavily yet have fathered children. Not drinking for him was particularly difficult because he and his friends think drinking is manly.

At the moment I know he hopes his sperm will improve because of the operation he had, but I worry that he may shut me out if it becomes clear that he won't be able to father a child. He would never share his feelings with me. Rather than talking about getting a divorce he would just push me so far away from him that we would drift apart. He wouldn't sit down and talk things over with me, instead he would go out with his friends rather than face me. He would feel a failure and want to call it a day.

Another problem has been created for me because he finds it difficult to handle feelings. It's not only difficult talking to him about what he is going through. If something upsets me I can't talk to him about how I feel because he doesn't respond. He also finds my job upsetting. I work with children which is great as far as I'm concerned, as a result I don't have any fantasies about children. Yet he thinks I must find the job very painful to do whereas the truth is that he finds my contact with children painful, but he can't admit this.

Another woman expanded on why she thought her husband had stopped talking to her at one point:

This period of time when he says he stopped communicating with me started with a vengeance after I miscarried. I think he felt responsible for that because of his abnormal sperm. I realised with hindsight that he became very withdrawn for what would have been the duration of the pregnancy.

He burst into tears at around the time the baby would have been born, it was as though he was discharging all those months of pain and grief. He asked for my forgiveness and said that he had been withdrawn because he felt he had caused all my pain. He therefore avoided becoming intimate with me because he didn't want to risk any further hurt and loss such as another miscarriage.

During those bad times he seemed to try and find fault with me and our relationship. He used to say we would both be better off with other partners and would then go on about finding other women attractive, but didn't pursue this further.

Once he started to share all his feelings of pain with me, our relationship improved. It was a healing time. If things hadn't changed I think I would have left him.

Another woman disagreed about how quickly her husband had recovered from the shock of his diagnosis:

It took much longer than he thought. It was very difficult for him in the beginning and I had to constantly bring up the subject if I wanted to discuss it. He never willingly brought it up. I had to pull everything out of him because he clammed up completely for at least the first two months. For my part I felt incredibly frustrated because he wouldn't let me help him. He just pushed me away, but once he started talking and opening up he recognised there were painful feelings inside him. But I think it cost him a lot to look at them.

This point was emphasised by another woman:

Men enclose themselves and find it hard to analyse their feelings and easy to shut off from them. The downside of this approach is that everything can suddenly burst out into the open at once and that can be frightening.

Counsellors' views

Comments from those who work with men may also shed light on the male experience. There was talk about men suffering in silence and being unable to express their feelings.

These sentiments were expressed in an article. Dr Lee who has counselled over 200 infertile men said that they bottle up their feelings. Getting at them was like trying to prise open an oyster and once done a torrent of emotions flowed out. He also said infertile men had certain characteristics, such as a refusal to initially admit to a problem and a refusal to talk about sexual activity. Dr Lee wanted to explore whether men were like this as a result of infertility or had been like this to start with (Steven, 1991).

Counsellors I spoke to claimed men had to handle special problems. The professionals had various theories about what men were coping with and why they coped in the way they did. One person picked up the issue of identity:

Male fertility is a symbol of sexual potency. If it is compromised there is a very real threat to a man's identity and he feels powerless. He is coping with the loss of potential and feels his ability to control the world is threatened.

The need to be active and in control was often mentioned:

> Men are used to running around trying to solve problems. In infertility they try to sort out the medical treatment and get proper information, but often they end up flapping around aimlessly in the wind. There isn't much for them to do because the doctors handle everything. The woman is all taken up with trying to get pregnant and the man becomes confused because there is no role for him.

Another thought concerned upbringing. Men need to solve problems because they are brought up to see the world in terms of their own autonomy rather than relationships with others. Scheduled sex and intrusive medical treatments could rob a man of his sense of independence and make him angry because he feels powerless.

The consequences of men ignoring feelings and being rational and logical were described by one counsellor. This was in the context of vasectomies but illustrated the male coping strategy:

> They make decisions with their heads rather than their hearts and think it all through in a methodical fashion, never envisaging that things could go wrong or that feelings could get in the way of their rational calculations. The thought that they might ever need to get the vasectomy reversed doesn't enter their heads and they can become incredibly angry when their plans go awry and they need to get this done.

The ability to deny feelings kept cropping up:

> People need to express feelings as a means of working through what is happening to them, but men find this difficult to do. Women are more able to absorb grief and sadness when their own fertility is affected yet men seem unable to do this. They deny these emotions and pretend everything is fine, then they agree to options such as adoption and DI whilst still ignoring their own feelings about their infertility. But they are storing up problems for themselves in the long term by doing this. They can self-destruct because of all these pent-up feelings. It's not uncommon for them to react strongly by perhaps drinking heavily or becoming violent. They may become sick or direct their anger at clinic staff.

Several counsellors emphasised the point that men do not confide in others and do not want to share their problems. 'They are less likely to admit to problems and ask for help in dealing with them', according to one person. If they share their predicament with male friends they risk disappointment according to Dr Lee. Those friends may rebuff them either by joking about the problem or offering to help them out (Steven, 1991).

The only role the man has, according to one counsellor, is to support the woman, but he can get fed up with what he sees as the woman's obsession with infertility. Eventually he can experience a crisis because of all this:

> He has no role to fall back on. The only one is coping with his own feelings and his partner's, but he is not trained to do that. So he feels useless and tries to refocus onto other areas such as work. His relationship can go into crisis because he is unaware of his own needs. He should be saying to his partner, 'slow down, give me time to think about all this', but he doesn't. What worries me is, what happens to him in the longer term? I think he may have to pay a price for being emotionally illiterate.

Yet on a brighter note the point was made that those who can adapt to what has happened and accept the losses they have suffered, can find exciting new ways forward.

A consensus?

Overall the comments from women and counsellors paint a picture of men being unable to cope well with the consequences of their infertility. The main reason given for this is that feelings are bottled up and avoided. Talking about the problem is the last thing that men want or are able to do and they expect to be able to cope without any support.

I felt many of these points surfaced in my discussions, but there were a mix of experiences though a common strand linked them. There was frustration at the lack of control over events and strategies were not often deliberately adopted but became recognisable as such on reflection.

Infertility could unleash painful feelings and several people did speak of having to confront changes in themselves as a result. They wrestled with the consequences of infertility. For others it seemed a relatively uncomplicated business. These men tended to be those who now had children and saw infertility as a closed episode, the worst times were over for them and coping had been a short-term business. Those in the first group had been through a more protracted experience which required greater adjustment. James and Brian eventually felt obliged to face up to feelings of inadequacy rather than evade them, but they were the exceptions.

What was dealt with and how was it managed? These two issues were often indistinguishable. Coping with the woman's needs for example, was also a coping strategy. Having said that, several points emerged from my interviews. Different things had to be dealt with at different times. In earlier chapters I looked specifically at how men coped with medical tests and treatments and other people's reactions to their infertility. These experiences all meshed together when interviewees talked generally about how they coped.

Some of them seemed to be coping with practical issues whereas others were struggling with intangible matters such as feelings and life plans. What was noticeable was that a good number of them said they coped by dealing with the woman's needs rather than their own, as in Luke's case. His experience however, conflicts with the idea put forward by some counsellors that men are unable to perform this role. (Of course whether Katie felt supported by Luke is another matter.) Yet he seemed hesitant and slightly guilty about even admitting he had his own needs. Others received support from partners and this proved useful in helping them face the experience.

Interviewees often seemed to think they were coping not with the loss of their fertility but with the possibility that they could not be parents and the failure to give their partners children. They did not often seem sad about their infertility but seemed to be looking for distractions in the waiting period before they became parents. Once this happened they hoped their problems were at an end. The picture as to whether men were storing up problems for the future, as suggested by one counsellor, was unclear. Only one marriage had broken down but it was probably too early for most to look at the long-term effects of their coping strategies.

Emotions caused problems though this was not the case for everyone. For those troubled by them there was uncertainty about how to tackle them. Uncomfortable feelings were shoved aside if possible and often only came out into the open at the woman's insistence. Underpinning this was a sense that feelings should not be shown and should be kept in check, adding weight to women's and counsellors' views that men find emotions hard to handle. The difficulty could be as in Martin's case that he stopped communicating with his partner and this only aggravated the situation.

There was also talk about being active and in control of events, a point mentioned by counsellors. Men also turned to activities which they felt broadened horizons and helped them to think of things other than infertility.

My impression was that most interviewees hoped that the experience would be a brief one that was quickly resolved. To start with most had devoted time and energy to coping with medical issues rather than getting involved in lengthy self-analysis. This picture was reinforced at a meeting I attended where men were talking about their infertility problems. Their main concern seemed to be about hunting out the latest medical information, and talk about how lives might be or have been changed by infertility was noticeably absent from conversations. Yet these were early days for the majority of them.

The different issues that men seemed to be addressing, are spelt out in more detail by Woollett in her study of how people manage infertility. Virtually everyone was trying to cope by looking at how life plans had been disrupted by infertility. Trying to regain a sense of control by seeking out medical help was a common strategy. Searching out reasons for infertility was also commonplace.

Other issues were raised less often. These included trying to develop a positive identity, looking at reasons for wanting children, considering the possibility of a childfree life, reassessing life goals and ways of getting them. She notes:

> There were considerable individual differences in the coping strategies employed, but there were no systematic differences in concerns or strategies of men or women, in cases in which cause of infertility lay with man, woman or when cause was unknown, in infertility with a first or subsequent child, where infertility was the primary problem or secondary to another problem.
>
> (1985: 476)

Coping strategies are also described by Stanton. She lists the following methods. Confrontive coping (fighting for what I want), distancing (carrying on as if nothing had happened), self-controlling (keeping feelings to oneself), seeking support (talking to others), accepting responsibility (I brought the problem on myself), escape-avoidance (hoping a miracle would happen), planful problem solving (making an action plan and following it) and positive reappraisal (changed in a good way as a result) (1991).

Are some coping methods better or more successful than others? This thought occurred to me during the various discussions. There is no easy answer to this because it all depends how success is defined. There may be clues, and some methods of coping may be more appropriate for certain stages of the man's experience.

Researchers talk of avoidance and approach coping techniques; the former are designed to avoid the problem and the latter to deal with it. On reflection I think my interviewees were trying to use approach techniques. Most were not burying their heads in the sand throughout the experience though this may have happened at times, particularly in the early stages.

Rather than labelling either set as good or bad, Stanton suggests they may have different uses. Avoidance strategies for example, may be more helpful in the short term when everything seems out of control. Trying to solve the problem at that point when there is little opportunity of control may be counterproductive. However, dealing with the problem may be more productive for chronic controllable problems. Not doing so may hold up the grief process that some think of as vital for successful adjustment to infertility. Drinking or eating too much in order to avoid the problem may cause additional complications and avoiding activities which remind the person of infertility may end up making the person more isolated. They are cut off from potentially rewarding situations (1991).

The idea that some strategies are better than others seems to be a powerful one despite the point that they may serve different purposes and be useful at some times but not others.

One study, for example, linked outcomes to coping methods. Snarey reported that 'although infertility is often a temporary problem, these early responses affect men's happiness in middle age, their marriages and whether they eventually have children, adopt or remain childless' (1988: 61).

His research involving 300 men looked at how they cope with infertility generally. They were interviewed over a period of years to see what happened to them. All chose a substitute for parenting after finding out there was some sort of a fertility problem. For example, 63 per cent spent time on activities such as home improvements, 25 per cent spent time with other people's children, 12 per cent on self-centred ones such as body building. Snarey says that none of those men who used self-centred substitutes adopted children.

He also claims that this had longer-term results. Two thirds of those who used self-centred methods were divorced by mid life whilst those who had used child substitutes early on were more likely to have happy marriages later on. Snarey claims there is a link between the coping method used and 'generativity' – the stage in life when older people begin to show concern for the next generation. Generativity is seen as vital to personal satisfaction in later life. None of those who used self-centred methods showed clear evidence of generativity in later years. The upshot of all this is that he urges men to look at their initial coping strategies. 'Their choices could be something they have to live with for a very long time' (1988: 62).

Whether the few men I spoke to who had found comfort in having contact with other people's children are destined for long-term happiness as opposed to those who did not use such substitutes is a moot point. More powerful because it has been around for a long time is the idea that successful coping means dealing with powerful emotions such as grief. If this is blocked, depression can set in. This was one of the points that was at the forefront of my mind during my interviews. Infertility counsellors I spoke to talked about the need to work through grief and the importance of grieving comes up in many books and studies. Stanway, for example, says 'grief after the diagnosis of infertility has to be worked through just as does grief at any other time' (1986: 168).

Woollett also concludes in her study that amongst other things successful coping strategies 'depend on the point that people have reached in their infertile history and the degree to which they have mourned their loss and are not closely associated with demographic or treatment variables' (1985: 482).

Grief is seen as central to the infertile person's experience. It is a peculiar type of unfocussed grief. Mahlstedt explains that it is like grieving over a soldier reported missing in action. She also says that men may be upset but be unable to show feelings because of social conditioning (1985).

When I discovered several interviewees did not see it this way, I thought they must be denying their feelings. Others express caution. The ideas that say people go through predictable stages of emotion and need to work through these for successful adjustment, have not been fully evaluated. Both these ideas assume that all infertile people are similar to each other and that those who adjust successfully use the same coping methods. This view minimises individual variation and scant attention is given to the different ways that people manage infertility hurdles (Stanton and Dunkel-Schetter, 1991).

My initial assumption that some men might be coping more successfully than others seems unwise. Indeed the idea that there can be any standard prescription for successful coping may be suspect. At the very least how you define success seems open to much debate. The point at which success is measured may also be relevant, as illustrated by Snarey's study (1988).

On closer inspection each man may cope differently because of a number of factors. An inexhaustive list of these would include the issues that he thinks he is dealing with, his previous coping experience, his background, the support systems around him, social conditioning, the importance of father-hood for him, and he may change coping tactics over time. The theme of 'variation' is one that runs throughout this book.

The need to deal with certain issues or to cope in particular ways may only arise for some men at certain times in their infertility experience. Not everyone will, for example, automatically examine their goals and values. They may succeed in treatment early on and not experience repeated failures of conception. Others may leave parenting issues in the hands of fate or God (Clark *et al.*, 1991).

Meanwhile far more exploration is needed of how people generally cope with fertility problems and specifically how men cope when their fertility is compromised. My interviewees had different coping mechanisms and it would be naive to think that men all cope in the same way for the sorts of reasons outlined.

14 Support

Men on occasion looked for support though this was not true for everyone.

SUPPORT IS BASICALLY UNNECESSARY

Mike felt capable of handling any problems himself:

> The bad times were when my wife was very depressed when she failed to become pregnant each month, but I never seriously thought about approaching a self-help group or going for counselling. I wasn't that bothered. We were reasonably self-contained as a couple and I felt that we would only have negative things in common with others in a support group.

> The point is that I think I represent Mr Average with an average infertility problem. The mental problems I've come up against haven't crushed me and I think men probably find them easier to cope with than women. After all, the maternal instinct is more powerful than the paternal one. Men can find other activities to throw themselves into so I don't really feel they need that much support.

Stephen objected to certain words:

> I don't care for the words 'help' or 'support' because they imply illness and an inability to cope. My wife and I helped each other during difficult times. We're a partnership that works and we found our solution which was adoption.

SOURCES OF SUPPORT FOR THOSE WHO WANTED IT

Partners

As seen in the last chapter, partners could be helpful. They might give direct or indirect support or a mixture of the two. Indirect support was reassuring, said Luke:

> Though I felt I was giving her a lot of support she also helped me in a less obvious way. She didn't reject me and also said that if I didn't want to go any further with donor sperm that would be all right. That was quite important for me because she was saying that our relationship rather than children was the most important thing in her life. It also helped that she reaffirmed me for the man I was. She didn't do this in an obvious way but made it clear she still found me sexually attractive and that was a great boost to my confidence. She didn't reject me physically or emotionally and we became closer because of the experience.

Families

Relatives and parents in particular were a potential source of support, but as discussed earlier on, the latter were often seen as unhelpful.

FRIENDS

They could be helpful though several men had no close friends. Male friends were approached cautiously for fear of being rebuffed by them. Female friends were seen as far more caring:

> The women have been great but the men hardly ever ask how I'm coping. I suspect most of them want to be more supportive but they can't be because of their upbringing. I think they also probably expect me to cope and don't want to be embarrassed by me if I appear not to be coping.

Brian described his experience of friends:

> My wife's friends are the closest ones I have, but I felt worried about burdening them with my feelings as they would then have had to deal with both of us. I decided to try and manage on my own.

> In the end things got really bad because I was so upset about giving my wife her injections and eventually she insisted that I ring her close friend. All my misery flooded out when I spoke to this person but she was very supportive. She understood our situation, the sort of person I was and why I found it so difficult giving the injections.

Matthew talked wistfully of the support his wife received from her female friend:

> I had no support and there was nobody I could talk to about my feelings.

The one person I could have shared them with was my wife's good friend. I know she would have been sympathetic, but she was a listening ear for my wife so I couldn't impose my problems on her.

Friends that were helpful sometimes supported the man's partner and not him though this was not always so. 'They were good to us both, particularly to me and would ask what was happening and wish me good luck. Little things like that help because you don't have to hide everything all the time.'

Work colleagues

This type of support was not mentioned much by most and Derek in particular had received rough treatment at the hands of his work mates. Employers could, however, be supportive on a number of counts. 'I was allowed time off work for clinic appointments without questions being asked.'

Brian's boss was sympathetic:

His wife had a difficult time with the birth of their last child and he was also thinking about having a vasectomy, so he was sensitive to what I was going through. I told him about my situation and he was very kind. He understood that I had personal problems, and that home comes first though I am committed to my work. Life was much easier for me because of his attitude.

Counselling and other forms of support

There was a reluctance to consider more formal sources of support. Matthew felt ambivalent about the whole subject. He thought he should be able to cope on his own and that talking about his feelings would be unproductive. Yet he wondered what might have happened had he talked about things earlier on. I was the first person he had talked to about his feelings since the discovery of his infertility in 1987:

I had nobody to turn to, didn't know of any places that could help me and felt unsupported. I was helping my wife but there was nothing for me. I would have liked a shoulder to cry on, a big sister to talk to even though nothing could be done about my feelings.

To be honest there was no chance of finding someone who could help me in my particular environment. I was brought up with two brothers and went to a male school. My male work colleagues are unsupportive. The only implicit help I received was from my wife because she didn't walk out on me. That knowledge was a comfort.

Perhaps I didn't look hard enough for other forms of help because I thought I should be able to cope on my own. If there had been somebody at the time who I could have confided in, perhaps those things that still irk me despite our two adopted children would have gone.

I think perhaps my irrational fear about people finding out about my infertility would have lessened if I had received some sort of help. Maybe I could have explored my feelings of dread about DI more fully. In that way I can see counselling might have been useful. Perhaps my fears would have become less frightening, but there's still a part of me that feels that such help wouldn't really have done any good.

Tim would have liked help at a later stage:

To start with I certainly wouldn't have wanted to talk to anyone professionally about my problems. It was vital I coped on my own. I needed to get my thoughts and feelings into a little bit of order before letting them out to anyone else. If help had been available in those early days I wouldn't have wanted it for these reasons, but it would have been useful later on.

Upbringing prevented one person asking for help:

You're conditioned to look after yourself and there is nothing in your background which allows you to think of getting help from anywhere else. Talking to someone else was initially quite out of the question though the idea has become more acceptable since I took a risk and started confiding in a friend.

Roger was bitter he had not received counselling during IVF attempts:

When my wife miscarried after IVF, I was ignored. The staff talked to my wife. I felt as though I didn't exist. There was no help for me and I had a hard time emotionally over the days following the miscarriage.

Experiences of counselling

Several people had been through counselling sessions with their partners in order to be considered for DI. These experiences were mostly seen as a waste of time. Wry remarks were made about the process being 'perfunctory and like rubber-stamping'. Alan wished the session had been more substantial and that counselling had continued afterwards:

I would have liked some emotional support once my wife started the inseminations and then became pregnant. It would have been good to have someone other than my wife to talk to about my various worries, for example, I had questions about the baby's health. As it was I had no real counselling. I suppose we could have tried to contact someone but we were so bound up with ourselves that we didn't think about this.

A handful of men had sought counselling support and found it useful. Luke explained why he had decided to try it out:

A friend actually suggested I do this. I'd been coping with my partner's investigations for several years before I found out I was infertile. By that point I was pretty knotted up so a friend suggested counselling. In the end I saw a therapist for about two years.

I wanted to look at all the strain I had been through and to examine my feelings of grief. Seeing a therapist did help to an extent but in a way the damage had already been done when I started the sessions. It would have been good to see someone before or at the start of medical investigations. I have a gut feeling that people who have these sorts of problems should get expert help straightaway with the psychological side of infertility. Men particularly need this to deal with feelings. I felt I had to explore my own with the help of a third party because there was nobody there for me. I supported Katie because I could see her need for it. She now acknowledges she didn't give me direct support though it is difficult for her to admit this. I didn't, however, know that I needed help earlier on and wasn't even aware of what feelings I had. I just pushed them down and ignored them. Seeing a counsellor although too late repaired some of the damage.

Chris was now seeing a counsellor since he had separated from his wife. He was bitter about the lack of such support earlier on when he and his wife were being investigated. 'It's only because of this help that I am able to tell you something of what I have been through.'

Self-help

Self-help groups provoked mixed responses. Most knew about them and liked receiving the groups' newsletters, but there was a certain wariness about getting too involved with the groups. One familiar point made was that men should cope on their own and Mike felt men were less hard hit by infertility than women.

Bruce thought he would be tainted by contact with a self-help group:

I think I felt I didn't need that much support most of the time. I did actually know about a support group and was given some of their literature but I felt that if I contacted them it would be like admitting I had a problem and I couldn't do that earlier on. At the bottom of it all, was a deep reluctance to accept help.

Ignorance kept men isolated:

> I felt incredibly lonely and managed on my own. I had no network of friends to share my feelings with and didn't know of any infertility support groups. Perhaps it would have been useful to have a formal group to turn to but I think I would have needed to be pushed into one.

Kevin felt he might be pushed in a certain direction if he became actively involved in a group:

> I felt the group was pushing the view that you should have a child by whatever means and at whatever cost. I would have liked to talk to someone who had come through the bad times in one piece. That would have been very encouraging, but none of them seemed to be looking at how you cope.

There were others who said self-help groups were useful because they cut down feelings of isolation. 'You find out there are lots of other men in the same position and that helps.'

Nobody had used a telephone helpline for advice and most seemed very uncertain as to whether they would do. One person felt it could be useful 'for practical help but not for dealing with feelings'. However, Bruce said he would use such a line if need be because he was more prepared to ask for help now:

> I struggled on my own with infertility all those years ago and found out the hard way that I needed to ask for help. I wouldn't make the same mistake again. Since then I've used a premenstrual helpline to ask for advice about my wife's symptoms. The advisers shared their experiences with me and were a big help. So I think if I had my time over again with infertility I'd definitely use a helpline.

Supporting others

There was a desire to help others starting out on the infertility experience or part way through it. Jeffrey explained he had been heartened by words of encouragement given to him and wanted to reciprocate this:

> We were waiting in the clinic one time and another man sitting there wished me good luck and wished me well. It was only a tiny gesture but it made me feel good. Because of that, I made an effort on a later occasion at the clinic to do the same for another man.

Several interviewees felt they had passed through the worst times and now wanted to share their experiences with other men. They felt they could do this by talking to me. Kevin was sad because he had tried to get a group of men together: 'I advertised for men with fertility problems but got no response. That's one of the reasons for talking about my experience now. I think it's important for men to acknowledge their infertility and not deny it.'

DISCUSSION

Not everyone wanted support and informal rather than formal systems of help were preferred.

Formal support had to be searched out. Help was wanted for specific events such as IVF, DI or coping with a partner's miscarriage. Counselling would have been useful at the beginning of the infertility experience according to some people. Though others theoretically agreed with this, they felt in practice they should cope on their own.

Partners provided the main source of support for most either directly or indirectly, but as discussed earlier in the book, men often felt they gave more support than they received back. Maybe people always think they give more than they receive, for in one study though both men and women reported giving each other equal amounts of support, women felt they gave more than they received (Abbey *et al.*, 1991). Support from other informal sources such as friends and family was patchy and men often felt they had to carefully select those they confided in. There was also envy of the support that some women received from female friends.

Men seemed rather vague about more formal support services (e.g. self-help groups, counselling) on offer. The comment was also made that there were insufficent support services. This experience may be commonplace. Counselling services for infertile people are patchy, at least in Britain (Harman, 1990), and tend to be directed at women, as previously discussed.

Yet men were ambivalent about whether they would have used them had they known about them. They wanted information about medical techniques but were dubious about the value of psychological help. Basically they felt either that they must cope on their own or that such services could not help them. Mike also said that he did not need support because he was not that distressed by his infertility.

The reluctance to take up offers of help was evident in the fertility helpline report. The vast majority of calls were from women. The report concludes:

the average low call rate from men sadly confirms the continuing significance of the traditional cultural taboo whereby society wrongly links fertility to virility, believing that to admit to a fertility problem is to indicate a virility problem. With such unfortunate social conditioning, it takes a strong and brave man to seek advice – even anonymously via a telephone helpline.

(Dickson, 1991: 3)

The reluctance to seek help, in particular counselling, may affect women as well as men. Researchers pointed to one study where only a minority of couples offered counselling accepted it. Possible reasons for this low response may be that the problems experienced by people are not as severe as suggested, that people see counselling as threatening, and that other forms of support may be found (Edelmann and Connolly, 1986).

There is also research which suggests that men may be particularly ambivalent about using counselling and other forms of help. Women seem more willing to seek social support (Dunkel-Schetter and Stanton, 1991). Another piece of research found that most people favoured counselling before DI and a third of couples thought it should be compulsory, but men tended to resist the idea of compulsory counselling. This may be because they do not want to talk about their own infertility or are more hesistant about seeking out social support than women (Klock and Maier, 1991). Berg and Wilson reported that though a majority of men felt psychological services were needed, only a much smaller number would have used them (1990).

This reluctance to seek help came up several times in my discussions. Support services were fine in theory but when it came to the crunch several men said they would not seek help despite the difficulties they had been through. Why might this be so?

One popular explanation is the one often quoted about the link between virility and fertility. Men may also not feel the impact of infertility for a while. Some of those I spoke to now recognised with hindsight that they had been distressed, but did not think they were at the time. They may also think fertility problems will be quickly resolved and so not see the potential for distress in the future.

A familiar theme was put forward by another counsellor. Men feel panic when dealing with feelings and this makes them loth to seek help even from their partners. She had taken phone calls from men who were trying to gauge what their wives felt, by talking to her:

> I think that some of the men are scared of talking to their wives because they fear rejection. They are scared of the woman's feelings and less obviously so of their own. They find it difficult to voice their anxiety and pain and so find it hard asking for help.

Men may be trapped inside a shell of invulnerability. They think they must manage on their own and find it difficult admitting they have problems. They have been brought up not to feel, to deny their emotions and to be dominant with a high need for achievement. They can express acceptable manly feelings of rage and anger rather than unmanly ones of failure and rejection, and asking for help may make them feel inadequate (Heppner and Gonzales, 1987).

This observation is confirmed by Rappaport when he discusses how men react to offers of counselling help in various situations. They do not want it, especially if they feel insecure because they think they are losing control. They have been brought up to make decisions, focussing on the rational, concrete and practical, but this is at the expense of their feelings (1984).

This may explain why men were ambivalent about asking for help, yet they may be missing out by not getting formal support, particularly counselling. Increasingly it is seen as a good thing (Pfeffer and Quick, 1988). Counselling can allow people to explore alternative options or ways to parenthood as well as looking at other issues such as how identity may be affected (Clark *et al.*, 1991). There is a suggestion in one piece of research that men who are receptive to the idea of counselling, are better adjusted. Men who wanted counselling appeared to have better marital relationships than those who didn't, amongst couples waiting for IVF (Shaw *et al.*, 1988).

Such services may also be particularly important for infertile men. More marriage difficulties were reported in one study by both men and women when the man had fertility problems. If this is so, support services may be particularly useful (Connolly and Cooke, 1987). Possibly this is because the emotional burden on wives is reduced if infertile men are helped to find other sources of support, and relationships can improve as a result (Abbey *et al.*, 1991). Some men (and women) may particularly need help and may show some of the following warning signs. Parenthood is very important for them, they are preoccupied with why they are infertile, they cope by avoiding the problem and are dissatisfied with available support systems (Dunkel-Schetter and Stanton, 1991).

However, the assumption that all infertile people and therefore men need support in the form of counselling needs further research. Many of the claims made for the benefits of counselling have not been systematically evaluated suggest Edelmann and Connolly. More information is needed about whether some people adjust more easily than others to infertility and if so what their coping strategies are (1986). As discussed in the last chapter, the idea that successful adjustment only happens when feelings are expressed needs more evaluation.

Yet most of those I spoke to did want some sort of support. They had been through periods of isolation and felt abandoned at times. The problems of being a man in terms of finding it difficult to ask for help emerged in some interviews and Matthew in particular spent time talking about his dilemmas. One part of him felt there was no point talking about his feelings, he was stuck with them and there was nothing to be done. Yet, another side of him regretted that he had never had the opportunity during the early part of his experience to talk about his needs and feelings. This was one of the reasons why he had decided to talk to me. He wondered whether counselling might have made his feelings less threatening and disturbing. Basically the main message that came through from his comments and others was ambivalence about the usefulness of formal support systems and a sense that help was not deserved.

15 Resolution

What did the men now feel about themselves? Infertility had marked their lives in varying degrees and certain strategies had been adopted to deal with it. Were they reconciled to their infertility and if so how did they know this and what did this mean for them? Was infertility always with them or could it be shrugged off and left far behind?

ACCEPTED INFERTILITY

There were those who said they had no choice but to accept the situation. They felt they had received an absolute diagnosis. They produced no sperm and that was the end of the matter. Tim for instance, said he accepted it, 'it's a fact like my crooked nose which can't be ignored'. Julian was adamant. 'I accepted it immediately. There's no point sitting around dwelling on the fact, that only makes you depressed. So I got on with my life.'

Roger said he did not rush around searching out medical cures for his condition. This was evidence of the fact that he had accepted his infertility, and Andrew thought the issue was clear cut. 'The proof of my acceptance is that I had the semen analysis done, took the results on board and have agreed to DI.'

Feelings had basically been resolved once Bruce's first adopted child arrived. Before that he felt he hadn't really accepted his infertility. 'That was one of the reasons I didn't join the self-help group because at some level I couldn't accept what had happened and say I was infertile.'

Matthew's remarks were tinged with a little sadness:

The actual infertility doesn't bother me, I've got no sperm and that's it. Occasionally I have an idle thought, I look at our adopted children and wish they were mine, but it's not a big issue. Time heals everything and my feelings have become easier. Sometimes I panic and have this nightmare scenario. What if something awful happened to the children?

Everything would come flooding back and I'd have all the old problems again of trying to create a family.

Brian felt he had accepted his diagnosis of sperm problems. 'That fact alone was something I could accept. I can't do anything about it apart from wearing baggy pants and soaking my testicles in cold water. It's out of my control.'

UNCERTAIN ABOUT ACCEPTANCE

Most men however, were uncertain about what state they were in now. They might start by saying the issue was clear-cut, but reveal other feelings about their fertility later on in the conversation. Some harboured thoughts of fatherhood. Peter for instance, felt his sperm had improved since the varicocele operation and hoped he might become a father. John was overjoyed at being a parent since his wife had given birth. Donor sperm mixed with his own had been used and infertility issues were at the back of his mind:

I don't really think about it now. It was a minor hiccup. My wife needed a bit of help to get pregnant, that's all. My infertility is not a problem, it's a fact that I have accepted. I haven't chased after medical treatments because being a biological father isn't the most important thing for me.

Yet later on he explained that because mixed sperm had been used, it was possible though improbable that he might be the father. 'You give the weaklings a sporting chance of getting in and send the cavalry in afterwards.'

Mike knew his sperm had fertilised his wife's eggs in early IVF attempts, so it was possible he might have been able to father a child. This thought emerged in the interview:

I produced a good sample which was then mixed with donor sperm and my wife became pregnant after that insemination. I preferred the idea of being able to father my own children, but the idea wasn't vital for me. It's more important for my wife. (In fact I was the one to bring up the question of donor sperm.) There is a possibility I could be the father but I'd need to have a blood test to sort this out but as far as I can see it would serve no purpose to have one. It's more important for my wife to think I'm the natural father though maybe deep down I would also like to believe this.

Ambivalence marked Luke's feelings:

I may or may not be the father. At the moment those thoughts about my fertility are in the background. I'm just very excited about the baby, but obviously that question mark will remain and I may have to consider having a blood test in the future. I guess I haven't accepted my infertility deep down. The crunch will come if we decide to try for another baby in the future, then my fertility is going to be examined again.

Derek said he could never accept that he was infertile. 'I have sperm and perhaps someday one will come up trumps.'

Jeffrey produced no sperm but also felt unable to accept his infertility. He was thrilled his wife was pregnant after donor sperm had been used, but said:

> The thought is still there in the background after all these years. Why haven't I got any sperm? If I go to my doctor about other things I normally ask for the latest news of male infertility treatments. If one came up in the next couple of years I'd go for it because I haven't accepted that this is the end. If I could have my own child I would definitely have one.

Later he said perhaps he had accepted his infertility:

> Because the baby is on the way. It's got in the way of the original sad thoughts and some of the pressures have been eased. I suppose I have got over some things though others can still upset me like the lad at work and his unpleasant remarks.

Finally he repeated but with a slightly different emphasis:

> I would still consider a new treatment, it wouldn't be right if I didn't because I want my own child. If nothing comes along, then so long as this baby is all right I won't miss having my own child so much. I just don't know, if we have a second child that will probably be the end of it. I don't think I would chase after medical treatments just for the sake of it.

Acceptance implied too easy a process for some. Coming to terms reluctantly with infertility was a better description of what happened. There were no easy answers so this was all you could do according to Kevin:

> I have come to terms with my infertility. I think I have accepted the fact (though it's been difficult) that I can't have my own children because I've got no sperm. I genuinely believe I can't father a child. That's clear-cut, but I could never accept that I can't be a dad and have children to care for. If I had I wouldn't be considering options like DI or adoption.

Laying painful feelings to rest had been difficult for Alan. Two years had elapsed since his diagnosis and he and his wife now had a baby after donor sperm had been used. He said he never felt infertile in an emotional sense but felt odd and strange. 'Something was mechanically wrong with me.' Infertility had been an obstacle which had to be overcome. 'I now feel like any normal bloke', yet he added:

> I accept it more now, but I'd really like to know why I have no sperm so

I could come to terms with it. Not knowing why is the worst part of it though our baby makes life more bearable.

Later on he said:

I think I've accepted it fairly well. Deep down I know it's one of those things I won't find out about unless I go in for massive investigations. Even then I still might not find out why I'm infertile, so why go through all that? Time heals wounds and things do get better. I felt that as soon as my wife became pregnant.

For Brian it was the other things linked to infertility which were hard to come to terms with. He could accept his infertility but 'the treatments are hard to accept. My wife has had to go through pain because of me and that's hard to swallow'.

DISCUSSION

Ideas about acceptance, coming to terms with infertility and resolving it are tied to the notion that infertility is a crisis to be worked through. In order to adapt successfully to the experience, a process must be worked through. Infertility means recognising there is a loss and mourning it.

Ultimately, the message is that men need to go through certain stages so as to move on. Stanway, for example, says people should not consider options such as adoption unless they have been through a recovery process. Men in particular 'say that they never really come to terms with their infertility – indeed there is no treatment for the long-term pain' (1986: 168).

The Houghtons make the following observations:

Not a great deal is known about the way in which a childless person comes to terms with his or her childless state, and is enabled to work towards an alternative view of life, or a lifestyle that offers some of the rewards that are comparable to those experienced in the bearing or bringing up of children.

(1987: 125)

Trying to understand what men felt about such matters was no easy task. My interviews were often marked by a confused air when talk turned to this area and Jeffrey's thoughts illustrate the dilemmas he keenly felt. There were no uniform experiences amongst interviewees about issues of resolution, apart from feelings of pain, isolation and uncertainty.

The clearest feelings tended to come from those who felt the business was over and done with; they had or were about to become parents. More often than not these men also had an absolute diagnosis. They had zero sperm counts and had been told nothing could be done for them. Yet this was not always so and the question 'why' still haunted Jeffrey and Alan. Brian who had an uncertain diagnosis of 'sperm problems', also felt he had accepted his infertility, though others with a similar diagnosis were more perplexed and uncertain about what such a diagnosis meant.

There was no obvious sense of working through stages of grief for most, though such ideas were familiar to a few men because of the research they had done.

What came up from the discussions is that infertility is not experienced as a permanent fixed state. Feelings about it shift over time and different diagnoses have different implications for fertility, so affecting resolution issues.

The concept of infertility was difficult to handle for most. It was a baffling idea particularly as some men suspected they had been fertile in the past. A couple of others knew their sperm had fertilised eggs during IVF. Robert said this 'made me feel better', perhaps it made him feel fertile. Martin was full of excitement because his wife was pregnant by him, but it was too soon to say how this event had affected his sense of fertility or whether his past experience would always make him feel infertile.

If such doubts remain, they may never be totally extinguished. As Luke pointed out, his fertility would again be under review in the future if he and his partner decided they wanted a second child. Past memories might come flooding back, reviving old anxieties. The same is probably true for Martin.

With the passage of time, some men became parents. This was seen as a blessing and much pain then melted away, but a dull ache remained as time passed for those still struggling to create families by various means. Only a couple of them were contemplating a childless future. James was facing up to this prospect with much heartache and uncertainty and the challenge was to find other ways to fulfilment.

How did men know if they had accepted their infertility? They were understandably a little hazy about how to evaluate or measure acceptance. Often they talked about coming through bad times to better ones. The pain had gone or eased and some also pointed to whether they were seeking medical treatments or had accepted alternative ways of becoming fathers. Kevin said he could accept never being a father but could never accept not being a dad (a parent).

The issue was linked I think to how far they felt their fertility had been damaged or lost and whether it could be restored. Increasingly men may be faced with more questions about this as further medical solutions are offered to them. Meanwhile men took different stances on this point. Some were intrigued by such prospects whilst others felt there was no point pursuing them because the whole process would just be dragged out with no clear conclusion at the end.

Ultimately I wondered how much men valued their fertility. (One counsellor had said they cherish it dearly.) For most this was an intangible concept and more often than not they concluded it was not vital though some seemed to harbour secret longings for fatherhood. Despite this uncertainty, Luke had tried to determine how vital fatherhood was for him whilst looking at other important areas of his life.

Examining life goals and reordering them may be a beneficial exercise. None of my interviewees had done this in a formal way, though beliefs and thoughts about fatherhood did crop up in most conversations. Taking this a step further may prove useful. Analysing parenting goals may allow people to find other ways to fulfilment (Clark *et al.*, 1991). This can lessen heartache. Hanging onto goals which cannot be achieved can be distressing because the person remains in a permanent state of infertility.

An examination of aims may lead to the realisation that they can be rearranged in order of importance or that there are other ways of achieving them. Re-examining ambitions can also be useful because the individual may be 'freed from seeing the failure of conception as a failure to achieve happiness or maintain a sense of self-worth'. Not everyone will analyse their goals. Some may never accept they cannot have children and invest considerable time and effort trying to conceive their own child. Others may minimise the undesirable implications of childlessness, whilst others may have a child relatively quickly after treatment (Clark *et al.* 1991: 171).

These ideas may account for why some men seemed to feel they had got to grips with infertility whilst others did not. Opting for adoption or DI rather than being a quick fix solution that denies the original problem may be a sensible way forward. But it may be important to know what is lost and what is gained by restructuring life plans; DI means, for example, accepting the father's genetic makeup is lost (Clark *et al.*, 1991).

Such options may be plausible ones for those men less strongly attached to the need to be biological parents. Feelings of lack of confidence may be checked by building up other life interests. Men's investment in the role of father may be sufficiently flexible to allow them to explore other ways of creating a family or filling the gap produced by a childfree relationship (Congress of the US, Office of Technology Assessment, 1988a).

These options may, however, be unsuitable for others whose values are different. Imposing uniform solutions on people is inappropriate.

These ideas seem useful because they encourage the idea of difference which characterised many of my conversations. There is no automatic assumption that all things will be equally important to all people and that there are standard solutions to the problem. Starting from each man's standpoint and looking at what is important for him and going from there may be the best way of understanding what he is experiencing. Whether men can ever leave the experience far behind them seems unclear. There are probably always going to be reminders of infertility in the future. An illustration of this is Bruce's adopted child throwing out the remark 'you're not my real father'. But the sense of being fertile or infertile may no longer be uppermost in men's minds as time passes and they adapt in their own ways to the challenges posed by infertility. Yet as Lottridge explains, though the pain of infertility lessened in his first marriage when he adopted a child, he again confronted it when his marriage broke up and he remarried. He concludes that though he has an adopted son and now a lovely baby daughter, 'I am still an infertile man. I have resolved most of my feelings and I accept my infertility, but I will never, fully, be reconciled to it' (1988: 42).

16 Couples

When I started my research for this book I was ticked off soundly by one doctor. He said that it was the couple not the individuals in that relationship who go through the infertility experience. My desire to focus primarily on what infertile men went through and their feelings made no sense to him. He poured cold water on my idea of exploring the male viewpoint.

He raised a vital and complex area of debate which cropped up throughout my conversations. At times men would talk of 'we' rather than 'I' during discussions, so I asked them for their thoughts on this area. What differences if any were there?

NO DIFFERENCE

A few men felt there was no difference. Stephen, for example, said though it was initially his problem 'we coped with it'. He and his wife were a partnership.

THERE ARE DIFFERENCES

Most, however, felt there were differences because of certain factors.

The diagnosis

Joint or sole infertility could affect the experience according to Andrew:

> I'm the infertile one so I've had to work through the problem for myself in a way that my wife has not had to do. She is fertile as far as we know, even though the DI attempts have so far been unsuccessful. If she does find out she has a fertility problem, then she'll have painful things to work through. Meanwhile there is this difference because I'm infertile and she is apparently fertile. We're out of step with each other.

Tim agreed life was easier when he and his partner were jointly infertile. 'It was much better once her problems came to light. We were both to blame and I felt less guilty. We both felt more comfortable with the situation.'

A point was made about the special nature of one type of diagnosis:

> Finding out I had no sperm was a dreadful shock. Straightaway I was hit between the eyes because the outlook was so bleak. Those feelings were peculiar to me and I had to struggle with them on my own. I think women don't often face such a stark diagnosis when it comes to their fertility.

A diagnosis of male infertility could cause tension between partners. 'At some stages she's been quite angry with me. It's a sort of frustration she's directed at me. I understand that and try not to feel guilty about the whole business.'

The physical experience

Partners had a more painful experience. Men did not go through the physical experience of failed conception:

> She suffered each month with her period, all that disappointment. I felt sad as well but it must be different for the woman. It's a more drawn out business for her and she has that physical reminder each month of loss.

Miscarriage also separated the sexes. A few men told me how they had stood helplessly on the sidelines. They cared very much about what was happening and could be 'cut to the core'. Despite this there was no support directed towards them and they tended to suffer in silence.

Medical treatment

This area was often mentioned. Feelings of exclusion and marginality were commonplace. Jeffrey and Bruce had been specifically shut out from preliminary medical consultations. The following comments convey a sense of the distress felt. 'I was disregarded from the outset and ignored by the doctor.' 'Forget it was the message the doctors gave me. I had no role to play except that of trying to support my wife.'

Interviewees said they felt unhappy and uncomfortable seeing their partners go through certain painful procedures. 'It was awful seeing her go through five IVF attempts even though by then we knew she too had some sort of a problem, so I didn't feel quite so guilty.' The discomfort stemmed from feeling useless. 'I'm just the onlooker who provides sperm from time to time.' Brian's misery was compounded:

Our experiences are different. She's being treated for my problem and it's unsettling knowing that. Not only is she having these treatments because of me, but I have to give her the awful injections. Sometimes she gets annoyed with me because she feels she's putting more effort into getting a child than I am. She thinks I'm not doing enough though she knows I'm doing all I can. The problem is there isn't much I can do to improve my sperm. She understands this but gets angry at times about the lack of help for male infertility.

Upbringing

Comments were made about how men and women have different experiences because of social conditioning. Matthew explained:

We differed on one significant point. She saw her future not in terms of a career but as being a wife and mother. That dream was threatened by my infertility. She was beginning to realise she was good at her job, but had taken it on the basis that she would leave when she became pregnant. That wasn't going to happen so she had to rethink her future.

For me it was less difficult. I had my job and was more interested in my career. I remember her saying that it was all right for me because I had my work but she had nothing to hold tight to.

Upbringing was also responsible for men's isolation. 'It's far more difficult for men to speak about infertility. They just can't be open about it. That fact makes them more isolated and separates them from women.'

Biology

Biology inevitably meant the sexes had divergent experiences according to several interviewees. Men tended to subscribe to the view that women have a stronger desire for pregnancy and childbirth. 'She became focussed on getting pregnant in a way I could never do.' Brian went into some detail about men's and women's different preoccupations:

My wife's drive is for children, mine for sex. It sounds strange but I didn't understand this for some time and it became a bone of contention between us. I felt pushed away when we made love and eventually found out why this was happening. She resented me getting my way when she wasn't getting her way. I was having sex and satisfying my needs but she wasn't getting a baby out of it. There was an imbalance. That's not to say I don't want children. I do, but the drive is less urgent for me than for her. I have a quieter need to provide guidance for my children as they grow up and help them make a success of their lives.

This difference caused problems between us. I felt a strong pressure from my wife to have sex when she was ovulating. That made me anxious and sometimes I couldn't perform. She in turn couldn't understand why I was able to make love easily at other times in her cycle. Once I understood that my strong sex drive was the same as her desire for children things eased because we understood each other better.

It's an important difference. At one point, Lucy was rather upset because I hadn't offered her a divorce in recognition of what she was perhaps going to lose. I had never thought about it like that and thought she was getting all the sex she wanted. Even though I was vaguely aware of the idea that having children is very important for women, I never realised how upset my wife was. I had my own selfish needs to satisfy and wasn't going to let go of her that easily.

Generally there was no exploration of why men felt women had a stronger drive for children. It was a biological fact, an instinct. Inevitably there were different responses as a result. 'I think women have deeper feelings about children. That makes them react in a different way to a man. The female instinct does seem to be stronger though men have to cope with feelings of inadequacy.' Women were thought to have a stronger parenting desire. 'I do care and want a family, but I think I could probably have coped better than my wife if we had decided on a childfree existence.'

The biological clock also sharpened the experience for the woman: 'She wanted to go through pregnancy and childbirth but was aware of getting older and was worried her childbearing years were running out. There wasn't the same sense of urgency for me.'

Jeffrey, however, disagreed with the view that it is women rather than men who have the basic drive for children. Men were born to reproduce and had a strong instinct to have children.

Coping with needs

Because of biology, many men felt a woman was more distressed by the prospect of childlessness. She was entitled to be upset and deserved support. Luke expressed a common sentiment. 'I bottled up my feelings to look after her.'

The man still, however, had needs, as Matthew emphasised:

The couple has needs and so does each person in that partnership, but the couple's needs are subservient to your own. You can never really know exactly what the other person feels. After all, you think for yourself ultimately, and your most private moments are your own.

Brian saw it this way:

> Yes, both of us are involved in trying to have a family, but the problems that come up are ones we handle in our own way and react differently to. DI for example, is not a problem for me but it is for my wife.

Kevin emphasised being out of step with his partner:

> I needed time to think things through and wanted her support. Of course she wasn't the infertile one and reacted differently to begin with. She was very matter of fact about my infertility and talked about various alternatives like DI quite early on. She wanted things to happen whereas I wanted time to make sense of what had happened to me. There was a gap between us because she didn't have to cope with feelings about the loss of her own fertility.

Support

There was a tendency to think women received more support. Consequently several men talked of feeling isolated and were jealous of the support their partners received from various people. Roger thought that neither he nor his wife had received much support but, 'I think my wife talked regularly and at some length to her mother about what was going on'.

Luke made a special plea for assistance:

> Help is particularly needed from the man's viewpoint. There is so little research into male infertility that people don't understand it and there are fewer treatment options available. This all makes it more difficult to cope with on the mental side. We also need support because of not being good at talking about our feelings. I had little help and that was why I eventually went to a therapist. My partner couldn't give me what I needed because she was grappling with her own separate feelings.

WOMEN'S THOUGHTS

I've added in a few comments from women which I think are illuminating.

The physical experience

This was commented on:

> I was pushing to get things sorted out. I felt dreadful as every month passed

but I think my husband would have waited longer to get the ball rolling. I think I was probably far more conscious of time passing than he was. The pain of not having a baby was more immediate and physical for me.

Coping and support

There were mixed feelings about this. Comments were generally about men clamming up and being unable to share their feelings. They worried that men would be unable to cope.

Women did not seem to feel supported by their partners (despite some men feeling they had supported the woman). Instead they talked of suppressing their own needs to support men. Feelings of anger, frustration and protectiveness ran through their thoughts:

I think he's coped quite well really. He's been prepared to talk about it which is unusual for a man. But I think looking back that at the start I shelved quite a few of my own needs because I wanted to help him.

There was quite a lot of guilt around and I was worried about telling him what I felt for fear of hurting him. It was difficult for him when he found out he was the one with the problem because I think women are brought up to believe they are the ones who will be infertile. We're told our equipment is complicated and likely to go wrong.

I did feel angry sometimes and felt bad about this because I knew it was irrational. The difficult bit was telling him how I felt but it took a long time to do that. We were both bickering a lot and it got to the point where we had to talk about my resentment.

We both looked for help from friends. That worked for me but not for him. Male friends just seemed to shut off from the whole thing. I also had to persuade him we needed to see a counsellor. I felt he wasn't actively looking for this support. He would come home and not talk about his infertility and I had to keep at him to get him to say what he was feeling. From my viewpoint I felt annoyed at the way men neglect each other. I had to get support not only for myself from friends but also for him in an indirect way. In the end I told him I just couldn't manage to support him as well as me. We had to see a counsellor and that helped a lot.

And:

I tried hard not to be angry with him and to work through the options with him. I could have ranted and raved but I tried to calm down. The whole experience was more urgent for me I think. I was the one who pushed to get things going whereas he would have been quite happy to let things ride. I started to drag up memories of past boyfriends, and thought of having sex with them as a way of getting a child, but that was abhorrent. The treatment experience has also been different for us. I'm the one who has had to make an upfront commitment to take drugs and have my body interfered with. I felt he wasn't doing enough at times. The least he could do was give me my drug injections, but he found that a problem. I got frustrated because I couldn't support him as well as myself.

The difference in experiences narrowed as time passed:

At the start, I thought what will he feel? He didn't react violently or emotionally, perhaps he didn't really understand the diagnosis. I wanted to talk to him and find out what he was thinking but didn't want to make a big deal out of it. I also remember rushing through various options in my mind at the beginning and thinking I would have to be strong for him. I also worried because I knew there was nobody else he could talk to apart from me. That was a big responsibility.

As time went by we started sharing things. I think the biggest difference is that I felt a huge range of emotions from the start and wanted to talk to him about them. He was slower to open up and when he did I found it difficult dealing with his feelings because I've always been the one who could cry knowing he would remain calm. It was unnerving trying to support him though I wanted to do this. Looking back I think we did cope differently at the beginning but luckily we've always been in basic agreement about the issues that faced us.

COUNSELLORS' THOUGHTS

Two points were made about men's and women's experiences which seem worth mentioning. Firstly, one person thought that men will walk away from a relationship rather than face up to the problem. The second was to do with fertility:

I think this means different things for men and women. The most important thing for a man is the sense that he is fertile. None of the treatments presently available generally alter his status. I think he feels that if he has sperm he is fertile and so assumes the woman is infertile. If he has no sperm he is more likely to accept his infertility. If I could say to all men with fertility problems that there was some magic ingredient that would make them fertile, they would be relieved. Thinking they are fertile is very important to them, but women want to know not only that they are theoretically fertile but that they can get pregnant and have children. I suspect that in about a third of the couples I see, the man would be glad if his partner said let's stop trying for a child. He wouldn't then have to continually face possible failure.

DISCUSSION

The idea that it is important to treat the couple rather than the individuals in that relationship is popular. This stems from the medical treatment of infertility. 'Fertility is the product of interaction between two people and so the infertile patient is in effect the infertile couple' (Congress of the US, Office of Technology Assessment, 1988c: 4).

Menning explains why infertility should be seen as the couple's problem from a psychological perspective. Each person in the couple has a strong interest in investigations and treatment, regardless of who turns out eventually to have the problem. If both the man and woman visit the doctor together at the outset, then power tends to be equalised. 'They gain courage and assertiveness from each other's presence and will often negotiate their needs more honestly right away' (1980: 318).

This approach seems to make sense as it takes two to make a baby. Yet the emphasis on the infertile couple rather than the individuals in that unit may have a downside. Differences can be glossed over and 'a fiction of cosy consensus' may be created (Pfeffer and Quick, 1988: 18).

The majority of my interviewees felt their experiences differed in significant respects from their partners. Various reasons were offered for this state of affairs. The nature of the diagnosis and whether the woman also had fertility problems changed experiences. The man might have to work through feelings his partner would never meet if he was the only one with the problem. There was the point made about a diagnosis of no sperm. Women would not often receive an equivalent diagnosis and so would not know how painful it was.

Several men said they felt isolated, marginalised and invisible during medical investigations. This was ironic because though they had the problem they were not normally being treated for it (and their experiences suggest that, contrary to what doctors claim, the couple is not always treated). This feeling sometimes led to another one: guilt. Partners were having a rough time because of the man's infertility.

The sexes care about different things according to one counsellor. The man treasures the idea of his fertility, but the woman does not only want to know that she is fertile. She wants to go through pregnancy and childbirth. Certainly, men tended to favour the view that women deserved more support because their loss was greater. Women would be harder hit by the prospect of possible childlessness (though few men, as seen in the previous chapter, seemed to think their own fertility was vital).

For their part, women mentioned feelings of urgency in a way that men did not. The result might be that she rushed ahead of the man, exploring solutions, as in Kevin's case.

The sense that women suffered more resulted in men feeling they had to cope by supporting their partners. Some but not all (notably Kevin) ignored their own needs in the process, thinking they must focus on the woman's needs. Their own feelings might just complicate matters. Yet others were unaware they had any feelings of note at that stage or said they had none, as in Mike's case.

Meanwhile women did not seem to feel they had been particularly supported in any way and worried about how men would cope. They also seemed to feel they would have to shoulder the main burden of coping and supporting the man through the experience whilst dealing with their own feelings.

Several of them remarked that their partners clammed up about feelings. Women took this as an ominous sign because they felt men needed to get their feelings out into the open. But one woman remarked how uncomfortable she initially felt when her partner did start to unburden himself. Overall there seemed to be a mismatch between perceptions of support. Men thought they supported their partners, yet women did not seem to feel this and instead thought they supported men. Ironically, men said they did not voice their feelings because they did not want to burden women. Yet this may well have been what women wanted, to know what the man was feeling rather than putting up with his silences.

Differences in experiences between the sexes emerge in other studies. One such (where female infertility was the main diagnosis) found that women wanted to talk about infertility more than men (Brand, 1989). Mahlstedt makes a point about the way men and women may cope with infertility generally (rather than tied to a diagnosis of male or female infertility). Couples can sometimes become polarised because infertility affects them differently. She says that a man often copes with pain by keeping it to himself and concentrating on his partner. The woman wants to talk to him about her pain but because he feels powerless to stop it, he may avoid listening to her. A spiral can develop with the woman becoming more vocal in order to attract her partner's attention and with him retreating and becoming quieter. Ultimately the woman may feel abandoned by the man.

The silence may imply not that he feels nothing but that he is not used to expressing emotions. Or it may be, Mahlstedt adds, that he is silent because children do not have the same meaning for him as for his partner.

She also points to specific differences that relate to male infertility. The man has to deal with treatments and people's attitudes towards his infertility. He feels responsible for creating the problem and thinks he must support his partner. The woman may experience mixed feelings, angry at times and supportive at others, whilst still having to cope with her own feelings of loss (1985).

Stanton's research (again female infertility was the main diagnosis) found that most men and women think the sexes cope differently. Women talk more about their feelings, and infertility was also seen as more distressing for women. Such perceptions may magnify differences whilst ignoring similarities in experiences and a gap may open up between the pair. There can be problems if each partner thinks their coping method is right and the other's wrong (1991).

The conclusion about gender differences is that more research is needed. Past studies have looked far more at infertile women than men and few studies have attempted to untangle the differences that may be due to sex and those due to the type of diagnosis received (Dunkel-Schetter and Stanton, 1991).

Reviewing my discussions, men clearly felt they had different experiences. Reading between the lines, there were also similarities and a blurring of the man's and woman's experience which blunted a sense of difference – at least from a distance. Men talked like women about having feelings of pain, loss and loneliness. Kevin, for example, spoke of powerful feelings and disturbing dreams, and some talked of distress when seeing babies and children. The passage of time seemed to bring some partners closer together once they started sharing their experiences with each other. Infertile men may share experiences in common not only with women but with men who are fertile but whose partners are infertile. They may all have to contend with feelings of inadequacy and loss, struggle with how to cope with these feelings and how best to support their partners.

A few distinctive differences however, stand out in my mind when the infertile man's experience is considered. One is specifically related to a diagnosis of male infertility and was mentioned by men whose partners were apparently fertile. They blamed themselves for the couple's childlessness. Men also felt neglected by the medical profession and guilty that their partners had to suffer painful treatments as a result. Men did not often have to contend with the pain of treatment themselves but perhaps wished they had suffered. Some but not all may find the idea that they are infertile highly upsetting, though as seen there was a good deal of ambivalence on this point. Men were not sure how important this concept should be to them, consequently they tended to downplay any sense of loss. They were reluctant to voice their feelings and needs because of guilt and a sense that their loss was not that great. They seemed to find it easier to attend to the woman's needs, but could pay a high price for this and become peculiarly isolated.

17 The way forward

What words of advice did men have for others setting out on the road they had travelled along and how could male infertility services be improved?

TREATMENT

Advice about medical help tended to dominate responses. Seek out the best, said Jeffrey. He also bemoaned the fact that services were so impersonal. Luke felt that getting checked out straightaway was important and prompt diagnosis was vital:

> They just took my fertility for granted at the beginning because I told them a previous semen sample (taken for another purpose) had been normal. A second more diligent clinic insisted on checking my sperm before going ahead with GIFT. If the check had been done at the beginning, then maybe my partner would not have had to undergo a minor operation and been given a fertility drug.

There was a similar plea:

> Question doctors who assume it's the woman's fault because the man may well have a problem. Doctors concentrate on investigating the woman because they think they can treat her but not you. Don't just give your semen sample to your wife to take to the hospital. Make sure you're involved from the start in investigations by going along to consultations.

Others stressed the need to hunt around for information and not be fobbed off by doctors who said nothing could be done. John for example, insisted it was vital to get information and take control:

> You may feel hopeless to start with so get the necessary facts and find out what choices there are. I know it's not easy to do this in the health service

and that we were fortunate having private help. But the point remains that you should find out what you can about available options.

Alternative approaches

As a result of his experience, Martin felt that attention to diet and lifestyle paid dividends. High-tech procedures worried him:

> I don't think that IVF is the solution to male infertility. High-tech medicine may save lives but I don't think it restores or guarantees good health. Other approaches which look at the whole person seem more sensible to me rather than ones which tinker with bits of you. We ended up looking at what we were eating and drinking, how much stress there was in our lives. I feel vindicated by this approach because I've now got my wife pregnant. I feel great. It's like a victory for the common man over technology gone haywire.

More medical research needed

There was sadness and bitterness about the medical treatment of male infertility. Women were being unnecessarily treated. Brian put it this way:

> The emphasis has been on the woman for years. There are precious few treatments for male infertility so it's my wife who has been treated rather than me. She has all the drugs while I stand around like a spare part. Yet she doesn't have the problem. There have been five years of uncertainty and it's only now that the problem of my poor sperm is being looked at. I've suffered as a result of all this, because my chances of having a family have been reduced. More research is needed to help people like me.

Luke wondered why doctors were clueless:

> They don't have a clue about sperm problems, so they look at the woman to try and get round the problem. They don't take much notice of the man. Why this should be I don't know, but I can't accept that women's rather than men's bodies are easier to manipulate. I guess the problem stems from the fact that gynaecologists dominate infertility services. On the whole they're just not interested in men.

Reduce stress levels

Brian made a plea for stress to be reduced. 'It may harm sperm, and doctors need to do all they can to put the man at ease and reduce his stress levels. Otherwise the whole thing becomes counterproductive.'

COPING IDEAS

Time

Slowing down was important, said Kevin. He needed time to understand what he felt about his infertility. He also said that he and his partner had developed a policy of not telling their families about what was happening 'until we then had a chance to think things through properly. We were worried they might lean on us in some way'.

Robert also felt time was needed:

> You mustn't rush things, slow down and see what you really feel about everything. It's difficult doing this because the spotlight is on the woman and her needs and she may be moving faster than you, but I have done it. I don't think you should ignore your feelings.

Tim agreed:

> The biggest mistake we made was to rush ahead with a physical plan of action without thinking through the mental side first. It's not sensible having a plan of campaign in this situation. I had to face up to my anger at having no target for my frustration. I know everyone reacts differently to infertility but it's important to understand just how difficult the whole experience is. You can't fix your feelings on anything other than a fuzzy idea of nothingness. You have to be aware of this and talk it through, but still it's tricky because there is nothing to get hold of.

Motives for fatherhood

Mike felt reasons should be looked at:

> I think you need to get down to basics and ask yourself how important it is to have a family and, specifically, your own children. If you feel it's essential to have them, then you need to do what you can to improve your sperm. You can take a wider view if your first priority is a family rather than your own children and you need to explore your feelings. Mine have changed over time and I now think that having a family is more important than a narrow insistence on having my own children.
>
> You can also take comfort from the fact that it's how you care for children that makes you a man. Not the actual fathering of them.

Support

Tim would have liked some counselling help after the initial period of coping on his own:

> We might then not have rushed into the medical treatments. It would have helped to talked sensibly about the consequences of my infertility, to look at our expectations of children and the importance of biological children.

Others echoed these thoughts. Julian, for example, felt that some sort of counselling would have helped:

> When I was ill with cancer, the doctor told me what I was likely to go through and what the treatment side effects were going to be. So I think it would have been helpful to do the same thing with my infertility, to look at what was happening and what the alternatives were. Nobody offered us counselling and we didn't think about it.

Finding out how others have coped could help, said Kevin:

> It's important to know that you will come through the experience in one piece. I would have found it useful to talk to another man who had been through it all. He would hopefully have reassured me that my feelings are normal and that things will get better.

Isolation was a reason for contacting other men in a similar position:

> You need to find men in your position. I think most of the time I felt pretty alone as I didn't know of anyone else in my situation. Now I belong to a support group, I can see how common the problem is and that helps put things in perspective. I know it can happen to anyone. Talking to someone who has been through it can be useful because you get an idea of what you might have to face. I would have liked to unload all my problems onto someone knowing that there would be no comeback from doing that.

KEEP TRYING FOR A FAMILY

Perseverance was the advice given by men who had families. Children took away the pain of infertility. Mike explained 'we just kept on trying a combination of things and finally struck lucky'.

NO EASY ANSWERS

There was also hesitation about what words of comfort or advice to offer other men. The way forward was blurred for some interviewees. There was not much that could be done to prepare a man for the experience said Roger:

There is nothing to help you. My wife supported me to an extent and perhaps a counsellor might have done. The main thing is that you are not alone, but I don't think I would have wanted to know in advance how painful this was all going to be.

Brian felt the opposite and added in some other points:

I would have liked to know at the beginning that it was going to hurt deeply and badly for a time. Knowing other men out there have a problem helps. It's good to know you're not a freak, that you're normal. You may feel guilty or inadequate thinking you have failed when you should have succeeded. Some men handle their problems and others don't. It can help to talk about all these things.

Others felt the whole experience was so bizarre that it was almost impossible to know what would be of help. 'It's a problem to say how you can get over what has happened and there are no clear solutions to it.' Andrew recommended an unquestioning acceptance of infertility:

There's no point trying to make sense of it. This sounds strange but it does help. For example, if you ask yourself why me, you could equally ask why not me? Currently most of us don't know why we have a problem and you need to take this on board and accept that nobody understands much about male infertility.

I don't think you can hand out standard advice. I had no sperm and was lucky because you can't clutch at straws with that diagnosis. But what you go through and how you react is a purely individual thing. However, I think it can help to talk to someone else at times, but when you're going through it all, you're so tied up with the problem that it's difficult to know what advice would be best at that stage.

Matthew had some stark advice:

You're on your own. No matter who you talk to, in the end you have to cope on your own. I know this is not a very comforting thing to say but I think we find our own way and I don't think anything I could say would make men feel better. I could say look at me I have two adopted children now, but I don't think that would be very helpful because we know that not everyone will manage to end up with a family. I would be seen as someone who has gone through and come out the other side, that doesn't help someone meanwhile cope with painful feelings. I also don't think men would benefit from hearing about the negative feelings I've had. Most people don't want to know in advance that something is going to be incredibly painful.

EDUCATION

A few people said schools could help matters by teaching boys about reproduction. 'They should be taught about male reproduction and fertility and infertility. All we were taught about was female reproduction'. And, 'you need to get rid of people's ignorance by teaching boys about their own bodies and the things that can go wrong when they want to have children later on'.

DISCUSSION

Inevitably much comment was about medical services. This was understandable as many experiences had been coloured by it. Much advice was to do with practicalities. How to get the best help, the importance of information, the need to be aware of self-help measures for men with sperm problems.

The advice largely emphasised ways of getting a family. Guidance on what feelings to expect and how to deal with them was more tentative or absent. This reflected men's ambivalent and varied ideas about feelings best illustrated by Matthew's remarks. Others seemed to have largely missed such feelings and so had no advice to give. The prospect of childlessness and how men might deal with that was also largely absent from most conversations.

One feeling was familiar. Isolation pervaded experiences. Breaking through this by sharing experiences with other men was seen as a useful exercise. Getting counselling help was also another way of cutting down barriers and making men feel less set apart.

Aside from words of advice, most hoped that medical services for male infertility would improve and that more research would be carried out into it. They wanted greater access to counselling services and some were hopeful that education could play a part in helping men.

The outlook

So what are the prospects for men in the future, particularly on the medical front? Despite the gloom that has surrounded male infertility, there are glimmers of light on the horizon. Some of these are to do with recognising there is a problem, rather than actual developments.

Prevention rather than cure is an idea, though in its infancy, that is now on the infertility agenda for men. There is increasing speculation about whether certain factors may affect sperm quality, e.g. smoking, environmental toxins, acute and chronic infections. Undescended testicles need to be treated as quickly as possible (Derek was bitter that he had not been treated until his teens). However, prevention is currently difficult because the 'factors that contribute to abnormal or too few sperm, for example, are largely unknown' (Congress of the US, Office of Technology Assessment, 1988c: 4).

The report therefore advises couples to allow time to achieve their reproductive goals. It also identifies the need for more information on male fertility and suggests this be done in America by setting up a survey of male reproductive health.

In terms of medical services, more interest is being shown in male fertility. There are doctors now who have a stronger interest in the subject. The growth of andrology is evidence of this and is an encouraging step forward. In the mid-1980s Schirren wrote about the training of andrologists and the need to bring young people into the field (1985).

Still there is a long way to go. Clinics are more geared towards treating female rather than male infertility (Congress of the US, Office of Technology Assessment, 1988b). One American doctor explained to me that urologists still mainly evalute men though there are increasing numbers of non-urological andrologists, but he said that male reproductive biology and andrology are poorly taught in American medical schools. He commented that a decade ago, only 6 per cent of one hundred schools surveyed had a significant programme in this area and felt this hadn't changed much in the intervening years.

Services, at least in the private British medical sector, are starting to appear more male-orientated. Diagnostic andrology services are being set up in some clinics. In the health service, there is talk of having a reproductive-medicine speciality which would include disorders of male reproduction. The stumbling block for the time being seems to be that gynaecologists still largely determine the treatment approach to male infertility. IVF is offered as a solution to male infertility (Pfeffer and Quick, 1988) and though it has given more information about sperm fertilising ability, is not a treatment designed to cure sperm defects. It is essentially a bypassing technique.

Currently one specialist described British services for male fertility and sexual dysfunction to me as being rather 'ad hoc'. Clinics may be unable to deal with any sperm delivery problems such as impotence or ejaculatory disorders. He also pointed to another practical problem. Obstetric and gynaecological departments which deal with men do not often have the facilities to treat them, particularly if surgery is needed. He wondered whether a number of super-specialised departments capable of dealing with complex problems will develop in the future. Yet he thinks it unlikely that such comprehensive centres of excellence will exist at a local level, so couples may have to travel some distance to them.

On the research front there is recognition that more study is needed into male infertility. Various policy issues for US congressional action on infertility are set out in the American government report. One option talks of expanding federal support for research into male infertility. This is needed because too little is known about sperm problems and 'efforts on prevention and treatment are largely guesswork'. Such research could identify risk factors that are currently unknown and would have the added bonus of developing male contraceptives (Congress of the US, Office of Technology Assessment, 1988c: 29). More specifically research is needed to further understanding of sperm capacitation and ability to penetrate the various parts of the egg (Walker, 1992).

Unsurprisingly, given the above, problems persist on the diagnostic and treatment front. The semen analysis is still the mainstay of male investigations throughout the world. There is a growing awareness that it needs to be properly done and that good-quality laboratory services are vital. Those that deal with IVF or andrology will have to develop quality control systems (Byrd, 1992).

The World Health Organisation also developed standard techniques for semen analysis in 1980. This initiative should help reduce variation in test results due to lack of standardisation, but Moghissi and Leach writing from an American standpoint, paint a slightly depressing picture. 'Despite their simplicity, only large clinics and specialised centers have adopted these standards. Other physicians and hospitals continue to use antiquated methods and substandard techniques to analyse semen' (1992: 438).

Australian practice suggests a halfway house. The Fertility Society of Australia told me that private pathology groups analyse semen but there is no standardisation of tests amongst them at present. However, the groups exchange information, slides and specimens for internal and external quality control.

On the treatment side, micromanipulation is hailed as an exciting recent development (Moghissi and Leach, 1992). Kelami also points to this plus other techniques such as IVF and surgical procedures for taking sperm out of the epididymis, but says other approaches have been less successful (1992).

Whether high-tech approaches are the way forward in the longer term is unclear. Several of my interviewees felt uneasy and unhappy about techniques such as IVF because they treat the woman not the man, yet IVF is increasingly being used to get round sperm problems. This may affect the development of other approaches, a possibility envisaged by Pfeffer with respect to general basic infertility services. She warns, 'there is a danger that those gynaecologists most enthusiastic about the new techniques will feel free to invest even more heavily in them to the detriment of existing facilities used to investigate and treat infertility' (1987: 90–91). In the context of male infertility, high-tech approaches may gobble up resources that could otherwise have gone to research.

Of course there are new developments which directly involve the man. An example of this is the removal of epididymal sperm whilst the man is under general anaesthetic. But the woman does not escape medical treatment as IVF is still performed to try and give the sperm every chance of fertilising her eggs.

Men also said they would have liked the chance to see a counsellor (though whether they would have taken the opportunity is another matter). As seen, the importance of counselling is increasingly recognised for people with infertility problems. Various types of services are considered by the American government report. It concludes that one in particular merits serious attention (though no clinics in the study used it). Each member of the couple would see a counsellor from the outset to explore a range of issues, and further help would be offered along the way (Congress of the US, Office of Technology Assessment, 1988a).

In Britain there has been a change that may help some men. People seeking help for certain licensed treatments such as IVF or where donated eggs or sperm are used should have the chance to get counselling help to explore treatment implications (Human Fertilisation and Embryology Act 1990). Clearly this help is of a limited nature because it only applies to licensed treatments and people who are not going through such treatments may also want counselling.

Much of this chapter has been about medical developments and associated concerns. Men's experiences were not just about these matters, but they were of vital concern to men, adding a particular flavour to the discussions. Everything else often seemed of secondary importance. Hence the attention given to them here. The messages from most though not all were that they wanted to be involved in medical checks, have their problems acknowledged and if possible have treatments directed at their problems. Though this may be pie in the sky for most at the moment, male infertility is inching its way up the medical agenda and any developments in the search for a male contraceptive pill will benefit infertile men.

Perhaps the brightest spark on the skyline is a shift in social attitudes. The secrecy surrounding male infertility is evaporating. There have been a spate of media programmes on the subject prompted by the latest high-tech medical approaches and a report on declining sperm counts (Connor, 1992). One British television chat show had men talking about their fertility problems and the presenter claimed this was the first programme to do so ('The Time The Place' 30 March 1992). Such media interest surely reflects a change in society's attitude towards male infertility.

18 Parting thoughts

The tiny number of men whose voices fill this book all saw male infertility as a problem. At the least it was a challenge to be overcome as the man struggled in his quest to create a family. This they had in common with each other and the fact that they had all recognised there was a question mark over their fertility.

Aside from that, their experiences varied enormously. When I asked myself 'why' I found a huge list of factors that might account for this variation such as type of diagnosis, past personal history and so on. Those factors I traced out, help, I think, show why men saw the problem differently, reacted to and coped with it in diverse ways, and the list I drew up of factors was by no means an exhaustive one.

Each man had a special perspective. This was not rigidly fixed but shifted at times during the course of the interview. Experiences however, did fall into rough groupings which I sketched out, with the groups overlapping on certain points.

But I think there is a fundamental distinction that divided men. In one camp there was the man who worried about how infertility might affect his chances of having a family and how his partner would react to him. These were his main anxieties. Others were additionally concerned with certain emotions. Brian for instance, had been deeply hurt by his diagnosis and was wounded by it in a way that someone like John seemed not to be. James was still struggling with the changes he sensed in himself as a result of his infertility.

The thoughts, feelings and practical issues that my interviewees faced up to are not all unique to infertile men. Anyone touched by infertility regardless of sex and whether they themselves are infertile, may struggle with thoughts about the importance of parenthood, the fear of being set apart from those with families, and feelings of inadequacy.

Yet men, regardless of whether they are infertile or not, can have particular problems to contend with. Motherhood is almost thought to be a right for women at the present time and they are seen to be more deserving of support if this prospect is denied them. Men, on the other hand, may find it difficult to know how important the loss of fatherhood is to them and not know how to voice any feelings they have about this. Upbringing and social conditioning can militate against men expressing feelings of sadness. That message clearly emerged in several conversations, with some expressing regret but resignation at this state of affairs.

Yet those currently faced with a question mark over their fertility can get twisted up in a special experience. The often quoted point about the link between virility and infertility may make men feel they have to remain silent, though I felt this point was not as important as is often made out. More notable from my viewpoint was a sense of marginality amongst those undergoing medical investigations. The man stood on the sidelines feeling useless, looking on as his partner was treated instead of him.

In addition, he may blame himself for not being able to give his partner a child, and blame himself for the sometimes painful treatments she endures. Yet little attention from any quarter may be directed to what he is feeling, and anyway he may not know what he feels, particularly since the message is that the woman is entitled to be upset but not the man. If he feels sad he may push this emotion away because he is unsure what he has to be sad about. If he is aware of feelings he may not reveal them to the woman for fear of upsetting her. He feels guilty, so deserves no help and thinks he can best support the woman by remaining silent. Yet ironically she may want the man to open up and tell her what he is going through. Instead he neglects himself when he should be tending to his own needs. This would help him as well as his partner.

Of course these perceptions are my interpretations of experiences. Some of my interviewees would challenge them and say I had misunderstood what they told me. Yet I feel on balance that these were the unseen strands that linked interviews together.

These thoughts are also based on a highly select group of men. There must surely be all sorts of other experiences that are not covered in this book. Many men may not accept they have a fertility problem and may not face up to the challenges posed by infertility. Others may accept they are infertile but not see the experience as problematic in any sense.

Further exploration is needed into the male experience. Meanwhile those stories recounted here show how a few men saw and coped with the experience of being infertile and how I interpreted their stories.

Appendix: self-help groups

Australia

Concern for the Infertile Couple
P.O. Box 412
Subiaco, Western Australia 6008
Tel.: 619–381–9313

Britain

CHILD
Suite 219
Caledonian House
98 The Centre
Feltham, Middlesex TW13 4BH
Tel.: 081–893–7110

ISSUE, The National Fertility Association
509 Aldridge Road
Great Barr, Birmingham B44 8NA
Tel.: 021–344–4414

United States

Resolve
1310 Broadway
Somerville, Massachusetts 02144
Tel.: 617–623–0744

References

Abbey, A., Andrews, F. M. and Halman, L. J. (1991) 'The importance of social relationships for infertile couples' well-being', in A. L. Stanton and C. Dunkel-Schetter (eds) *Infertility Perspectives from Stress and Coping Research*, New York: Plenum Press.

Abse, D. W., (1966) 'Psychiatric aspects of human male infertility', *Fertility and Sterility*, 17, 1: 133–9.

Aitken, R. J., Richardson, D. W. and Clarkson, J. (1984) 'Assessment of the fertilising capacity of human spermatozoa', in W. Thompson, D. M. Joyce, J. R. Newton (eds) *IVF and DI Proceedings of the Twelfth Study Group of the Royal College of Obstetricians and Gynaecologists*, November.

Alikani, M. and Cohen, J. (1992) 'Advances in clinical micromanipulation of gametes and embryos: Assisted fertilisation and hatching', *Archives of Pathology & Laboratory Medicine*, 116, 4: 373–8.

Austin, C. R. (1976) 'Biological basis of insemination, sperm transport, capacitation and fertilisation', in M. Brudenell, A. McLaren, R. Short and M. Symonds (eds) *Artificial Insemination Proceedings of the Fourth Study Group of the Royal College of Obstetricians and Gynaecologists*.

Balerna, M. and Piffaretti-Yanez, A. (1992) 'Semen analyses in the nineties: Some reflections on their context, importance and limits', in G. M. Colpi and D. Pozza (eds) *Diagnosing Male Infertility: New Possibilities and Limits*, Basel: Karger.

Ballantyne, A. (1991) 'Test-tube success gives infertile men hope', *Sunday Times*, 10 November.

Barber, R. (1992) 'The fight to be a father', *Good Housekeeping* magazine, February.

Barker, G. H. (1986) *The New Fertility*, London: Adamson Books.

Barratt, C. L. R., Chauhan, M. and Cooke, I. D. (1990) 'Donor insemination – a look to the future', *Fertility and Sterility*, 54, 3: 375–85.

Bellina, J. and Wilson, J. (1986) *The Fertility Handbook: A Positive and Practical Guide*, London: Penguin.

Bents, H. (1985) 'Psychology of male infertility, a literature survey', *International Journal of Andrology*, 8: 325–36.

Berg, B. J. and Wilson, J. F. (1990) 'Psychiatric morbidity in the infertile population: A reconceptualisation', *Fertility and Sterility*, 53: 654–61.

Berger, D. M. (1980) 'Couples' reactions to male infertility and donor insemination', *American Journal of Psychiatry*, 137: 1047–9.

Bishop, S. (1991) 'Cancer and the kindest cut', *Independent*, 26 March.

Blizzard, J. (1977) *Blizzard and the Holy Ghost*, London: Peter Owen.

Bradbury, P. (1985) 'Desire and pregnancy', in A. Metcalf and M. Humphries (eds) *The Sexuality of Men*, London: Pluto.

Brand, H. J. (1989) 'The influence of sex differences on the acceptance of infertility', *Journal of Reproductive and Infant Psychology*, 7: 129–31.

Bromham, D. R., Balmer, B., Clay, R. and Hamer, R. (1988) 'Disenchantment with infertility services: A survey of patients in Yorkshire', *British Journal of Family Planning*, 14: 3–8 .

Byrd, W. (1992) 'Quality assurance in the reproductive biology laboratory', *Archives of Pathology & Laboratory Medicine*, 116: 418–22.

Carlson, N. L. (1987) 'Woman therapist: Male client', in M. Scher, M. Stevens, G. Good and G. A. Eichenfield (eds) *Handbook of Counseling and Psychotherapy With Men*, Beverly Hills and London: Sage.

Christie, G. L. and Pawson, M. E. (1987) 'The psychological and social management of the infertile couple', in R. J. Pepperell, B. Hudson and C. Wood (eds) *The Infertile Couple*, Edinburgh: Churchill Livingstone.

Clark, L. F., Henry, S. M. and Taylor, D. M. (1991) 'Cognitive examination of motivation for childbearing as a factor in adjustment to infertility', in A. L. Stanton and C. Dunkel-Schetter (eds) *Infertility Perspectives from Stress and Coping Research*, New York: Plenum Press.

Clements, D. (n.d.) 'A process of understanding' in *Collection on the Male Perspective*, produced by Resolve (American self-help group).

Congress of the US, Office of Technology Assessment (1988a) 'Infertility: Medical and social choices', vol. iv, 'Social and medical concerns', February.

—— (1988b) 'Infertility: Medical and social choices', May.

—— (1988c) 'Infertility: Medical and social choices, summary', May.

Conkling, W. (1991) 'From infertility to fatherhood: New techniques can increase the odds for conception', *American Health: Fitness of Body and Mind*, Jan.–Feb.

Connolly, K. J. and Cooke, I. D. (1987) 'Distress and marital problems associated with infertility', *Journal of Reproductive and Infant Psychology*, 5: 49–57.

Connor, S. (1992) 'Mystery of the vanishing sperm', *Independent on Sunday*, 8 March.

Cook, R., Parsons, J., Mason, B. and Golombok, S. (1989) 'Emotional, marital and sexual functioning in patients embarking upon IVF and AID treatment for infertility', *Journal of Reproductive and Infant Psychology*, 7: 87–93.

Cooke, I. D. (1988) 'The future', in C. L. R. Barratt and I. D. Cooke (eds) *Advances in Clinical Andrology*, Lancaster: MTP Press.

Cozens, J. (1992) 'How you both can cope with your feelings', *Good Housekeeping* magazine, February.

David, A. and Avidan, D. (1976) 'Artificial insemination donor: Clinical and psychologic aspects', *Fertility and Sterility*, 27: 528–32.

Dickson, J. (1991) 'The fertility helpline, statistical synopsis of first annual report', produced by Issue, the national fertility association, 12 October.

Doyal, L. (1987) 'Infertility – a life sentence? Women and the national health service', in M. Stanworth (ed.) *Reproductive Technologies: Gender, Motherhood and Medicine*, Cambridge: Polity Press.

Doyle, C. (1991) 'The unjust cost of parenthood', *Daily Telegraph*, 23 July.

Dubin, L. and Amelar, R. D. (1972) 'Sexual causes of male infertility', *Fertility and Sterility*, 23, 8: 579–82.

Dubois, T. E. and Marino, T. M. (1987) 'Career counseling with men', in M. Scher,

M. Stevens, G. Good and G. A. Eichenfield, *Handbook of Counseling and Psychotherapy with Men*, Beverly Hills and London: Sage.

Dunkel-Schetter, C. and Lobel, M. (1991) 'Psychological reactions to infertility', in A.L. Stanton and C. Dunkel-Schetter (eds) *Infertility Perspectives from Stress and Coping Research*, New York: Plenum Press.

Dunkel-Schetter, C. and Stanton, A. L. (1991) 'Psychological adjustment to infertility: Future directions in research and application', in A. L. Stanton and C. Dunkel-Schetter (eds) *Infertility Perspectives from Stress and Coping Research*, New York: Plenum Press.

Edelmann R. J. and Connolly, K. J. (1986) 'Psychological aspects of infertility', *British Journal of Medical Psychology*, 59: 209–219.

——(1989) 'The impact of infertility and infertility investigations: Four case illustrations', *Journal of Reproductive and Infant Psychology*, 7: 113–19.

Eliasson, R. (1976) 'Assessment of male fertility, introduction', in M. Brudenell, A. McLaren, R. Short and M. Symonds (eds) *Artificial Insemination Proceedings of the Fourth Study Group of the Royal College of Obstetricians and Gynaecologists.*

Ferris, A. (1991) 'A baby at any cost?', *Options* magazine, November.

Fort, M. (1990) 'Sperm wail', *Guardian*, 4 September.

Fraser, L. R. (1992) 'Requirements for successful mammalian sperm capacitation and fertilisation', *Archives of Pathology & Laboratory Medicine*, 116, 4: 345–50.

Gardner, M. J., Snee, M. P., Hall, A. J., Powell, C. A., Downes, S. and Terrell, J. D. (1990) 'Results of case-control study of leukaemia and lymphoma among young people near Sellafield nuclear plant in West Cumbria', *British Medical Journal*, 300: 423–34.

Gillie, O. (1986) 'The return to potency', *Sunday Times*, 11 May.

Glover, T. D., Barratt, C. L. R., Tyler, J. P. P. and Hennessey, J. F. (1990) *Human Male Fertility and Semen Analysis*, London: Academic Press.

Green, J. (1988) 'The baby we can't have', *Guardian*, 28 December.

Greer, G. (1984) *Sex and Destiny: The Politics of Human Fertility*, London: Pan.

Gregson, S. (1988) 'Male infertility', *Practitioner*, 232: 1265–6.

Hall, L. A. (1991) *Male Sexuality 1900–1950*, Cambridge: Polity Press.

Hamblen, E. C. (1960) *Facts for Childless Couples*, Springfield: Charles C. Thomas.

Hammen, R. (1944) *Studies on Impaired Fertility in Man with Special Reference to the Male*, Copenhagen: Einar Munksgaard.

Hammond, K. R., Kretzer, P. A., Blackwell, R. E. and Steinkampf, M. P. (1990) 'Performance anxiety during infertility treatment: Effect on semen quality', *Fertility and Sterility*, 53: 337–40.

Hargreave, T. B. (1983) 'Non-specific treatment to improve fertility', in T. B. Hargreave (ed.) *Male Infertility*, Berlin: Springer-Verlag .

Hargreave, T. B. and Nillson, S. (1983) 'Seminology' in T. B. Hargreave (ed.) *Male Infertility*, Berlin: Springer-Verlag.

Harman, H. (1990) 'Trying for a baby', a report on the inadequacy of NHS infertility services by the shadow health minister, House of Commons.

Heppner, P. P. and Gonzales, D. S. (1987) 'Men counseling men' in M. Scher, M. Stevens, G. Good and G.A. Eichenfield, (eds) *Handbook of Counseling and Psychotherapy with Men*, Beverly Hills and London: Sage.

Hite, S. (1981) *The Hite Report on Male Sexuality*, London: Macdonald.

Hodgkinson, L. (1983) 'The men who queue at the female clinics', *The Times*, 26 January.

—— (1991) 'Reversing up a one-way street', *Independent*, 3 September.

Holder, D. (1992) 'Primagravidas in their prime', *Guardian*, 23 January.

Holman, T. (n.d.) 'A fragile sense of hope', in *Collection on the Male Perspective*, produced by Resolve (American self-help group).

Hotchkiss, R.S. (1945) *Fertility in Men*, London: Heinemann.

Houghton, D and Houghton, P. (1987) *Coping with Childlessness*, London: Unwin Hyman.

Hudson, B., Baker, H. W. G. and deKretser, D. M. (1987) 'The abnormal semen sample', in R. J. Pepperell, B. Hudson and C. Wood (eds) *The Infertile Couple*, Edinburgh: Churchill Livingstone.

Hull, M. G. R. and Glazener, C. M. A. (1984) 'Male infertility and in-vitro fertilisation', *Lancet*, ii: 231.

Hull M. G. R., Eddowes, H. A., Fahy. U., Abuzeid, M. I., Mills, M. S., Cahill, D. J., Fleming, C. F., Wardle, P. G., Ford, W. C. L. and McDermott, A. (1992) 'Expectations of assisted conception for infertility', *British Medical Journal*, 304: 1465–9.

Hull, M. G. R., Glazener, C. M. A., Kelly, N. J., Conway, D. I., Foster, P. A., Hinton, R. A., Coulson, C., Lambert, P. A., Watt, E. M. and Desai, K. M. (1985) 'Population study of causes, treatment, and outcome of infertility', *British Medical Journal*, 291: 1693–7.

Humphrey, M. (1986) 'Infertility as a marital crisis', *Stress Medicine*, 2: 221–4.

Humphrey, M. and Humphrey, H. (1988) *Families with a Difference*, London: Routledge.

Interim Licensing Authority (1991) The sixth report.

Issue (1989/1990) 'Male infertility and Chinese medicine', postbag section, produced by Issue, the national fertility association, Winter.

—— (1991a) 'Survey results', No. 21.

—— (1991b) No. 22.

Jackson, B. (1984) *Fatherhood*, London: George Allen & Unwin.

Jackson, M. H., Malleson, J., Stallworthy, J. and Walker, K. (1948) *Problems of Fertility in General Practice*, London: Hamish Hamilton.

Jenkins, P. (1991) 'I'm fine really', *Achilles Heel* magazine, Summer.

Jequier, A. M. (1986) *Infertility in the Male*, Edinburgh: Churchill Livingstone.

Jequier, A. M. and Crich, J. (1986) *Semen Analysis: A Practical Guide*, Oxford: Blackwell Scientific Publications .

Johnston, D. R. (1963) 'The history of human infertility', *Fertility and Sterility*, 14, 3: 261–72.

Jones, M. (1991) *Infertility, Modern Treatments and the Issues They Raise*, London: Piatkus.

Jones, M. H. (n.d.) 'Beautiful desire led to this?', in *Collection on the Male Perspective*, produced by Resolve (American self-help group).

Kaufman, S. A. (1969) 'Impact of infertility on the marital and sexual relationship', *Fertility and Sterility*, 20, 3: 380–3.

Kedem, P., Mikulincer, M., Nathanson, Y.-E. and Bartoov, B. (1990) 'Psychological aspects of male infertility', *British Journal of Medical Psychology*, 63(1): 73–80.

Keith, J. M. (1991) 'Microinsemination and related micromanipulation methods', *Issue*, 21, produced by Issue, the national fertility association, Spring.

Kelami, A. (1992) 'Male infertility now and in the 1990s', in G. M. Colpi and D. Pozza (eds) *Diagnosing Male Infertility, New Possibilities and Limits*, Basel: Karger.

Kempers, R. D. (1976) 'The tricentennial of the discovery of sperm', *Fertility and Sterility*, 27, 5: 603–5.

Kingman, S. (1991) 'Drug offers hope to infertile men', *Independent on Sunday*, 24 March.

Klock S. C. and Maier, D. (1991) 'Psychological factors related to donor insemination', *Fertility and Sterility*, 56: 489–95.

Landesman, C. (1991) 'Glad to be dad', *Guardian*, 26 March.

Laurance, J. (1982) 'The moral pressure to have children', *New Society* magazine, 5 August.

Laws, S. (1990) *Issues of Blood*, London: Macmillan.

Lazarides, L. (1992) 'Before they've even been conceived', *Everywoman* magazine, February.

Leese, H. (1988) *Human Reproduction and In Vitro Fertilisation*, Basingstoke: Macmillan Education.

Lilford, R. J. and Dalton, M. E. (1987) 'Effectiveness of treatment for infertility', *British Medical Journal*, 295, 6591: 155–6.

Lottridge, S. S. (1988) 'One man's infertility', in E. S. Glazer and S. L. Cooper *Without Child: Experiencing and Resolving Infertility*, New York: Lexington Books.

Lyndon, N. (1990) 'Bad mouthing, why the way women talk about men is still hurting all of us', *Sunday Times* magazine, 9 December.

McAllister, N. (1991) 'Bursting the bubble', *Guardian*, 4 April.

MacFarlane, A. (1986) *Marriage and Love in England 1300–1400*, Oxford: Basil Blackwell.

McGrade, J. J. and Tolor, A. (1981) 'The reaction to infertility and the infertility investigation: A comparison of the responses of men and women', *Infertility* 4: 7–27.

McKie, R. (1991) 'Gene breakthrough heralds male pill and infertility cure', *Observer*, 13 October.

McLaren, A. (1984) *Reproductive Rituals: The Perception of Fertility in England from the Sixteenth to the Nineteenth Century*, London: Methuen.

MacLeod, J. and Gold, R. Z. (1952) 'The male factor in fertility and infertility: effect of continence on semen quality', *Fertility and Sterility*, 3, 4: 297–315.

MacNab, T. (1984) 'Infertility and men: A study of change and adaptive choices in the lives of involuntarily childless men', unpublished doctoral dissertation, Fielding Institute, Berkeley, California.

Mahlstedt, P. P. (1985) 'The psychological component of infertility', *Fertility and Sterility*, 43: 335–46.

Mann, T. and Lutwak-Mann, C. (1981) *Male Reproductive Function and Semen*, Berlin: Springer-Verlag.

Mason, M.-C. (1990) 'How Steven finally became a father on', *Daily Telegraph*, 27 November.

—— (1991) 'Pick the best sperm, then egg them on ', *Independent*, 29 October.

Mathieson, D. (1986) 'Infertility services in the NHS: What's going on?', report prepared for Frank Dobson MP, shadow minister of health.

Menning, B. E. (1980) 'The emotional needs of infertile couples', *Fertility and Sterility*, 34, 4: 313–19.

Miall, C.-E. (1985) 'Perceptions of informal sanctioning and the stigma of involuntary childlessness', *Deviant Behaviour*, 6(4): 383–403.

Mihill, C. (1991) 'Road monitor tracks sperm', *Guardian*, 23 September.

Moghissi, K. S and Leach, R. (1992) 'Future directions in reproductive medicine', *Archives of Pathology & Laboratory Medicine*, 116, 4: 436–41.

Moncur, A. (1987) 'Steady drinking can ruin your sex life', *Guardian*, 3 April.

Moorehead, C. (1984) 'The paternal triangle', *The Times*, 11 April.

Mosse, J. and Heaton, J. (1990) *The Fertility and Contraception Book*, London: Faber & Faber.

Neuberg, R. (1991) *Infertility*, London: Thorsons.

Newill, R. (1974) *Infertile Marriage*, London: Penguin.

Osherson, S. (1986) *Finding Our Fathers*, New York: Free Press.

Owens, D. (1982) 'The desire to father: Reproductive ideologies and involuntarily childless men', in L. McKee and M. O'Brien (eds) *The Father Figure*, London: Tavistock.

Owens, D. J. and Read, M. W. (1984) 'Patients' experience with and assessment of subfertility testing and treatment', *Journal of Reproductive and Infant Psychology* 2: 7–17.

Pantesco, V. (1986) 'Nonorganic infertility: Some research and treatment problems', *Psychological Reports*, 58: 731-7.

Parry, V. (1991) 'Male infertility: a neglected issue', *Options* magazine, January.

Pfeffer, N. (1985) 'The hidden pathology of the male reproductive system', in H. Homans (ed.) *The Sexual Politics of Reproduction*, Aldershot: Gower.

—— (1987) 'Artificial insemination, in-vitro fertilisation and the stigma of infertility', in M. Stanworth (ed.) *Reproductive Technologies: Gender, Motherhood and Medicine*, Cambridge: Polity Press.

Pfeffer, N. and Quick, A. (1988) *Infertility Services: A Desperate Case*, The Greater London Association of Community Health Councils.

Pfeffer, N. and Woollett, A. (1983) *The Experience of Infertility*, London: Virago.

Philipp, E. (1984) *Overcoming Childlessness: Its Causes and What to do About Them*, London: Hamlyn .

Prentice, T. (1984) 'Birth of new hope for men who can't be fathers', *The Times*, 20 August.

—— (1988) 'Anguish of the sterile husbands', *The Times*, 20 April.

Rappaport, B. M. (1984) 'Family planning: Helping men ask for help', in J. M. Swanson and K. A. Forrest, *Men's Reproductive Health*, New York: Springer.

Reynolds, E. and Macomber, D. (1924) *Fertility and Sterility in Human Marriages*, Philadelphia and London: W. B. Saunders & Co.

Richards, M. P. M. (1982) 'How should we approach the study of fathers?', in L. McKee and M. O'Brien (eds) *The Father Figure*, London: Tavistock.

Richman, J. (1982) 'Men's experiences of pregnancy and childbirth', in L. McKee and M. O'Brien (eds) *The Father Figure*, London: Tavistock.

Royal College of Obstetricians and Gynaecologists (1976) *Artificial Insemination Proceedings of the Fourth Study Group*, M. Brudenell, A. McLaren, R. Short and M. Symonds (eds).

Saaranen, M., Suonio, S., Kauhanen, O. and Saarikoski, S. (1987) 'Cigarette smoking and semen quality in men of reproductive age', *Andrologia*, 19(6): 670–6.

Sandmaier, M. (1991) 'Male infertility: New tests, new options', *Working Woman* magazine, January.

Schellen, A.M.C.M. (1957) *Artificial Insemination in the Human*, Elsevier Publishing Co.

Schirren, C. (1985) 'Andrology – origin and development of a special discipline in medicine: Reflection and view in the future', *Andrologia*, 17(2): 117–25.

Shaw, P., Johnston, M. and Shaw, R. (1988) 'Counselling needs, emotional and relationship problems in couples awaiting IVF', *Journal of Psychosomatic Obstetrics & Gynaecology*, 9: 171–80.

Short, R. (1976) 'Assessment of male fertility', discussion in M. Brudenell, A. McLaren, R. Short and M. Symonds (eds) *Artificial Insemination Proceedings of the Fourth Study Group of the Royal College of Obstetricians and Gynaecologists.*

Simon, A, Younis, J., Lewin, A., Bartoov, B., Schenker, J. G. and Laufer, N. (1991) 'The correlation between sperm cell morphology and fertilisation after zona pellucida slitting in subfertile males', *Fertility and Sterility*, 56, 2: 325–31.

Small, M. F. (1991) 'Sperm wars', *Discover* magazine, July.

Smith, E. (1991) Interview with the Ross family in *Hello* magazine, 6 April.

Smith, G. (1990) 'The crisis of fatherhood', *Achilles Heel* magazine, April.

Smolev, J. and Forrest, K. A. (1984) 'Male infertility', in J. M. Swanson and K. A. Forrest (eds) *Men's Reproductive Health*, New York: Springer publishing.

Snarey, J. (1988) 'Men without children', *Psychology Today*, March.

Snowden, R. and Mitchell, G. D. (1981) *The Artificial Family*, London: George Allen & Unwin.

Snowden, R. and Snowden E. M. (1984) *The Gift of a Child*, London: George Allen & Unwin.

Snowden, R., Mitchell, G. D. and Snowden, E. M. (1983) *Artificial Reproduction: A Social Investigation*, London: George Allen & Unwin.

Spark, R. F. (1988) *The Infertile Male: The Clinician's Guide to Diagnosis and Treatment*, New York: Plenum Medical.

Stanton, A. L. (1991) 'Cognitive appraisals, coping processes and adjustment to infertility', in A. L. Stanton and C. Dunkel-Schetter (eds) *Infertility Perspectives from Stress and Coping Research*, New York: Plenum Press.

Stanton, A. L. and Dunkel-Schetter, C. (1991) 'Psychological adjustment to infertility: An overview of conceptual approaches', in A. L. Stanton and C. Dunkel-Schetter (eds) *Infertility Perspectives from Stress and Coping Research*, New York: Plenum Press.

Stanway, A. (1986) *Infertility: A Common-Sense Guide for the Childless*, Wellingborough: Thorsons.

Steven, C. (1991) 'Out for the sperm count', *Guardian*, 7 June.

Sutkin, L. C. and Good, G. (1987) 'Therapy with men in health-care settings', in M. Scher, M. Stevens, G. Good and G. A. Eichenfield (eds) *Handbook of Counseling and Psychotherapy With Men*, Beverly Hills and London: Sage.

Tracy, C. (1991) 'Vasectomy – seven years on', *Achilles Heel* magazine, Summer.

Turner, B. S. (1984) *The Body and Society*, Oxford: Basil Blackwell.

USA Today, (1991) 'Lifestyle change may help', February.

Vaughan, P. (1972) *The Pill on Trial*, Harmondsworth: Penguin.

Walker, A. (1990) 'Pentoxifylline – a new hope for poor semen', *Issue*, The National Fertility Association, Summer.

Walker, R. H. (1992) 'College of American pathologists' conference xx on new developments in reproductive biology: Summation and recommendations', *Archives of Pathology & Laboratory Medicine*, 116: 442–3.

Wardle, P. G. (1990) 'Treatment of male infertility', *Prescribers' Journal*, 30, 3: 124–30.

Welford, H. (1990) 'Millions of sperm, but still no baby', *Independent*, 4 September.

Winston, R. (1989) *Getting Pregnant*, London: Anaya.

Woollett, A. (1985) 'Childlessness: Strategies for coping with infertility', *International Journal of Behavioural Development*, 8: 473–82.

Wu, F. (1983) 'Endocrinology of male infertility and fertility', in T. B. Hargreave (ed.) *Male Infertility*, Berlin: Springer-Verlag.

Yovich, J. (1991) 'Pentoxifylline for male factor infertility', *Issue*, The National Fertility Association, No. 23.

Yovich, J. L. and Matson, P. L. (1988) 'The treatment of infertility by the high intrauterine insemination of husband's washed spermatozoa', *Human Reproduction*, 939–43.

Name index

Subject index